Cavalier Generals

Cavalier Generals

*King Charles I and His Commanders in the
English Civil War 1642–46*

John Barratt

Pen & Sword
MILITARY

First published in Great Britain in 2004 by
Pen & Sword Military
an imprint of
Pen & Sword Books Ltd
47 Church Street
Barnsley
South Yorkshire
S70 2AS

ISBN 1 84415 128 X

A CIP catalogue record for this book is
available from the British Library

Typeset in Bulmer by
Phoenix Typesetting, Auldgirth, Dumfriesshire

Printed and bound in Great Britain by
CPI UK

Pen & Sword Books Ltd incorporates the imprints of Pen & Sword Aviation,
Pen & Sword Maritime, Pen & Sword Military, Wharncliffe Local History,
Pen & Sword Select, Pen & Sword Military Classics and Leo Cooper.

For a complete list of Pen & Sword titles please contact
PEN & SWORD BOOKS LIMITED
47 Church Street, Barnsley, South Yorkshire, S70 2AS England
E-mail: enquiries@pen-and-sword.co.uk
Website: www.pen-and-sword.co.uk

Contents

Preface

PERHAPS inevitably, the victors in Britain's Civil Wars of 1638–1651 have received much greater attention than their defeated opponents. While there have been a number of studies of such luminaries of the Parliamentarian cause as Oliver Cromwell and Sir Thomas Fairfax, Sir William Waller, and Sir William Brereton, the Royalists, with the inevitable exceptions of Charles I, Prince Rupert and Montrose, have been less well served.

This book looks at the careers, personalities and battles of a dozen Royalist commanders during the First Civil War of 1642–46. It attempts to assess their performance and their impact on the Royalist cause, and examines in more detail a key battle of their career.

My selection, while including most of the major commanders and some who are undeservedly less well known, is inevitably a personal one, and I am conscious of the ghosts of omitted Cavaliers such as 'Blind Harry' Hastings, Sir William Vaughan –'the Devil of Shrawardine' – and the fearsome Charles Gerard peering angrily over my shoulder. I hope that one day they too will find their chronicler.

Any researcher into seventeenth-century history will be both amused and irritated by the many vagaries of spelling and punctuation in use at the time. For the sake of ease and consistency here, I have, in all but one example, which deserved quoting in its original form, put the words of my commanders and their contemporaries into modern English.

Thanks are due to a large number of individuals and institutions for their unfailing help and advice. The staff of the Sydney Jones Library, University of Liverpool, the British Library and the Bodleian Library, Oxford, have, as ever, been highly efficient in coping with my demands. Rupert Harding and the team at Pen and Sword have helped with ideas and encouragement in putting this book together, while Derek Stone has produced maps to his usual high standard.

Over the years, many researchers into the English Civil War have provided invaluable information and assistance. Among them are Ivor Carr, John Lewis, Les Prince, Stuart Reid, Keith Roberts, Dave Ryan, John Tincey and Alan Turton. Some of their research and discoveries may be found in this book: the inevitable mistakes and omissions are mine.

John Barratt
June 2004

Auldearn

INVERNESS ✕ Alford

✕ ✕ ABERDEEN

INVERLOCHY ✕ PERTH
Tippermuir ✕

INVERARY
Kilsyth ✕
GLASGOW EDINBURGH

Philliphaugh ✕

NEWCASTLE

Marston
Moor
✕ YORK
LEEDS
BRADFORD ✕
Adwalton Moor ✕ HULL
WAKEFIELD PONTEFRACT

LIVERPOOL

CHESTER NEWARK
Nantwich ✕

✕ Naseby

WORCESTER
Ripple ✕ ✕ Edgehill

GLOUCESTER OXFORD
STOW

BRISTOL
✕ Newbury LONDON
✕
Langport ✕ Roundway ✕ Cheriton
Down

Stratton ✕
LYME
EXETER

✕ PLYMOUTH
Lostwithiel

·THE·
·CIVIL·
·WAR·

DDG
2004

Chronology

1639
Charles I defeated in First Bishop's War with Scotland

1640
Second Bishop's War
20 August	Scottish Covenanting army invades England
28 August	Covenanting victory at Battle of Newburn
16–26 October	Hostilities ended with Treaty of Ripon
1 November	'Long Parliament' meets
11 November	Impeachment of Strafford

1641
15 February	Triennial Parliament Bill calls for a Parliament to be called at least every three years
12 May	Strafford executed
24 June	'Ten Propositions' of Parliament propose curbing royal powers
22 October	Outbreak of rebellion in Ireland
1 December	'Grand Remonstrance' of Parliament presented to king

1642
January	Attempt by king to arrest 'Five Members' fails; Charles leaves London
February	Queen Henrietta Maria goes to Holland to raise munitions and men
5 March	Parliament passes Militia Ordnance to take control of militia from king
18 March	King establishes Court at York
1 June	King presented with Parliament's 'Nineteen Propositions' proposing further drastic curbs on royal powers
18 June	King rejects 'Nineteen Propositions'
June	First arms and officers from Continent reach Royalists
2–3 July	Navy declares for Parliament
15–27 July	First siege of Hull ends in Royalist failure
2 August	Goring surrenders Portsmouth to Parliament
22 August	King Charles raises standard at Nottingham signalling official outbreak of Civil War
23 September	Prince Rupert defeats Parliamentarians at Powicke Bridge
23 October	Battle of Edgehill; Royalists win marginal victory
12 November	Rupert storms Brentford; advance on London halted at Turnham Green; Royalists retreat to Reading and Oxford

1643
19 January	Hopton repulses Parliamentarian invasion of Cornwall at Braddock Down
February	Queen and munitions land at Bridlington
2 February	Rupert takes Cirencester, clearing communications between Oxford and the West

19 March	Royalist victory at Hopton Heath in Staffordshire
3 April	Rupert storms Birmingham
7–21 April	Rupert takes Lichfield. First mine to be used in England is exploded
25 April	Earl of Essex takes Reading
16 May	Cornish Royalist victory at Stratton
21 May	Goring captured at Wakefield
14 June	Rupert's Chalgrove raid disrupts Parliamentarian operations in Thames Valley
30 June	Newcastle defeats Northern Parliamentarians at Adwalton Moor
4 July	Battle of Lansdown; Western Royalists fail to defeat Waller in inconclusive action
13 July	Wilmot defeats Waller at Roundway Down
26 July	Rupert storms Bristol
6 August– 4 September	Siege of Gloucester
1 September	'Cessation' agreed between Ormonde and Irish Confederates frees English troops in Ireland to fight for king
2 September	Earl of Newcastle lays siege to Hull
4 September	Prince Maurice takes Exeter
20 September	First Battle of Newbury; king fails to defeat Earl of Essex
25 September	Solemn League and Covenant signed between English Parliament and Covenanting regime in Scotland
October	Prince Maurice takes Dartmouth
11 October	Royalist defeat at Winceby
12 October	Newcastle raises siege of Hull
13 October	Contingent of English troops from Ireland land in North Wales
13 December	Royalists take Beeston Castle in Cheshire
26 December	Lord Byron lays siege to Nantwich

1644

19 January	Scottish army invades England in support of Parliament
25 January	Sir Thomas Fairfax defeats Byron at Nantwich
3 February	Scots fail to take Newcastle-upon-Tyne
19 February	Action at Corbridge; Langdale raids Scottish horse quarters
4 February	Rupert appointed President of Wales and Captain General in Wales and the Marches
29 February	Parliamentarians under Sir John Meldrum lay siege to Newark
7–8 March	Indecisive action between Newcastle and Scots at Bolden Hills
21 March	Prince Rupert relieves Newark
23 March	Indecisive action between Newcastle and Leven at Penshaw Hill
29 March	Hopton and Firth defeated by Waller at Cheriton
11 April	Belasyse defeated at Selby
22 April	Allied armies lay siege to York
25 May	Rupert storms Stockport
28 May	Rupert storms Bolton
11 June	Rupert takes Liverpool
29 June	Charles I defeats Waller at Cropredy Bridge
1 July	Rupert relieves York
2 July	Battle of Marston Moor; Rupert and Newcastle defeated
16 July	York surrenders
21 August	Royalists defeat Essex at Beacon Hill (Lostwithiel campaign)

31 August	Royalists defeat Essex at Castle Dor (Lostwithiel campaign)
1 September	Montrose defeats Covenanters at Tippermuir
3 September	Skippon and Essex's foot surrender at Lostwithiel
13 September	Montrose defeats Covenanters at Aberdeen
18 September	Lord Byron defeated at Montgomery
20 October	Newcastle-upon-Tyne falls to Scots
27 October	Second Battle of Newbury; Parliamentarians fail to defeat Charles I
November	'Leaguer' of Chester begins
6 November	Prince Rupert appointed Lieutenant General of Royalist forces
9 November	'Third Battle of Newbury'; Oxford Army relieves Donnington Castle
19 December	House of Commons passes Self-Denying Ordnance to create New Model Army

1645

2 February	Montrose defeats Argyll at Inverlochy
18 February	Grenville fails to take Plymouth
19 February	Maurice relieves Chester
22 February	Parliamentarians take Shrewsbury
2 March	Langdale relieves Pontefract
4 April	New Model Army formed
22 April	Rupert defeats Massey at Ledbury
9 May	Montrose defeats Covenanters at Auldearn
10 May	Royalist Council of War at Stow on the Wold decides strategy for Naseby campaign
30 May	Rupert storms Leicester
14 June	Battle of Naseby; Oxford Army defeated
2 July	Montrose defeats Covenanters at Alford
10 July	Battle of Langport; Goring and Royalist Western Army defeated
23 July	Fairfax takes Bridgwater
15 August	Montrose defeats Covenanters at Kilsyth
10 September	Rupert surrenders Bristol; dismissed by king
13 September	Montrose defeated at Philliphaugh
24 September	Charles I defeated at Rowton Heath
13 October	Langdale and Northern Horse defeated at Sherburn

1646

3 February	Byron surrenders Chester
16 February	Hopton defeated at Torrington
12 March	Royalist Western Army surrenders at Truro
21 March	Astley and last major Royalist field army surrenders at Stow on the Wold
5 May	King Charles surrenders to Scots at Newark
31 May	Huntley and Montrose disband Scottish Royalist forces
24 June	Surrender of Oxford to Fairfax
19 August	Surrender of Raglan Castle

1647

16 March	Surrender of Harlech Castle, the last Royalist garrison in mainland England and Wales

Chapter One
All the King's Generals

ENGLAND in the mid-seventeenth century was a hierarchical society, and though the outbreak of civil war in the summer of 1642 divided influential sections of society between king and Parliament, the great majority on both sides had no desire to overturn the nation's basic fabric.

This innate conservatism was reflected in the initial choice of commanders for the opposing armies. Both Royalists and Parliamentarians preferred, unless unavoidable, to appoint generals drawn from the 'natural' ruling class of aristocrats and gentry. During the first year of the war, of six Royalist regional commanders, five were leading magnates of the areas concerned, and the sixth, Lord Capel, came from the same background, and was appointed to command on the Welsh Border because of the lack of any suitable local figure.

The Parliamentarians, to only a slightly lesser extent, followed the same policy. However, by the end of 1643 both sides were coming to recognize that the nobly-born commanders had largely failed in their task. Of the Royalists, only the Marquis of Newcastle, in the north of England, retained his old command. By force of circumstance, rather than through choice, king and Parliament recognized the need to give greater responsibility to less nobly-born men who had practical experience of warfare or had proved their ability since the outbreak of fighting.

A popular misconception is that the armies of the English Civil War consisted almost entirely of amateurs who learnt the art of warfare by hard experience as they went along. This is a major over-statement. Although there was no standing army in Britain, the religious wars which had been in progress on the Continent throughout the period had attracted thousands of men from the British Isles, mainly, though not entirely, fighting for the Protestant cause. For many young English gentlemen, a few years' service with the long-established English Brigade in the Netherlands was seen as a normal part of their education.

For many others, particularly younger sons with no prospect of inheriting the family estates, the life of a soldier became a full-time career. Hundreds of Englishmen, and even greater numbers of Scots followed this course, serving with most of the major European armies. On the outbreak of Civil War many of these, either scenting profitable employment or through personal conviction, returned home and enlisted with king or Parliament.

1

The result was that most regiments raised in the opening months of the war contained at least a sprinkling of officers with previous military experience of some kind. While most of the rank-and-file may have had no more than some form of training with their local Trained Band, there were enough veterans available to fairly rapidly inculcate them with military basics.

However in 1642, on the Royalist side, only the king's principal field force – known to historians as the 'Oxford Army' – had professional soldiers in most of its key positions. None of the regional commanders, with the partial exception of the Earl of Newcastle, had any previous experience, and this would be amply demonstrated by their inadequate performance during the first year of war. By the end of 1643 a process had begun by which men from slightly humbler backgrounds, but with greater military experience and proven ability, began to assume more senior commands. The trend was paralleled in the Parliamentarian armies, and ultimately, with the formation of the New Model Army in 1645, carried further than in the Royalist forces.

The majority of the king's most able generals were men with military experience prior to the war. Of the thirteen individuals discussed here, only King Charles and Newcastle were relative military innocents on the outbreak of war. Of the rest, Princes Rupert and Maurice, Sir Richard Grenville, George Goring, Jacob Astley, Henry Wilmot and the Earl of Forth were effectively professional soldiers. John Byron, Ralph Hopton and Montrose had more limited, but significant, previous experience. This pattern was echoed among the rest of the king's senior commanders.

The reasons for their appointments varied. Although they had some European service behind them, Prince Rupert and Maurice owed their rapid rise initially to their royal birth, and both were arguably eventually promoted too far. Men like Newcastle, Byron, Montrose and Hopton were important more for their regional and local influence than for their previous military experience, though that was an added advantage. Forth, Goring, Wilmot and Astley were professional soldiers appointed for their expertise and experience. Sir Richard Grenville, ever the exception, was a thoroughgoing professional soldier who also had huge influence in his native Cornwall.

It is worth spending a little time in examining the role of a seventeenth-century general. Few specialized in the modern sense. Though each might have individual talents – Rupert, Maurice, Goring, Wilmot and Byron as cavalry commanders, Astley in leading foot – a Civil War army commander was expected to fulfill a variety of responsibilities. In theory, all of the Royalist generals came under the ultimate command of King Charles I as Captain General. In practice, because of the slowness and uncertainty of communications between Oxford (Royalist capital for most of the war) and the more distant regions under Royalist control, most commanders enjoyed a great deal of independence. Newcastle in the north was indeed recognized as having authority virtually equal to that of the king. While Charles and his Council of War might issue general strategic directives or wishes, they could have little control over frequently fast-moving operational matters. Given this, and the defects of Charles's own personality, it was easy for an independently-minded general like Goring or Grenville to operate largely to his own agenda. Even in the north Newcastle had little direct control over some of his more distant commanders, such as the Earl of Derby in Lancashire and 'Blind Harry' Hastings, Lord Loughborough, in the Midlands.

It was normal practice, before a general took any major decisions, for him to consult a Council of War made up of the senior officers in his command. Yet there was no onus on a general to follow the advice given to him. Prince Rupert, for example, often ignored or overrode the suggestions of his subordinates, with disastrous results at Marston Moor, and perhaps Naseby. The king's own Council of War was frequently so riddled with dissent as to be ineffective.

This degree of independence was a major test of a commander. Some, like Rupert, were not in any case 'team players' and flourished best when operating away from the king's direct control. Others, such as Prince Maurice, and to a lesser extent, Ralph Hopton and John Byron, faltered when given near-absolute authority. Some among our subjects, principally Goring and Grenville, exploited such situations for their own benefit.

Few generals had all-round ability. Rupert, Wilmot and Maurice were primarily cavalry commanders. Rupert had some success in army command, and was a notable strategist, but Maurice fared badly in higher command. Byron proved to possess the qualities required in a successful cavalry commander and governor of a besieged town, but was less suited to lead a field army. Goring was one of the outstanding cavalry leaders of the war, but a disastrous army commander. King Charles proved, apart from a brief interval in 1644, unsuited for the role of Captain General, and has a major responsibility for the Royalist defeat.

Of our generals, perhaps Astley and Montrose fared best. Astley displayed all-round competence in most roles he was asked to fill, while Montrose, though not without significant weaknesses, proved a generally capable independent commander in a testing situation.

As well as leading their troops in the field, Civil War generals were frequently expected to run the military administration of the areas under their command. This involved them in the delicate task of maintaining good relations with civilian authorities and populations. The Royalists, with less territory under their undisputed control than their opponents had, found this increasingly difficult as the war went on. In the short term, some of our generals, notably Rupert, Astley, Newcastle and Hopton, had qualified success in this role, though eventually their demands grew too great for the limited resources available. Others, like Byron, were usually on uneasy terms with the civilians who came under their control. Goring and Grenville, among our examples, had the usual disregard of professional soldiers for civilians, and placed the well-being of their troops above all else. Montrose regularly ravaged actual or potentially hostile territory, partly in an attempt to ensure its inhabitants' obedience and partly, lacking a secure base, as the only way in which he could maintain his soldiers.

Civil War armies, and consequently the battles in which they were engaged, were generally smaller than contemporary Continental examples. Only a handful of engagements of the First Civil War – Marston Moor, Edgehill, the two

Newburys and perhaps Naseby, approached the scale of some of the battles of the Thirty Years War. Consequently it was often possible, at least until his vision was obscured by the dense clouds of smoke produced by the use of black powder, for a general to be able to survey the entire battlefield. Before fighting began, usually in consultation with his senior officers, a general would deploy his troops, normally in accordance with a battle plan drawn up at the start of the campaign, and give orders for the broad conduct of the battle. However, once fighting actually began, a commanding general's ability to influence the course of events was usually limited. There were no clear rules regarding where he should position himself. While subordinate generals commanding foot or horse would be stationed with their own troops, a senior general often had a less clear role. Sometimes, as with Charles I at Naseby, he would be with his reserve, but it was common for him to become closely involved in the fighting. Rupert, at both Edgehill and Naseby, charged with his horse, while at Marston Moor neither he nor Newcastle were able to gain overall control of events.

It was in any case difficult for a commanding general in the fast-moving confusion of pitched battle, and usually with only a small staff, to exercise overall control. Most demanding in such situations was the role of a cavalry commander. He needed to be able to spot and exploit fleeting opportunities in battle, and the post might therefore seem more suited to younger men, like Rupert, Maurice and Goring. But in practice there were a number of successful older cavalry commanders. For the Royalists both Lord Byron and the 60-year-old Sir William Vaughan did well, while the best-known example of all is of course Oliver Cromwell.

Physical fitness was almost essential for a Civil War general. As well as fighting in battle, a commander had to be able to withstand the rigours of long marches in all kinds of weather. Rupert was well-known for his physique and strength, and King Charles overcame childhood disabilities to prove himself able to stand up to arduous campaigning. Other generals, however, found their careers ended or blighted by illness or injury. Prince Maurice was struck down by serious illness on at least two occasions during the war, and Ralph Hopton seems never to have regained his confidence after being injured in a powder explosion. Rather more prosaically, the elderly Earl of Forth, a notorious imbiber, eventually succumbed to the effects of gout, deafness and a fall from his horse. Goring's great talents declined largely because of the effects of drink, although he also suffered from lameness and possibly attacks of malaria contracted in Europe.

With most armies relatively small, there were plenty of opportunities for a commander to display his qualities of personal leadership, which might sometimes be enough to change the course of an action. So George Goring, noted for his readiness of mind in an emergency, was able to stem the advance of Cromwell's horse at Second Newbury by leading a well-timed counter-charge. Rupert was in the thick of the action on a number of occasions, though his intervention at Marston Moor, where he temporarily rallied his own fleeing Regiment of Horse with a cry of: 'Zwounds, do you run? Follow me!' was ultimately in vain. Byron was in his element in small-scale, hand-to-hand encounters. The elderly and unflamboyant Jacob Astley encouraged his foot at Edgehill with a well-chosen prayer. Montrose was able to rally wavering troops on more than one occasion, although King Charles's passive and remote personality made little impression on fleeing soldiers at Second Newbury and Naseby.

Despite their frequent involvement in fighting at close quarters, fatalities among Civil War generals were fairly rare. Although several of our subjects – including Maurice, Grenville, Byron and Wilmot – were wounded on one or more occasion, none were killed. Only one Royalist army commander – the 1st Earl of Northampton – was killed in action, although losses among officers at brigade level and below were much heavier. This was due in part to the inaccuracy and unreliability of firearms. Rupert, who was only wounded in the final days of the war, on more than one occasion escaped injury when an opponent's pistol misfired. Commanding generals probably often wore better body armour than inferior officers, making edged weapons less effective against them, or, being mounted, were able to get clear of difficult situations. Significantly most injuries seem to have occurred to the head, if a helmet was lost, or to the thighs or legs, unprotected by armour.

Ultimately, a general's success rested largely upon how he was viewed by his men. Rupert and Maurice were admired and emulated by the younger officers and men who served under them, mainly because of their dash and bravery in action. Goring and Wilmot gained popularity through a combination of charm and good fellowship. Montrose had their charisma and personal magnetism without their wild living. Hopton, Grenville and to a lesser extent Byron, though tough disciplinarians, were known to endeavour to take care of their soldiers' needs. The dour and fearsome Langdale won the devotion of his Northern troopers by sharing their hardships and their stubborn independence. Charles, as always, was lacking in the necessary qualities. His officers might revere his role as monarch, but few had warm affection for the man, while his common soldiers hardly knew him.

One of the most enduring popular historical legends is of the plumed and ribboned roistering devil-may-care 'Cavalier'. It is interesting to consider just how few of our commanders actually fitted that image. Astley and Forth were hard-bitten professional soldiers, with little of the romantic about them. Byron was noted for his learning and love of books, as was Newcastle. Hopton was a devout and solid middle-aged man. Montrose had considerable charisma, but was no roisterer. King Charles's private life was exemplary, and his inspirational qualities virtually nil. Prince Maurice was regarded by many as boorish, while Rupert, often held up as the epitome of the Cavalier of legend, while certainly brave and dashing, was apparently generally restrained in his personal life, fairly humourless and intolerant of dissent.

Only three of our subjects seem even partly to conform to the popular image. Grenville, with his love of sparkish dress, and sardonic wit, has some resemblance to a dark version of the legend. Goring certainly possessed in abundance the charm and love of wild living, but he lacked generosity of spirit and loyalty of character. Closest of all, perhaps, was Harry Wilmot, that slightly buffoonish figure, who loved horses, drink, women and good fellowship, who fought with foolhardy bravery, quarrelled and duelled, and through all the trials and tribulations of a chequered career, remained to the end a dedicated if sometimes confused servant of the House of Stuart.

Chapter Two
King Charles and Lord Forth

THE sculptor Bernini is said to have commented of a portrait of Charles I that he had never seen a face 'which showed so much greatness, and withal, such marks of sadness and misfortune'. Charles seemed to have been born to misfortune. A delicate and sickly child, with a stammer which he never fully overcame, Charles, as second son to King James I, had never been expected to ascend the throne. Only the unexpected death of his charismatic elder brother, Prince Henry, in 1612, thrust him into a role for which by character and training he was singularly ill-equipped.

Few who knew Charles doubted either his sincerely-held beliefs or his good intentions. By nature deeply religious, serious and a patron of the arts, Charles, through sheer determination, overcame physical disadvantages to become a skilled horseman, who during the Civil War rode hundreds of miles in all weathers. Few questioned his personal courage either. Although never a fighting soldier, Charles invariably displayed calmness and resolution on the battlefield, while his conduct at his trial and execution in 1649 won admiration from eye-witnesses.

Unfortunately Charles never developed any real skills in relating to those outside his close intimate circle. His natural shyness was masked by an aloof formality which often seemed cold indifference. Small and slight, and always impeccably dressed, Charles maintained the dignity and aura of monarchy, but gave it little warmth or appeal. His underlying lack of self-confidence and his poor personal skills made Charles rely heavily on the judgement of his current favourite, or to be unduly influenced by the views of the last person he spoke with, and to be duplicitous in order to avoid unpleasant confrontations. This made for intrigue and unclear policy in peace, and lack of firm decision-making in war.

Although usually deeply loyal to the handful of people whom he really trusted – his wife, Queen Henrietta Maria, his first favourite, the Duke of Buckingham, Strafford (for whose execution by Parliament Charles never forgave himself) and, until 1645, his nephew, Prince Rupert – Charles never developed many other close relationships. He tended to treat the service of others as a right, not as something to be earned and nurtured, and the queen warned her husband: 'If you do not take care of those who suffer for you, you are lost.'

Approach to war

Charles's actions in the years leading up to Civil War lie outside the scope of this study, except in so far as they impinge on military matters. Most of the king's policies were influenced by his belief in the Divine Right of Kings – that monarchs were appointed by, and ultimately only answerable to, God. This led to the development of a centralized, paternalistic system of government which eventually attempted to dispense with the services of a frequently obstructive Parliament and became known as 'Personal Rule'.

As a result of unsuccessful foreign adventures, legally dubious methods of raising revenue, and above all, a religious policy which could easily be misrepresented by opponents as an intention to reintroduce Catholicism, Charles managed to alienate many of the country's most influential interest groups.

Matters came to a head in 1638 with the king's attempt to impose the English Prayer Book on his predominantly Presbyterian kingdom of Scotland. The result was a national uprising, and two brief conflicts – known as the Bishops' Wars – ensued after the king's attempts to impose his will by force. The two wars provided Charles, as nominal Captain General (commander-in-chief) of the English army, with his first practical military experience. They were an object lesson in how not to fight a war, but the problems encountered provided invaluable lessons for some of the king's future Civil War commanders, if not necessarily for Charles himself.

The humiliation of defeat in the Bishops' Wars brought confrontation between the king and his English opponents much closer. The crisis had forced him to recall Parliament, which, sensing its advantage, pushed through increasing numbers of measures that would remove most of the monarch's real powers.

The war begins

By the summer of 1642, thanks in part to a reaction by many moderates against the Parliamentarian radicals' more extreme proposals, Charles had increased his support. As violence spread, Civil War was formalized by the raising of the Royal Standard at Nottingham on 22 August.

Almost as much as in medieval times, a monarch was expected to provide personal leadership. On 23 October, the morning of the Battle of Edgehill, Charles told his troops: 'your King is both your cause, your quarrel and your Captain!' One modern writer suggests that he actually welcomed the outbreak of war:

> Ultimately Charles found war a simple answer to a complex problem; it brought the relief that always seemed to come from action. War was direct; it did not engender the same sense of guilt that compromise produced; it was a matter of black and white, of friend and foe.[1]

Charles himself stated baldly at the start of the war; 'My aim is to fight for my crown and my dignity'[2], and in October, before Edgehill, an eyewitness remarked: 'I never saw the King look better, he is very cheerful'.

But this perhaps over-simplifies Charles's complex personality. Politically, he had no aim other than to vanquish his opponents. But he found the reality of war horrifying. He was sickened by the carnage of Edgehill, and he repeatedly attempted, usually ineffectively, to ameliorate its worst effects, sometimes with adverse effects on Royalist strategy. In August 1643, for example, aghast at the high casualties suffered in Rupert's recent successful assault on Bristol, he forbade a similar attempt on Gloucester. On several occasions, the king tried to moderate the more ruthless actions of his commanders.[3] He would spasmodically attempt to curb the indiscipline of his troops, finding theft from churches particularly offensive, and order efforts to care for the sick and wounded, though he was often unable to provide the resources for this to be done properly. He also disliked the suffering of what he regarded as the deluded soldiers of his opponents. When, in September 1644, the unpopular and pompous Secretary at War, Sir Edward Walker, jested about the rough handling administered by Royalist troops to Parliamentarian soldiers captured at Lostwithiel, the king retorted angrily: 'Fie upon you. That was ill-said and worse done!'[4]

'Pater Rottwein'

Despite his lack of experience, the outbreak of war automatically made Charles Captain General of the Royalist forces. Charles took this duty, like most others, extremely seriously, marching with his army on campaign and presiding regularly over his Council of War. He did, however, recognize his own inexperience. The well-tried solution, which Charles adopted, was to appoint a Lord General (in modern parlance a Chief of Staff) who would act as his military adviser, and be responsible for much of the day-to-day control of the army.

Charles's first choice was the Earl of Lyndsey, an elderly courtier whose military experience was well in the past. Lyndsey probably recognized his limitations. It is usually suggested that he resigned in a huff on the morning of Edgehill in protest at Prince Rupert's interference in the deployment of the army, but it may well be that Lyndsey was not unwilling to go.

His replacement, who would serve Charles during the next two critical years, was an altogether more able and colourful character. Patrick Ruthven was a prime example of that ubiquitous seventeenth-century military figure, the Scottish professional soldier. Born in 1573, the son of a minor Scottish gentleman, Ruthven followed many of his contemporaries in opting for a military life. In 1606 he left Scotland to enter Swedish service, and by 1616 he was a colonel of Scots horse. Gustavus Adolphus knighted Ruthven following the battle of Dirschau (1627) and valued him not least for being 'one who could drink immeasurably and preserve his understanding to the last', and so extract information from the inebriated. It was because of his fondness for the bottle that Ruthven, a bluff, powerfully built ruddy-featured man, earned the nickname in Germany of 'Pater Rottwein.' Ruthven evidently had an eye for the ladies, marrying three times. His first wife is unknown, his second was the daughter of a Scottish comrade, and the third was a German lady, Clara Berner of Mecklenberg.

Ruthven was a skilled soldier, with a wide knowledge of siege warfare and pyrotechnics. In 1638, after being Governor of Ulm in Germany for several years, the mounting crisis in the British Isles led to Ruthven returning home to serve Charles I as Muster-Master in Scotland. In 1639, in recognition of his support, he was made Baron Ruthven of Etterick, and in 1639, as renewed fighting loomed, was appointed Governor of Edinburgh castle. The fortress was seen as vital, not only as a symbol of royal power, but as a means of dominating the city of Edinburgh. Ruthven believed the Covenanters would attack it prior to launching an invasion of England, and saw the castle as a threat to their rear if they crossed the Border. Knowing that the enemy had him under close watch, Ruthven stealthily reinforced his garrison by smuggling in, two or three at a time, troops disguised as sailors. Powder and arms were brought in hidden in beer casks.

Ruthven faced serious difficulties. Most of his garrison were Lowland Scots, of uncertain loyalty, and as they had to purchase their food supplies from the citizens, there was a good deal of fraternization. To add to his problems, part of the castle defences collapsed during the winter, and the Scots were unwilling to provide materials for their repair. As spring approached, tensions mounted, with the garrison suffering abuse whenever they left the castle.

Hostilities finally commenced in May 1640, when Ruthven's guns opened fire on the city, killing an estimated thirty civilians. Cut off from outside assistance, Ruthven held out until 15 September, when, without water, having suffered 200 casualties and himself stricken with scurvy which cost him most of his teeth, he surrendered.

He remained committed to the Royalist cause, and early in 1642 went to Germany, supposedly on a private visit, but actually to recruit for the king from among his old comrades-in-arms. He rejoined Charles at Shrewsbury in September, bringing with him twenty-two experienced officers, and was created Earl of Forth by a grateful monarch.

Forth (as he will now be known) spent several weeks training recruits, before being appointed Lord General on the morning of Edgehill. His first task was to assist Rupert and Sir Jacob Astley, Major General of Foot, in forming up the army in the Swedish style of deployment which they preferred to the Dutch formations advocated by Lyndsey.

During the next two years Forth would play an important, if not always clear, role in Royalist strategy. Contemporary sources tend not to differentiate between the decisions and actions of the king and those of Forth. Propagandists understandably gave most of the credit for success to Charles, while Forth was evidently a fairly reticent character. He was also not particularly well-liked by the king's civilian advisers and Clarendon painted an acidic portrait of the Lord General:

> The general, though he had been without doubt a very good officer, and had great experience, and was still a man of unquestionable courage and integrity, yet he was now much decayed in all his parts, and, with the long continued custom of immoderate drinking, dozed in his understanding, which had never been quick and vigorous; he having been always illiterate to the greatest degree that can be imagined. He was now become very deaf, yet often pretended not to have heard what he did not then contradict, and thought fit afterwards to disclaim. He was a man of few words, and of great compliance, and usually delivered as his opinion which he foresaw would be grateful to the King.[5]

Clarendon was writing about the situation early in 1644, when Forth's faculties may have deteriorated, but it appears that for most of the war he fulfilled his duties competently enough, handling the routine administration of the Oxford Army, and providing military advice when needed. He also, at least initially, acted as field commander, though the king took an increasingly active interest in these matters as the war went on.

The high command

Forth's tendency to keep a low profile assisted him in maintaining usually amicable relations with Prince Rupert. If he was frustrated by the wide powers which Charles conferred on his nephew, including the right of direct appeal to the king over the heads of the Lord General and the Council of War, Forth evidently kept his views to himself. Given the convoluted fashion in which Charles operated, he perhaps had no other option.

After the Royalist advance on London stalled in the autumn of 1642, Charles was faced with the unwelcome prospect of a long war. A more formalized chain of command was required for the expanding Royalist forces around Oxford. But the king, and by implication Forth, never established a clear system, instead leaving matters to evolve more or less in piecemeal fashion. A multitude of committees, often with ill-defined powers, gradually appeared, confusion which was mirrored in some of the commissions issued to individual commanders.

In theory overall control rested with the Council of War, headed by the king himself, the most regular attendee at its meetings, and with whom final decisions rested. The incomplete nature of the surviving records makes a full assessment of the Council's role impossible, but certain salient features are clear. Like similar councils of lesser commanders, it had no executive powers, and was intended to act as an advisory body to the king. In Oxford it customarily met in the king's quarters in Christchurch College, and on campaign wherever appropriate. Its membership varied, but normally consisted of the senior officers of the Oxford Army, the Lord General, General and Lieutenant General of Horse and the Major

General of Foot, and some civilian officials, together with currently favoured courtiers such as the king's cousin, the Duke of Richmond, who held no formal position in army or government. Also called on as required were various 'experts', usually lower-ranking army officers.

Generally numbering between ten and seventeen, the role of the Council varied according to circumstances. On campaign, where its numbers were generally fewer, it might meet on a daily basis to discuss logistical and immediate military questions. In Oxford, when military decisions were less pressing, meetings took place once or twice a week and were mainly administrative in nature. Increasingly, aspects of this work were hived off to other committees, whose actual standing was sometimes unclear.

The effectiveness of the Council of War was limited by two major factors. Its authority never really extended beyond Oxford and the West Midlands, and did not really operate at all in Newcastle's northern command, while regional commanders were not always co-operative. The Royalist Council of War would never achieve the overall control gained by the Parliamentarian Committee of Both Kingdoms in the later stages of the war.

This lack of authority was partly the result of communication difficulties, but the overriding factor was the king himself. All important decision-making revolved around Charles. Without his approval no significant order could take effect, and decisions were increasingly made by the king without reference to most, or at times any, of his councillors. In the intrigue-ridden Royalist Court the opportunities for cliques, interest groups or even forceful individuals to put their case directly to the king were endless. Charles's well-known tendency to be unduly influenced by his current favourite, and his preference for subterfuge and behind-the-scenes dealing, led to a dangerous lack of continuity and clear decision-making. Open discussion was increasingly replaced by intrigue.

In 1644 Arthur Trevor warned Prince Rupert: 'persuasion avails little at Court, where always the orator convinces sooner than the argument', while Queen Henrietta Maria, who after her arrival at Oxford in July 1643, took full advantage of what she criticized, chided the king that 'If a person speaks to you boldly, you refuse nothing.'

One result of the king's failings was growing enmity and division among his councillors. Initially the main problems were caused by Prince Rupert's assumption of powers and responsibilities outside his role as General of Horse. As the king's favoured confidante during the first year of the war, his views often held sway over those of the remainder of the Council. While some officers, such as Forth and Astley, seem to have been willing to go along with this, others including the ambitious Wilmot, Lieutenant General of Horse, and many of the civilian councillors, increasingly resented exclusion from decision-making.

Although Rupert was absent from Oxford for several weeks in the spring of 1643, on his return he resumed a dominant role in Royalist strategy, which continued until the arrival of the queen in July, and the aftermath of the capture of Bristol. The situation began to change after the decision of the king, supported by his Council of War, to lay siege to Gloucester. After Charles, fearful of a repeat of the losses suffered at Bristol, refused him permission to storm the town, Rupert withdrew from active direction of the siege, which passed to Forth. The latter, along with other experienced officers, assured the king that Gloucester would fall within ten days, but operations dragged on indecisively. It is difficult to apportion blame for this; the Royalists had supply problems and were hindered in their mining operations by bad weather, but there seems also to have been lack of drive. A characteristic episode took place after the Earl of Essex had relieved Gloucester early in September and had set off back on the road to London. Chafing to take up the pursuit, after waiting in vain all day for orders, an angry Rupert went in search of Charles, and found him, Forth, and the General of the Ordnance, Lord Percy, peacefully playing piquet in the king's quarters.

Throughout this period, Charles appears to have played a fairly passive role in military operations. At Gloucester he spent most of his time either in his quarters several miles from the siege works, or back in Oxford engaged with political affairs, nor is there any record of his playing an active role at the First Battle of Newbury in September, other than characteristically issuing an order after the battle to the Mayor of Newbury for the care of the wounded, without providing him with the necessary resources.

The disappointing outcome of the 1643 campaign caused fierce recriminations among the Royalist leadership. A more inspirational commander than Charles might have been able to rally his followers and restore morale, but the king allowed himself to be drawn into the factional in-fighting:

> no man was more disquieted by them than the king himself, who in his person as well as in his business, suffered all the vexation of the rude and petulant and discontented humours of the Court and army.[6]

1644: search for a strategy

With the departure to the north of Rupert early in 1644, the situation began to change. Charles was feeling more confident in military matters. In the previous year he had put forward some ideas for general strategy, labelled 'my own child', which seem to have been tacitly ignored by Rupert and Forth.

Early in 1644, following a series of reverses suffered in Hampshire by Lord Hopton, Forth, as an old friend, was sent to him, nominally on a private visit, but actually to exert a watching brief. Typically, Charles failed to define his role clearly. As Clarendon relates:

> And the earl of Brentford [Forth], general of the army, who had a fast friendship with the Lord Hopton, expressing a great inclination to make him a visit rather than to sit still in his winter quarters, his Majesty being very glad,

and cherished the disposition, and was desirous that so great an officer might be present in an army upon which so many of his hopes depended, and which did not abound with officers of great experience. [Hopton] was exceedingly revived with the presence of the general, and desired to receive his orders, and that he would take upon him the absolute command of the troops; which he as positively refused to do, only offered to keep him company in all expeditions, and to give him the best assistance he was able; which the lord Hopton was compelled to be contented with: nor could there be a greater union and consent between two friends, the general being ready to give his advice upon all particulars, and the other doing nothing without communication with him, and then conforming to his opinion and giving orders accordingly.[7]

This might have been a comfortable arrangement for those involved, but it was not an ideal way in which to direct a campaign, and the dual leadership, malfunctioning on that occasion because Forth had been stricken with gout, was one of the factors in the reverse suffered by Hopton's forces on 29 March at Cheriton.

Clarendon held Cheriton to have been a disaster for the Royalists, which:

broke all the measures, and altered the whole scheme of the King's counsels: for whereas before he hoped to have entered the field early, and to have acted an offensive part, he now discerned he was wholly to be on the defensive part, and that likely to be a very hard part too.[8]

This is an over-simplification. Cheriton had not been a major defeat in terms of casualties. Much more serious for Royalist plans was the intervention of the Scots on Parliament's side. Charles should have known the inevitability of this ever since the signing of the Solemn League and Covenant between Parliament and the Scottish leadership in the previous September, but, lulled by the optimistic forecasts of the Marquis of Hamilton, the king, in one of his major blunders of the war, had chosen to discount the possibility until it was too late. As a result, he had been forced to divert Rupert northwards, and the need to support the Marquis of Newcastle would absorb most of the veteran troops from Ireland intended to strengthen the Oxford Army for the 1644 campaign.

Rupert's departure did nothing to ease tensions in the Council of War. Forth remained as unassertive as ever, and Lord Wilmot, free of the prince's dominating presence, began to exert his own views, and was quickly at loggerheads with the king's civilian advisers. As usual, Charles was unable to resolve the situation. In April, in a flying visit to Oxford, Rupert put forward a defensive strategy for the south, by which the king would concentrate on holding the garrisons around Oxford with his foot, supported by raiding cavalry, until the prince could settle matters in the north and come to his support. Charles accepted Rupert's plan, although there were good grounds for doubting its feasibility, as the Oxford Army lacked enough foot to hold these outposts securely.

Clarendon, however, felt that:

If this counsel had been pursued steadily and resolutely, it might probably have been attended with good success. But as it was even impossible to have administered such advice to the king, in the strait which he was in . . . so it was the unhappy temper of those who were called to these councils that resolutions taken upon full debate were seldom prosecuted with equal resolution and steadiness, but changed upon new shorter debates, and upon objections which had been answered before; some men being in their natures irresolute and full of objections, even after all was determined according to their own proposals; others being positive, and not to be altered from what they had once declared, how unreasonable soever, or what alterations there were soever in affairs. And the king himself frequently considered more the person who spoke, as he was in his graces or his prejudice, than the counsel itself that was given: and always suspect, or at least trusted less to, his own judgement, than he ought to have done; which rarely deceived him so much as that of other men.[9]

To add to the confusion, freed of the rather intimidating presence of Prince Rupert, Charles was showing signs of taking a more active role in military planning, which quickly led to misunderstanding with Forth.

KEY ACTION: THE OXFORD CAMPAIGN, 1644

On 10 April 1644, the southern Royalist forces had held a rendezvous at Aldbourne Chase, where they totalled 6,000 foot and just over 4,000 horse. At this stage, prior to the discussions with Prince Rupert, it had been intended to take the offensive in the south against the Parliamentarian army of Sir William Waller, and to avenge the defeat at Cheriton. The Parliamentarians, however, planned to use the armies of Waller and the Earl of Essex in combination to attack Oxford. As they were estimated to have a total strength of some 20,000 men, the Royalist strategy was plainly impracticable. In an effort to build up the strength of the army, Forth had on 11 April recommended the evacuation of Reading which he, correctly, regarded as indefensible. This proposal was of course vetoed in the plan put forward by Rupert, but on his departure, his strategy was almost immediately abandoned, as the king, swayed as usual by the arguments of those present, changed his mind, and on 18 May ordered Reading evacuated.

By now Essex and Waller were on the move, and Essex occupied Reading on 23 May. Two days later the Royalists also evacuated Abingdon, south of Oxford. Once again there were sound reasons, but the king, who was now taking an increasingly active role in military decision-making, was incensed that Forth had carried out the evacuation without waiting for his confirmation. A rift between the two was averted by placing the blame on Lord Wilmot.[10]

Essex occupied Abingdon on 26 May, and over the next few days the Parliamentarian forces steadily closed in on Oxford. On 28 May Essex managed to cross the Thames at Sandford Ferry, three and a half miles below the Royalist capital, and next day marched to Islip, six miles to the north-east, where he established his headquarters. His next objective was to get across the Cherwell and attack Oxford from the north, but for three days his attempts to force a crossing were beaten off.

Waller meanwhile was responsible for operations to the south of Oxford. He too was held back for several days, but on 1 June he succeeded in crossing the Thames at Newbridge, and could now advance on Oxford from the south.

The news reached the king at 1pm on 2 June, and, guarded by his Lifeguard of Horse, Charles rode to his nearby manor of Woodstock, centrally placed for his commanders in the field, and called a Council of War. There were two choices left to him, neither attractive. He could either stand siege in Oxford, with only a couple of weeks' supplies, or try to break out to the west. The Council was apparently divided, and in a short break from deliberations, Charles, showing either considerable *sang froid* or lack of imagination, went hunting and killed two bucks.

By the time the Council was resumed later in the day, the situation had deteriorated further, with news that Waller's horse were now advancing north of the Thames. To avoid their being trapped, Charles ordered the foot defending the Cherwell crossings to pull back into Oxford. On the first of several occasions that summer, he spent the night in his coach in a field in the midst of his army, and next day returned to Oxford, where a final decision on his next move was now urgent.

> And now in human probability the Rebels had his Majesty, his Children, his Army, this City, and all those who with the hazard of their lives and expense of their fortunes had so long stuck unto his Majesty and the justice of his cause, even in their power and possession; and this [passage added by Charles I] was so much apprehended even by some of eminency, that at this time, his Majesty's yielding upon conditions to the Rebels, was proffered him by one and but one of those whom he privately consulted that evening (which was rejected with Scorn) about the Resolution which he then took.[11]

According to Clarendon, Charles, showing great resolution and coolness in this time of crisis, commented that 'possibly he might be found in the hands of the Earl of Essex, but he would be dead first.'[12]

Presumably working closely with Forth and Wilmot, Charles devised the high-risk strategy of breaking out of Oxford that night with the horse and 2,500 picked musketeers, slipping between the two encroaching Parliamentarian armies and heading west across the Cotswolds to Worcester.

Aided by feints by the rest of the Oxford Army towards Abingdon, which distracted Waller for a few critical hours, Charles, at 9pm on 3 June, 'that never to be forgotten evening', set off on his perilous march. Essex had failed to guard a critical crossing point of the River Evenlode between Bladon and Long Harborough. Once across this, the Royalists were out of immediate danger of being trapped, though not from pursuit. Throughout the next two days, the king, with only brief rests for himself and his weary troops, pressed on through rain squalls and hail storms, via Northleach, Burford, Bourton-on-the-Water and

Broadway, over the Cotswolds to Evesham, where they arrived on the evening of 5 June – 'which was the first night's rest of our Army'.[13]

From here, on a false report that Waller had reached Broadway in pursuit, the Royalists marched next day to the greater security of Worcester. Though he had evaded the Parliamentarian trap, the king still risked pursuit and destruction by the greatly superior Parliamentarian forces. He was saved by the blunders of his opponents and the decision of Essex, on 6 June, to leave the king to Waller, while he took his own army into the west.

It would be some days before the king at Worcester was aware of this unlooked for reprieve. On 9 June Rupert's friend, the Duke of Richmond, told the prince: 'we want money, men, conduct, diligence and good counsel.' With Waller now at Evesham, Charles continued northwards up the River Severn to Bewdley, sending some cavalry in a feint towards Bridgnorth as if he were planning to continue northwards to join Rupert.

In fact the Council of War was divided regarding its next move. A sub-committee, consisting of Forth, and half a dozen others, met over two days, but could not decide between the options of joining Rupert or returning to Worcester and then attempt to rejoin the remainder of the Oxford Army and bring Waller to battle. The decision was left to the king, who on 14 June, decided on the second option. On the same day he sent a fateful directive to Rupert, ordering him to relieve York and defeat the Allied armies besieging it as quickly as possible, and then return to join him. Charles, in the meantime, would 'make a shift (upon the defensive) to spin out time until you come to assist me.'[14]

Though the order would play a major part in bringing about the great Royalist defeat at Marston Moor, it at least represented a coherent strategy, and was probably the best option available. Shipping his foot back down the Severn to Worcester by boat, Charles moved rapidly. Waller had now marched northwards along the river to Stourbridge, and on an assurance that he was still there, the king on 16 June crossed the Avon again at Evesham, and by evening was back on the crest of the Cotswolds at Broadway. Early on 17 June he reached Chipping Campden 'where we had time to breathe and look about us.'[15]

The worst was over; on 17 June Waller, in belated pursuit, admitted to the Committee of Both Kingdoms that he could not overtake the king. On 21 June Charles joined forces with the rest of the Oxford Army, giving him a total of 6,000 foot and 4–5,000 horse, and could anticipate battle with Waller with some confidence.

For the moment, halted around Buckingham, the king's main concerns were once again dissensions among his own commanders, with Wilmot in particular growing steadily more dissatisfied.[16] An increasingly rancorous dispute regarding the feasibility of an advance on London, coupled with the offer of peace terms to Parliament, favoured by Wilmot, was ended by the arrival of Waller, who, on 29 June, in a scrambling encounter at Cropredy Bridge in Oxfordshire, was sufficiently mauled to put him out of action for the remainder of the summer.

The spring campaign had ended much more favourably for the king than had seemed likely at its outset. It is difficult to see, given the distractions of the war in the north, and the limited resources available in the south, that Charles could have adopted a more advantageous strategy. If he had partly been saved by the blunders of his opponents, the king, perhaps because he was free of the overpowering presence of Prince Rupert, had played a weak hand with considerable coolness and skill. It was probably thanks to Charles, more than any other single individual, that the Royalists avoided a major reverse, which, on top of Marston Moor, might well have proved fatal.

Victory in the west: Lostwithiel

With Waller out of action, the king and his Council had space to consider their next move, though, with confirmation of the defeat at Marston Moor, their strategy was once again in doubt. The decision to pursue Essex was reached for two reasons; firstly the lack of any more attractive alternative, and secondly the concern of the king for his wife and new-born daughter in Exeter.

On 12 July Lord Digby informed Rupert:

> There remains nothing for us to do but to go westwards, since your Highness have not had good fortunes in your late action, we should be cooped up and have no way out of Wales to the West. Prince Maurice has a gallant army, equal with Essex . . . If we get to join him before Waller overtake us, we shall be likely to crush him between us.[17]

Forth was becoming unsuited for the demands of active operations. In tribute to his services, on 27 May he had been created Earl of Brentford, but it may be that the demands of the next few weeks of arduous campaigning had proved a sore trial to the gout-stricken old man. Clarendon felt that:

> General Ruthven . . . both by reason of his age and his extreme deafness, was not a man of counsel or of words; hardly conceived what was proposed, and as confusedly and obscurely delivered his opinion, and could indeed better judge by his eye than his ear, and in the field well knew what was to be done.[18]

Charles had been planning to replace Forth with Prince Rupert, but events in the north meant that the change would not be effected until the end of the campaigning season.

While Charles had been sparring with Waller, Essex had continued his march westwards, Maurice falling back before him and avoiding action until he could be joined by the king. The Parliamentarian commander now made his fateful decision to continue west in order to relieve Plymouth and subdue Cornwall, thus obligingly placing himself in a trap. On 26 July the king and Maurice linked up near Exeter, having a combined strength of about 5,000 horse and 10,000 foot,

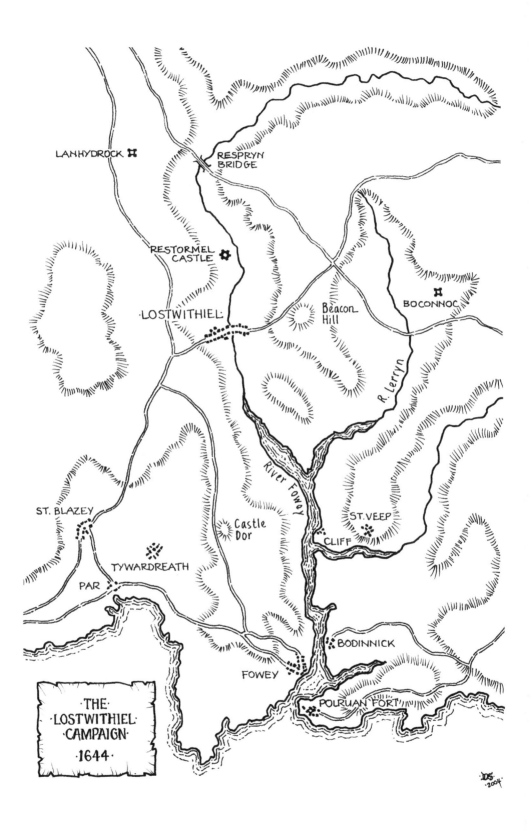

LANHYDROCK ✠

RESPRYN BRIDGE

RESTORMEL CASTLE ✿

LOSTWITHIEL

Beacon Hill

BOCONNOC ✠

R. Lerryn

River Fowey

ST. BLAZEY

Castle Dor

ST. VEEP

CLIFF

TYWARDREATH

PAR

BODINNICK

FOWEY

POLRUAN FORT

THE LOSTWITHIEL CAMPAIGN 1644

DS 2004

and outnumbering Essex by about two to one. By 10 August they had been reinforced by Sir Richard Grenville's small Cornish force, and had Essex completely hemmed in with his back to the sea, around Lostwithiel and Fowey. Nevertheless, the Parliamentarian commander still hoped to be relieved by land and supplied by sea, and excellent defensive terrain meant that his resistance was likely to be prolonged.

The Royalists were faced with a difficult operation, involving the supply of some 18,000 men, and the need to co-ordinate operations across a wide front. Details of how this was done are frustratingly scarce, but Forth's vast experience must have proved invaluable, especially in such matters as arranging for regular supplies of food and ammunition to be conveyed from Exeter and Dartmouth. Success was by no means total; the operation to reduce Essex lasted for almost a month, and as time went by there were increasing problems, with Royalist troops leaving the ranks to forage in the surrounding countryside. This was cause for concern; the king and his commanders were acutely aware of the need to keep the support of the Cornish population, and orders were issued against looting and straggling, with the death penalty threatened for transgressions, though it is unclear whether this was actually imposed.

Forth knew that an immediate frontal assault on Essex's positions was likely to be a costly business, and so during the following weeks the Royalists mounted a series of limited offensives with the aim of gradually confining the Parliamentarians into a smaller area, and denying them use of the port of Fowey. Continuing bad weather prevented Essex receiving supplies by sea, while a small relief column was repulsed in Somerset.

On 21 August, with active operations apparently largely directed by Prince Maurice, who as commander of the Western Army worked closely with Forth, the Royalists mounted a large-scale assault designed to clear the enemy from the commanding position of Beacon Hill, overlooking Lostwithiel. By the end of the day, meeting with little co-ordinated resistance from Essex, all objectives had been secured.

Although Charles and his commanders were aware from the reports of deserters of low morale among Essex's men, and that they were short of supplies and provisions, the Royalists were equally concerned about the continuing desertions among their own men, and the effects of prolonged exposure to cold wet weather. Although the king was anxious to strike a decisive blow, he was delayed for several days awaiting a re-supply of ammunition from Dartmouth.

It was not until 31 August that the Royalists were ready to strike, after suffering an annoying reverse when the Parliamentarian horse managed to slip through their badly extended cordon and reach the safety of Plymouth. The final stages of the fighting consisted of a series of closely-fought engagements in the small hedged fields to the north of Fowey, and a determined Parliamentarian stand on higher ground around the ancient earthwork of Castle Dor. This saw some of the most fiercely contested actions of the campaign, and Charles himself, in a notable departure from previous battles, was closely involved. With his Lifeguard he took part in the pursuit of the retreating Parliamentarian foot as they fell back towards

Fowey. He was close enough to witness one of the dramatic incidents of the day when at about 1pm:

> Captain [Edward] Brett led up the Queen's troop, and most gallantly in view of the King charged their foot and beat them from their hedge, killing many of them, notwithstanding their muskets made abundance of shot at his men: he received a shot in the left arm in the first field, and one of his men, La Plume, a Frenchman, killed, yet most gallantly went on and brought his men off . . . he retreated to be dressed, and the King called him and took his sword which was drawn in his hand, and knighted Sir Edward Brett on his horse's back.[19]

With Parliamentarian resistance obviously on the point of collapse, it is tempting to think that Charles was enjoying himself. At the end of the day, as firing died down, Captain Richard Symonds and the Lifeguard were:

> drawn into the next close but one, where his Majesty was . . . This night the King lay under the hedge with his servants in one field. The troops of Lifeguards lay in the next, it being very windy, and cross wind for Essex shipping of his men, and rained much and great storms.[20]

During the night Essex fled in a fishing boat, and next day, Phillip Skippon, commanding the abandoned Parliamentarian infantry, agreed to terms by which his men were disarmed and supposedly given safe conduct to Portsmouth. Much to the king's distress, the terms were dishonoured, with his troops, ignoring his own efforts to prevent them, looting the Parliamentarians as they marched off. Once the local country folk had taken their own revenge, less than half of Essex's foot eventually reached their own territory.

Rupert takes command

If Lostwithiel had been a high point for King Charles, the campaign leading up to the Second Battle of Newbury (27 October) saw him display some of his worst characteristics. Although he had agreed with Prince Rupert not to fight a battle until the latter could reinforce him and take over command from Forth, Charles then allowed himself to be persuaded by his newly appointed General of Horse, George Goring, and Lord Digby to advance to Newbury and take up a defensive position there with a greatly weakened army to face the combined Parliamentarian armies of Essex, Waller and the Earl of Manchester. Only the skill of subordinate officers, in particular George Goring and George Lisle, staved off defeat. Charles himself was once again close to the action, displaying, as after Lostwithiel, his unremarkable powers of personal leadership when he failed to rally some fleeing troops.

Forth was wounded in the action, but after receiving some hasty first aid in nearby Donnington Castle, he performed his last major service for the king by organizing, with Prince Maurice, a successful extrication of the Royalist army under cover of darkness.

Forth himself was less fortunate. During the retreat to Bath, a Parliamentarian commander, Colonel John Birch, received information that Forth was nearby with his wife and her maids in a coach, and, of particular interest, a wagon loaded with his personal effects, including plate. In a hasty charge the Parliamentarians routed Forth's escort, though Forth and his staff were able to escape into the surrounding fields. They were apparently not Birch's main concern. Riding on, he was able to capture the elderly Lady Forth, her coach and the baggage wagon, and bear them off in triumph to a highly embarrassed Earl of Manchester, who ordered their release, though not before Birch had quietly removed one or two pieces of plate for his personal use.

At about this time, Forth reportedly broke his shoulder in a fall from his horse, and on 6 November he resigned his command in favour of Prince Rupert. Clarendon, for all his dislike of Forth, did not view the change favourably:

> The army was less united than ever; the old general was set aside, and prince Rupert put into the command, which was no popular change: for the other was known to be an officer of great experience, and had committed no over-sights in his conduct; was willing to hear every thing debated, and always concurred with the most reasonable opinion; and though he was not of many words, and was not quick in hearing, yet upon any action he was sprightly, and commanded well.[21]

It is a fair tribute to this unsung old Scottish soldier to note that while under his command the Oxford Army never suffered a major defeat. Afterwards it never won a major victory.

Forth would not see active service again. Early in 1645 he went with the Prince of Wales to the west as one of his Council of experienced advisers. Accompanying the Prince to France in 1646 as his Chamberlain, Forth would continue to work for the Royalist cause, buying arms in Sweden, and in 1650 accompanying Charles II to Scotland. The Scottish Parliament declined to make use of his services, so Forth retired to Dundee, where he died on 2 February 1651.

Disaster at Naseby

For Charles the remaining months of the First Civil War were ones of steadily mounting disaster. The problems experienced when Prince Rupert had previously been with the Oxford Army resurfaced. He was now, at least in theory, in a position of overall authority, but the divisions among the different factions in the king's Council grew to new heights. As ever, Charles proved unable to resolve the differences, particularly those between Rupert and Digby, and his equivocal and ineffectual approach not only undermined much of Rupert's authority, but continued to prevent any clear-cut strategy being consistently followed.

Matters came to a head during the Naseby campaign, when the king's failure to follow an agreed strategy played a major part in the Royalist army being brought to battle on 14 June in a situation of disadvantage and against Rupert's wishes. Even during the battle Charles continued to equivocate. Left in effective command of the reserve, he attempted to commit it in support of the hard-pressed Royalist foot under attack by Cromwell. In reality it is unlikely that they could have affected the outcome, and Charles might well have been killed or captured. Certainly one of his attendants thought as much; the reserve were already showing signs of wavering when:

> The King . . . was even upon the point of charging the enemy, in the head of his guards, when the Earl of Carnwath, who rode next to him (a man never suspected for infidelity, nor one from whom the King would have received counsel in such a case), on a sudden laid his hand on the bridle of the King's horse, and swearing two or three full-mouthed Scots oaths said: 'Will you go upon your death in an instant?', and before his majesty understood what he would have, turned his horse round; upon which word ran through the troops that they should march to the right hand: which was both from charging the enemy or assisting their own men. And upon this, they all turned their horse and rode upon the spur, as if they were every man to shift for himself.[22]

Characteristically King Charles had once again failed to act decisively at a critical moment. His role in the battle ended in a disorderly flight from the field in which he narrowly escaped capture.

Charles and his cavalry spent most of the remaining months of the war in increasingly desperate quartering of the Midlands, Wales and the north, during which the king probably saw more of his kingdom and the lives of his ordinary subjects than he had in the rest of his reign. Militarily, however, it was largely irrelevant, especially following the defeat suffered by the Royalist horse at Rowton Heath on 24 September.

In May 1646, recognizing the inevitable, Charles I surrendered to the Scots. The military career of King Charles was over. For the most part it had been an undistinguished one. Only in the spring of 1644 had Charles really shown the firmness and resolution required of a successful commander. Otherwise, apart from some displays of personal bravery of a somewhat passive kind, he had utterly failed in the key responsibilities of a commander-in-chief to act with firmness and resolution, control and resolve differences among his subordinates, and stick to an agreed strategy.

Clarendon, perhaps a little too charitably, said of Charles:

> the most signal parts of his misfortunes proceeded most from the modesty of his nature, which kept him from trusting himself enough, and made him

believe that others discerned better who were inferior to him in those faculties, and so to depart often from his own reason to follow the opinions of more unskilful men . . . [23]

More realistically, in his lack of resolution, and his frequently disingenuous methods, Charles himself probably deserves the greatest share of blame for the Royalist defeat.

Chapter Three
Prince Rupert

According to the historian Richard Ollard:

> Rupert . . . personifies the concept of Cavalier . . . the image of Rupert is part of everyone's apprehension of the Civil War . . . Rupert's flawless courage on the battlefield was matched by a brilliance and boldness in strategy and tactics that no commander on either side surpassed.[1]

Prince Rupert, Count Palatine of the Rhine and nephew of King Charles I, arouses stronger feelings than any other Royalist commander. Rupert, with his abrasive, domineering and intolerant personality, was viewed with dislike and suspicion by many contemporaries. The prince's modern biographers, however, have virtually all succumbed to the romantic image of a dashing warrior prince, though not denying his imperfections of personality. Typical in their verdict are Richard Holmes and Peter Young:

> Close study of his career shows how little justified is his popular image as a mere swashbuckling *beau sabreur*. His fiery, temperamental pride and tactlessness should not be allowed to obscure his broad mastery of generalship. As a leader of cavalry he had few equals; he was perhaps less good at training and disciplining his Horse, but here he was hampered by the independence and parochialism of his subordinates. The same factors hindered him as an army commander.[2]

His most recent biographer, General Sir Frank Kitson, says of Rupert: 'He brought one of the sharpest intellects of the age to bear on military problems.'[3]

Rupert's dominating and intimidating personality is apparent in his portraits, two of which also illustrate the effects which the war had upon him. The saturnine young prince of 1642, with his dark hair and black armour, relieved only by a scarlet cloak, radiates arrogant self-confidence. But in William Dobson's less well-known uncompleted portrait of the winter of 1644, the effects of Rupert's first great failure at Marston Moor, and the suspicion of others which was gnawing increasingly at him, are apparent in the drawn features and dark-shadowed eyes.

It is the portrait of a man out of his depth, whose failings would ruin both himself and the cause he served.

Early life

Rupert was always destined for conflict. Born in 1619, the third son of Frederick, Elector Palatine and Elizabeth daughter of James I of England, he spent his childhood in exile in the Hague, where, reflecting his polyglot ancestry, Rupert became fluent in French, German, English and Dutch. His restless and hot-tempered personality earned him the nickname from his siblings of 'Rupert the Devil'.

As a member of a large and impecunious family in exile, it was clear that Rupert would have to earn his living as a soldier. As a result his education emphasized the military arts, with the experienced English professional soldier Jacob Astley among Rupert's tutors. Rupert became an excellent swordsman and marksman, and was noted for his height (6ft 4in), strength and savage temper, the latter partly redeemed by his charm and restless energy.

Rupert began his military career at the age of 13, in 1633, when he accompanied Prince Frederick-Henry of Orange to the siege of Rheinburg. In 1636, with his brother, Maurice, Rupert visited England, where he established a close bond with his uncle, Charles I, and Queen Henrietta Maria. In 1637 the young princes were in the thick of the action at the Siege of Breda, where Rupert made the acquaintance of later allies and enemies such as Henry Wilmot, George Goring and Charles Lucas.

Two years later, in 1638, Rupert had another significant encounter when he took part in an attempt to recover the Palatinate. Serving with the Protestant force under Rupert's brother, the exiled Elector, Charles Louis, was a Scottish professional soldier, James King. At Lemgo the army encountered an Imperialist force, and Rupert, leading an initially successful but over-extended cavalry charge, was taken prisoner. King was blamed for failing to support him, leading to a grudge which would later have momentous consequences.

Rupert spent the next three years as a prisoner of the Imperialists, profiting from his enforced inactivity by systematic military study and discussions with senior Imperialist commanders. During this time the prince also acquired the famous large white poodle, 'Boy', who would be almost as well-known as his master in the opening years of the Civil War.

General of Horse

Despite his relative youth – he was still only 22 – Rupert had already acquired a considerable military reputation, and, as Civil War loomed in England, King Charles, aided by Cardinal Richelieu of France, managed to negotiate Rupert's release. In December 1641 Rupert was back in the Hague. After assisting Henrietta Maria in purchasing munitions Rupert, accompanied by Maurice and a number of professional soldiers, including the Walloon engineer Bernard de Gomme and the French explosives expert Bartholomew la Roche, set sail for England in July 1642, and after an adventurous journey, joined his uncle at Nottingham in time for the formal start of the war. Despite a warning from the queen that she regarded Rupert as unsuitable for senior military command,[4] Charles immediately appointed Rupert as his General of Horse, upsetting a number of his older and more experienced commanders, such as Henry Wilmot, Commissary General of Horse, who was eight years Rupert's senior. Discontent was increased by the king's decision to allow Rupert the right of direct appeal to him over the heads of the Lord General and the Council of War.

Rupert saw the war in simplistic terms as a fight between his much-loved uncle and the rebels who threatened him. He also had the uncompromising approach to warfare typical of contemporary conflict in Europe. Rupert would gradually moderate both of these viewpoints, but in the interim they caused considerable problems both for himself and his uncle's cause. An early example came when Rupert demanded that the citizens of Leicester present him with £2,000 for the Royalist cause, warning that if they failed to deliver 'I shall tomorrow appear before your town in such a posture with horse, foot and cannon as shall make you know it is more safest to obey than resist his Majesty's command.' Not for the last time Charles was forced to repudiate his nephew's action (though he kept the money).

In another example of his uncompromising approach, Rupert was delegated by the king to deal with the refusal of some of the Leicestershire Trained Bands either to march with the Royalist army or surrender their arms.

> So the Prince, Prince Maurice and the Sheriff with a troop of dragoons asked if they would march. They said, nay. Whereupon the Prince clap'd his Pistol to the head of the man that spoke and then they all laid down and after their Example, Nottinghamshire and Derbyshire did the like.[5]

As General of Horse, control of the Trained Bands had nothing to do with the prince. Already, with his uncle's active support, he was extending his authority beyond his formal responsibility.

During the next few weeks Rupert, supported by experienced officers such as Patrick Ruthven and Henry Wilmot, was feverishly engaged in organizing and training the expanding Royalist cavalry arm. He had an early taste of success on 23 September at Powick Bridge near Worcester, when a forceful if improvised charge by the Royalist horse shattered their opponents.

There has been considerable debate about how far the tactics in which the Royalist horse were trained, and which brought them so much initial success, originated with Rupert himself. At the start of the war the Parliamentarian horse, and some of the regional Royalist horse, followed Dutch tactics which emphasized the use of firepower to disrupt an enemy attack before responding with a counter-charge. The tactics introduced by Rupert are often said to be derived from those used by Gustavus Adolphus of Sweden. This is not entirely correct, as shown by a comparison of Rupert's actions at Edgehill with Swedish tactics. At Edgehill, Richard Bulstrode wrote, Rupert:

> Passed from one wing to the other, giving positive Orders to the Horse, to march as close as was possible, keeping their Ranks with Sword in Hand, to receive the Enemy's Shot, without firing either Carbin or Pistol, till we broke in amongst the enemy, and then to make use of our Fire-Arms as need should require.[6]

Swedish tactics, however, differed:

> only the first or at most the first two ranks, when near enough to see the whites of the enemy's eyes, were to give fire, then to reach for their swords; the last rank however was to attack without shooting but with swords drawn, and to keep both pistols (or in the first ranks, one) in reserve for the mêlée.[7]

The Swedish attack still involved a brief halt to fire pistols, but Rupert was dispensing with this, and going straight into the mêlée, using his cavalry, armed and equipped as medium horse or 'harquebusiers' in the role given by military writers to heavy cavalry or 'cuirassiers'. This was probably partly an improvisation resulting from an initial shortage of firearms. A similar tactic, for this reason, had been employed by the Poles earlier in the century.

One other legend should be laid to rest. The Royalist horse were not indulging in a wild, hell-for-leather charge. They still advanced in 'close order' at no faster pace than 'a good round trot'. Part of the initial success of the Royalist tactics lay in the fact that they were probably easier for relatively raw troops to use than the Dutch methods favoured by the Parliamentarians. To be effective, the latter required well-trained and motivated troops, which initially the Parliamentarians often lacked.

As the war went on, the tactics of both sides converged. Cavalry actions became brutal slogging matches between similarly armed and trained bodies of horse. Rupert, however, continued to keep a close eye on Continental refinements in deployment and tactics, for example deploying bodies of 'commanded' musketeers among his horse to increase firepower.

Rupert's strongly-held views are frequently claimed to have resulted in a Royalist command crisis on the morning of the battle of Edgehill. According to the generally accepted version of events, the Royalist Lord General, the Earl of Lyndsey, resigned in protest when the king overrode his plan to deploy the army in the Dutch style, in favour of Rupert's preference for the more complicated Swedish formations. However, Lyndsey may have already agreed to give up his post to the vastly more experienced Patrick Ruthven, who, with the veteran Major General of Foot, Sir Jacob Astley, also favoured the Swedish deployment.

The outcome of Edgehill was a sweeping if uncontrolled victory for Rupert and the Royalist horse, though it was almost lost as a result of the rough handling received by the king's infantry. According to some accounts, Rupert wanted to follow up the narrow victory by a lightning thrust on London with a picked force of horse and dragoons, but this was vetoed by the king because of the fears of some of his civilian councillors that the result would be a massacre of citizens. Again it is not entirely clear what Rupert proposed, and the chances of success were not high.

Rupert played a leading role in the eventual unsuccessful advance on London which culminated in the action at Brentford and the stand-off at Turnham Green. A Parliamentarian spy gave a vivid picture of the prince:

> Prince Rupert took off his scarlet coat, which was very rich, and gave it to his man, and buckled on his arms, and put a gray coat over it, that he might not be discovered. He talked long with the King, and often in his communication with his Majesty, he scratched his head and tore his hair, as if he had been in some grave discontent.[8]

The onset of winter brought no respite for the restless prince, as he settled his cavalry into their quarters around Oxford, organized their training, and launched frequent raids on enemy outposts. He was often absent from Oxford, and his influence on the wider conduct of the war at this stage is difficult to determine. Rupert seems to have worked reasonably well with the Lord General, Ruthven, possibly because the latter tended to defer to him. The prince's relations with the king's civilian advisers were already tepid, and he had a brush with Secretary of State Lord Falkland over protocol. Rupert also made the acquaintance of his only consistent civilian ally at Court, the king's cousin, James, Duke of Richmond, with whose wife, on scanty evidence, Rupert is said to have had an affair.

Rupert's private life during the war is obscure. While not indifferent to the company of women, he never married, and, with his restless energy focussed on the war, possibly had little time for dalliance. Most of his biographers feel that Rupert's rather puritanical code of honour would have debarred him from a relationship with the wife of his friend, although contemporaries thought otherwise.

The prince had already begun to ruffle a number of feathers. His second-in-command, Henry Wilmot, seems to have disliked him from the start, and resented taking orders from Rupert, while many civilian advisers had been annoyed by the prince's behaviour in council. He had, said Sir Philip Warwick:

> a little sharpness of temper of body, and uncommunicableness in society or council, (by seeming with a pish to neglect all another said, and he approved not) made him less grateful than his friends wished; and this humour soured him towards the Councillors of Civil affairs, who were necessarily to intermix with him in Martial affairs.[9]

Rupert was most at ease in the company of soldiers, particularly ones who would not challenge his opinions. Men such as the steadfastly loyal Will Legge, the fierce Charles Gerard, and Prince Maurice formed the prince's closest circle. Other soldiers, like Lord Byron, did not always give Rupert the unquestioning support which he increasingly felt to be his due.

Rupert was always admired by his younger officers and men. One anecdote captures their mood:

> one day, on a very cold morning, [Rupert] tied a very fine laced handkerchief about his neck, which he took out of his coat pocket, and this appeared so becoming that all his mimics got laced pocket handkerchiefs and made the same use of them, which was the origin of laced cravats.[10]

Initially criticism of Rupert was muted by his military successes. On 3 February 1643 he stormed Cirencester, clearing Royalist communications with the west, and in March he was given a more extensive independent command, with orders to open up links with the Royalist north by re-taking Lichfield. In the process Rupert once again caused his uncle considerable embarrassment. On 3 April Rupert stormed the town of Birmingham, notorious for its Parliamentarian sympathies, and looted it thoroughly. Next day, as he left, much of Birmingham was set ablaze. Though the Royalists denied that the action had been deliberate, the result was a gift for Parliamentarian news sheets with headlines such as 'Prince Rupert's Burning Love for England Discovered in Birmingham's Flames'. Charles was forced to write his nephew an uncomfortable letter, urging him to:

> mingle severity with mercy, that your carriage and behaviour towards our subjects may gain upon their opinions, and take their affections rather than their towns . . . have a care of spilling innocent blood . . . but spare where you may destroy.[11]

Rupert was unconvinced, though he was thereafter generally more circumspect in actions which he clearly felt to be permissible under the rules of war.

Lichfield was taken in a bloody but effective operation in which Rupert exploded the first mine of its kind to be employed in England. But Essex's advance on Reading caused the king to recall Rupert urgently to Oxford. He proved unable to prevent the fall of Reading, and was evidently in a sour mood afterwards, judging by a letter from Secretary of State Sir Edward Nicholas:

> the King is much troubled to see your Highness' discontent, and I could wish that some busy-bodies would not meddle as they do with other men's offices, and that the King would leave every officer respectively to look to his own proper places, which would give abundant satisfaction, and quiet those that are jealous to see some men meddle, who have nothing to do with affairs.[12]

Rupert's temper was always improved by action. On 18 June he led a raid against Parliamentarian quarters in the Thames Valley, culminating in the celebrated encounter at Chalgrove Field. Here Rupert displayed his customary daring in combat. As the opposing forces deployed, separated by a hedge, a number of

Rupert's officers advised him to retreat, but the prince felt that the enemy would then fall on his rear, and, his short-fused temper igniting, exclaimed:

> This insolency is not to be endured! . . . His Highness facing all about, set spurs to his Horse and first of all (in the very face of the Dragoons) leapt the hedge that parted us from the rebels. The Captain and the rest of his Troop of Lifeguards (every man as they could) jumped over after him: and as about 15 were gotten over, the Prince presently drew them up into a Front until the rest could recover up to him. At this the rebel Dragoons that lined the hedge fled; having hurt and slain some of ours with their first volley.[13]

Rupert's military reputation had reached new heights, climaxed a month later by perhaps his most dramatic success, when on 26 July he stormed Bristol, England's second city. But the Royalists suffered heavy casualties in the assault, which horrified the king. As a result, in early August, when the Royalists moved against Gloucester, whose Governor, Edward Massey, declined to surrender as expected, Charles vetoed Rupert's proposal to make an immediate assault, preferring an orthodox siege.

Rupert had already caused his uncle some embarrassment with a dispute over the appointment of the Governor of Bristol,[14] and on this further rebuff he somewhat sulkily declined to take any responsibility for the conduct of the siege of Gloucester, (which technically should not have been his anyway) and confined himself to his duties as General of Horse.

Rupert was further soured by political developments. The arrival of Queen Henrietta Maria provided a serious rival for the ear of the king, and the prince, possibly aware of Henrietta Maria's opposition to his being given a senior command, made no effort to cultivate her favour. The queen was building up her own party at Court, which, favouring such officers as Wilmot, and courtier politicians like Lord George Digby and Treasurer John Ashburnham, was viewed by Rupert as a threat to his own position. As the queen's party wanted a more active prosecution of the war, it might have been in Rupert's interests to bury his grudges and ally himself with them, and Digby and Lord Percy, an ineffectual General of the Ordinance but a favourite of the queen, made efforts to cultivate Rupert's support, hinting that he might replace Forth as Lord General.

Rupert, however, suspicious of their motives, would have nothing of it, and by the autumn was convinced that Digby was his secret enemy.

Military developments caused further problems. The high hopes of the summer ended in an autumn of discontent. The Parliamentarian army of the Earl of Essex not only succeeded in relieving Gloucester, but avoided destruction at the First Battle of Newbury (20 September). Rupert, already angered by what he perceived as the lack of urgency of the king and Forth in pursuing Essex, had favoured fighting a defensive action at Newbury, but was over-ruled by the Council of War. The Royalists not only failed to drive Essex from his strong position, but met with uncomfortable evidence that the superiority of their cavalry was fast eroding.

This reverse led to fierce recriminations. Stung by criticism of his failure to prevent Essex relieving Gloucester, Rupert hit back by blaming Wilmot, for not intercepting Essex on his march to Gloucester, and (with rather more justification) Lord Percy for ammunition shortages at Newbury. To Rupert's alarm, Lord Falkland, killed at Newbury, was replaced as Secretary of State by George Digby. The dispute between Rupert and Wilmot was particularly unfortunate. In November Arthur Trevor, a political 'fixer' in Oxford who worked for both Rupert and the Earl of Ormonde, warned the latter:

> The army is much divided, and the Prince at true distance with many of the officers of horse.[15]

Charles, torn in loyalty between wife and nephew, as usual lacked the authority and resolve to settle the matter. A temporary solution was provided by the arrival of English troops from Ireland on the Welsh Border, and the need to re-organize the command structure there, and by the threat of a Scottish invasion of the north of England.

Command in the north

On 3 February Rupert, appointed as Captain General of North Wales and the Marches, though retaining for the present his title of General of Horse, left Oxford to take up his new command at Shrewsbury. He tackled an unsatisfactory situation with his customary drive and energy. He had a capable second-in-command, John, Lord Byron, and the two men worked energetically to re-organize finances, quarter, pay and equip reinforcements from Ireland, and rebuild the existing forces in the area which had recently been defeated at Nantwich (25 January). Rupert also replaced local civilian garrison commanders wherever possible by professional soldiers from outside the area.

The arrival of English veterans from the savage war in Ireland, and Rupert's own attitude away from the restraining influence of his uncle, saw an increase in the harshness with which the war was waged. There had already been one alleged massacre in the area (at Bartholmley) before the Prince's arrival,[16] and other examples followed, notably the ruthless campaign waged by Sir Michael Woodhouse along the Welsh Border, which included a massacre in cold blood of the surrendered garrison of Hopton Castle, and a near-repeat at Brampton Bryan, for which Rupert appears to have given at least tacit approval.

Rupert was receiving urgent pleas for assistance from a number of quarters. The worsted Lancashire Royalists led by the Earl of Derby were pressing for intervention in that county; the Marquis of Newcastle was calling for support against the Scots, and the king hoped for reinforcement by the Irish veterans in time for the summer campaign. Furthermore, Rupert's absence from and unpopularity in Court circles was limiting his share of available resources. On 6 March the cynical but realistic Arthur Trevor told Rupert that his remedy was to win a victory: 'for

I find no court physic so present for the opening of obstructions as good news.'[17]
Fortunately, Rupert had just obliged.

KEY ACTION: THE RELIEF OF NEWARK, 21 MARCH 1644

In February Sir John Meldrum, with about 5,000 Parliamentarian troops from the Midlands, laid siege to the key Royalist garrison of Newark upon Trent. If it fell communications between Royalist north and South would be severed. The local Royalist forces under Lord Loughborough were too weak to raise the siege, so on 7 March the king requested Rupert to assist. The prince ordered Loughborough to send 700 horses to Bridgnorth, to mount some of his musketeers, and on 12 March received another urgent request from the king to go to Newark's aid. The prince was at Chester, and sent Will Legge to Shrewsbury, to muster as many musketeers as possible and send them by barge along the River Severn to Bridgnorth. Rupert himself, with his own and part of another regiment of horse and three guns, met the 1,100 musketeers, under Major General Henry Tillier, at Bridgnorth on 15 March, and marched via Wolverhampton and Lichfield to Ashby-de-la-Zouch, gathering reinforcements. Joined at Ashby on 18 March by Loughborough, Rupert now had about 3,300 horse and 3,000 foot.

The Parliamentarians at Newark were not particularly concerned by reports of Rupert's activities. They believed Meldrum could both maintain the siege and beat off any relief attempt. But Meldrum was frustrated by dissensions among his commanders, which 'well nigh broke the heart of the poor old gentleman', and by mid-March the Parliamentarian Committee of Both Kingdoms was considering ordering him to abandon the siege. Meanwhile a detachment of Meldrum's men under Sir Edward Hartop bungled an attempt to block further Royalist reinforcements under George Porter, who joined Rupert at Ashby on 19 March.

The prince had arranged for Loughborough to have wide gaps cut in the hedgerows on a cross-country route from Ashby towards Newark, which would allow a speedy approach while avoiding guarded roads. By 20 March Rupert was at Bingham, only 10 miles from Newark. He planned an early start next day, swinging round to the south of Newark in order to cut Meldrum's line of retreat.

It was not until the night of 20 March that Meldrum learnt of Rupert's arrival at Bingham, and obligingly rejected suggestions that he should raise the siege. He believed he could hold off Rupert's attack using the natural defences of the River Trent and a fortified ruin called the Spital, which guarded the crossing by a bridge of boats into an area enclosed by arms of the river, known as the 'Island'. He concentrated the bulk of his foot there, on the right bank of the Trent, north-east of the town of Newark, from where they could retreat northwards if necessary.

Rupert resumed his march at 2am on the 21st. As his men formed up in the moonlight, Rupert, probably with an eye to boosting morale, told Will Legge that he had dreamt that Meldrum had been beaten. An advance party under Loughborough was sent to engage the enemy until the main force came up.

THE·NEWARK·CAMPAIGN·
1644·

SHREWSBURY

BRIDGNORTH

R. Severn

WOLVERHAMPTON

DUDLEY

Rupert

R. Trent

ASHBY·DE
-LA-ZOUCH

NOTTINGHAM

BINGHAM

BELVOIR

NEWARK

·NEWARK·
·21·March·1644·

R. Trent

The Island

Muskham Bridge

fort

Bridge of boats

Queen's Sconce

Rupert

NEWARK

Spittal

Meldrum

Tillier

Rupert

Beacon Hill

Just before dawn on 21 March Rupert and his vanguard occupied high ground known as Beacon Hill, about a mile east of Newark, chasing off a small Parliamentarian detachment. Below him he could see Meldrum deploying in front of the bridge of boats, with some foot, and a party of about 1,500 horse in two bodies in front of them. Colonel Edward Rossiter commanded the horse on the left, Francis Thornhaugh those on the right.

Rupert was eager for action:

> The Prince thus easily gaining the hill, increased his Highness' natural courage, upon his apprehension besides, of having many advantages upon a retreating enemy: whereupon 'Courage' says he, 'let's charge them in God's name with the Horse we have, and engage them till our Rear and Foot be march'd up to us.[18]

The Royalist horse were probably drawn up in three lines. The first consisted of Rupert's own Regiment and Lifeguard, about 650 men, commanded by the Prince himself. Loughborough and Porter formed the second line, with a small division under Charles Gerard in reserve.

At about 9am Rupert charged. On the Royalist right Richard Crane and Rupert's Lifeguard broke through Thornhaugh's men, who behaved poorly, and rode forward as far as the Spittal. On the Royalist left, however, Rossiter, doubling his files to six deep, counter-attacked, and caused Rupert some difficulty. The prince and a few companions were briefly surrounded and involved in fierce hand-to-hand fighting. Rupert was attacked by three opponents. He cut one down with his sword, while another was shot by his French aide, Mortaigne. The third grabbed Rupert by the collar, but had his hand cut off by William Neale. A counter-charge by Captain Clement Martin's troop of Rupert's Regiment, supported by Charles Gerrard, broke Rossiter's men, and Meldrum pulled his foot back to the shelter of the Spittal.

The Royalist foot now arrived, and Rupert sent Tillier to work his way along the river bank in an attempt to seize the bridge of boats, but he found it too strongly defended. For the moment Rupert confined himself to containing the Parliamentarians on the island, but during the afternoon he got about 500 horse across the river. Soon afterwards a sally by the Newark garrison took a fort on the far side of the island which controlled the exit at Muskham Bridge.

Trapped, with many of his men in a state of mutiny, Meldrum asked for terms. Those he was granted were surprisingly lenient. Next morning, after surrendering their guns and firearms, the Parliamentarians were allowed to march away. Rupert was left in possession of eleven guns, two mortars and 3,000 muskets, though his disappointed men attempted to loot the departing Parliamentarians, until beaten off by Rupert and his officers with drawn swords.

Although the Relief of Newark was greeted as a great victory, there was criticism that Rupert had allowed Meldrum to get off too lightly. Once re-armed, his army would be able to take the field again. But the Prince's supporters argued that he had achieved his aim of relieving Newark, and *Mercurius Aulicus* pointed out:

true though it was that the enemies were distressed, yet very wise Generals have not thought it safe to make such men desperate. Besides which, being now in the midst of their own Garrisons, they might possibly be relieved. And to confess the truth, the Prince's Horse were so over-marched, and his Foot so beaten off their legs, that he found his men less able for the present for this; in very truth too, the Rebels were more than was believed.[19]

As it was, Rupert's success led to a brief Royalist recovery of Lincoln, Gainsborough and Stamford.

The Relief of Newark was Rupert's single most outstanding achievement. Displaying a mastery of swift movement, and concentration of force at the decisive point, he had outwitted his opponents, and brought off a remarkable success. If he had been known for no more than this action, Newark would have ranked Rupert among the most notable commanders of the war.

'York March' and Marston Moor

Rupert urgently needed to complete his work on the Welsh Border, aided by an increased flow of resources following his victory. Working with almost frantic energy, Rupert did much to transform his command. Although he tried to work with existing civil authorities where possible, their interests were closely subordinated to military needs. At Chester, for example, Rupert supported Byron in blocking the appointment as Governor of Sir Francis Gamul, the desired candidate of the leading citizens. Instead the post went to Will Legge, that reliable and unquestioning intimate of Rupert, severely curtailing the role of the civil authorities in military matters. By the middle of May, as well paying a lightning visit to Oxford to resolve on a defensive strategy in the south, Rupert had prepared a field army of some 2,000 horse and 6,000 foot.

On 19 May he set out on his invasion of Lancashire, prior to relieving the Marquis of Newcastle in York. Although much of the Welsh Border was now in Royalist hands, their hold rested upon insecure foundations, largely, as Byron for one sensed, reliant on the personal presence of Rupert. If anything went amiss with his northern expedition, the entire edifice might come crashing down.

But the Lancashire campaign proceeded with Rupert's customary success. Described, rather brazenly in the circumstances, by Sir John Meldrum, now defending Manchester, as 'that fierce thunderbolt which terrifies the ignorant', Rupert forced a crossing of the River Mersey at Stockport, and on 28 May stormed Bolton, routing the Lancashire forces of Alexander Rigby. The 'Bolton Massacre' was one of the more notorious alleged atrocities of the war, with reports of hundreds of civilians, men, women and children, massacred. In reality, most of those killed seem to have been combatants, with quarter granted to many who surrendered.[20]

Rather more bloody was the assault on Liverpool, which after a fierce resistance was taken in a night assault on 11 June, during which a number of panic-stricken civilians were killed, and widespread looting took place.

With the port of Liverpool, the principal objective of the first stage of the campaign, in Royalist hands, Rupert could prepare to relieve York. Despite his success, he was evidently in a deeply disgruntled mood. The main reason appears to have been the decision by the king's commanders to jettison the agreed strategy in the south, with the result that Charles, faced by the combined armies of Waller and Essex, was soon in flight from Oxford and briefly considered taking refuge with Rupert in the north. Soon after the fall of Liverpool the Prince received the king's fateful and oft-quoted letter which can only really be read as an instruction to relieve York, at the same time defeating the Allied armies there, and coming to Charles's assistance as quickly as possible.[21]

On 29 June Arthur Trevor wrote from Chester that Rupert:

> by letter from court, understands that the king grows daily more and more jealous of him and his army; and that it is the common discourse of the Lord Digby, Lord Percy, Sir John Culpeper, and Wilmot, that it is indifferent whether the parliament or prince Rupert doth prevail; which did so highly jesuit prince Rupert, that he was once more resolved to send the king his commission and get to home. This fury interrupted the march ten days, but at length time and a friend, the best coolers of the blood, spent the humour of travail in him, though not that of revenge; to which purpose he hath sent his letter to the king for the removal of them from his council; and if this be not done, he will leave this war and sit down.[22]

However, while Rupert was probably incensed, it is more likely he was awaiting a re-supply of powder and shot from Bristol, and absorbing new recruits from Lancashire.

On 22 June, with an army of about 14,000 men, a mixed force of new levies and veterans, Rupert set out on the first stage of his 'York March' across the Pennines. If it had not been overshadowed by the disaster of Marston Moor following closely on its heels, Rupert's Relief of York would have won him even greater fame than his triumph at Newark. After halting for two days at Skipton, to rest his men and gain intelligence of the situation at York, Rupert advanced on 30 June to Knaresborough. Expecting a Royalist advance directly on York, the Allies pulled back to a defensive position on Marston Moor, west of the city. However, the prince, sending a cavalry screen along the York road to occupy their attention, swung north with the rest of his army to cross the River Ure at Boroughbridge, then east across the River Swale at Thornton Bridge, and thence down the east bank of the Ouse towards York, seizing intact a Parliamentarian bridge of boats at Poppleton. By the evening of 1 July, with the baffled Allies still standing helplessly on Marston Moor, York had been relieved.

But triumph was speedily followed by crushing disaster. A major cause of the Royalist defeat was the tortuous relationship between Rupert and the Northern Royalist commander, the Marquis of Newcastle,[23] a problem which, with more tact and patience, Rupert might have at least minimized. But he made other uncharacteristic errors as well. As his leading troops deployed on Marston Moor on the morning of 2 July, with the Allies hastily reversing the withdrawal they had begun towards Wetherby, the prince was anxious to bring them to immediate battle. There were two main reasons for this. The first was in obedience to what Rupert regarded as clear orders from the king to fight a battle as quickly as possible. Secondly he hoped to counteract the Allied numerical superiority by attacking them while they were still disorganized.

Opinions differ on whether an immediate Royalist attack would have gained the crushing victory which Rupert required. On balance it seems unlikely, but in any case the late arrival of the Northern foot from York left Rupert unwilling to risk an attack without them, and the inevitable criticism if it failed. When Rupert's old nemesis, James King (now Lord Eythin, and Newcastle's Lieutenant General), eventually arrived on the scene, he trenchantly criticized the deployment of the Royalist forces as being too close to the enemy. These dispositions were evidently intended for an offensive action, and the prince is again open to criticism, once the decision had been made not to fight that day, for failing to pull his troops back to a safer distance from the enemy.

Rupert's final fatal error, brought on perhaps as much by the strain of attempting to keep his temper with Newcastle and Eythin, as by any measured calculation, was his decision in the early evening to allow his troops to stand down, on the assumption that it was now too late in the day for the Allies to attack. More than any other factor, this tipped the scales against the Royalists and lost them what was a surprisingly close-fought battle.

Of Rupert's part in the actual fighting there is little relevant to say. He fought with his customary bravery, his beloved dog being killed in the fighting, but was never able to get to grips with the fast-moving situation. By midnight the 24-year-old prince was back in York, having lost his first major battle, and with it, arguably, the war.

Reaction to defeat

Rupert's conduct over the next few months did little to enhance his reputation. In the immediate aftermath of Marston Moor, he spoke confidently of rallying his men and resuming the fight. But this mood of optimism was quickly overtaken by bitterness and despondency. Rupert was still a young man, with little experience of failure, and his naturally suspicious and aggressive tendencies now seem to have deepened to the verge of paranoia. As usual, he required scapegoats for his failure. Newcastle and Eythin were obvious ones, and Rupert unsuccessfully attempted to have Eythin arrested for treason. For Marston Moor itself, Lord Byron, commanding the Royalist right, was blamed, on dubious grounds, for launching a premature charge.[24]

There remained a chance of prolonging resistance in the north, but, after spending a few weeks unsuccessfully attempting to rebuild his army at Chester, Rupert left responsibility in the area to Byron, and went to Bristol. Here he spent several weeks in at best, relative inactivity, and at worst, if a dubiously authentic letter from Trevor may be believed, in debauchery. One interpretation might be that the prince had suffered some kind of temporary breakdown as a reaction to his defeat, but the evidence is insufficient to reach a conclusion.

Certainly King Charles appears to have been concerned about his nephew's frame of mind. At the end of August an anonymous correspondent, probably the Duke of Richmond, assured Rupert that the king 'does not nor ever did believe you faulty in anything has fallen out there [the north].' However, in a hint of the dissension among Rupert's commanders which followed Marston Moor, he warned: 'It is given out here that your commanders are unsatisfied, because you have only private counsels, and never hear their opinions concerning your business.'[25]

Charles himself wrote to Rupert on 30 August:

> I send you herewith the possible remedies for those difficulties you sent me, which obstruct your advance of monies, whereby I am confident you will not only be contented, but likewise satisfied that I can do no more for your supply than I have done in this; and you will find the like care in the rest, as Digby will particularly inform you, whom I must desire you (for my service's sake, because he is a useful servant) so far to countenance as to show him a possibility to recover your favour, if he shall deserve it, which I hope he will; and if not, he shall repent it too late. Not doubting that for my sake, but you will make this and a greater experiment . . . I have an implicit faith in you.[26]

Digby was also rapped over the knuckles, and wrote to Rupert assuring him that no blame was attached to him for the defeat at Marston Moor, while the removal of two other arch-critics, Wilmot and Percy, also went some way to mollify the prince. Nevertheless, his enmity towards Digby remained, if for the moment superficially concealed. On 16 October Rupert confided somewhat incoherently in Will Legge:

> 'Digby and Rupert friends, but I doubt they trust one another alike. Digby makes great professions and vows to Rupert, but it will do no good upon him. Great factions are breeding against Rupert, under a pretence of peace; he being, as they report, the only cause of war in the kingdom. This party is found out, but no particulars proved. They will be, and then the King did promise to punish, or there will be no staying: which else Rupert is resolved to do, since the King's friends are in no very good condition, and he hath promised me fair; it is well if half be performed.[27]

Digby has traditionally been portrayed by sympathetic biographers of Rupert as an unscrupulous and accomplished conspirator, whose wiles were too great for the straightforward prince to fathom. In reality, Digby, whatever his faults, was undoubtedly loyal to the king, and does seem to have made some genuine attempts at reconciliation with Rupert. Rupert was equally capable of intrigue and character assassination. The aims and characters of the two men were ultimately irreconcilable, and the story of the next year would be one of deepening enmity between them. It was yet another example of a situation which the king should have taken firm steps to resolve.

Lieutenant General

A plan under spasmodic consideration since earlier in the summer was now concluded. The elderly and increasingly infirm Earl of Forth was replaced as commander of the Royalist armies by Prince Rupert. It may seem surprising that the 24-year-old prince, just after suffering such a crushing defeat, his already obvious character defects deepened by the consequences of failure, should be elevated to such a position of responsibility. It is difficult to regard the decision as anything other than a grave mistake. Whether the king had any doubts remains unclear, and he was in any case once more suffering from a guilty conscience, having disregarded Rupert's advice not to fight a battle until he joined him with reinforcements, and as a result almost suffering disaster at the Second Battle of Newbury (27 October).

On 6 November the Prince of Wales was appointed 'first Captain General of all our forces.' This was a purely honorific title made on Rupert's recommendation. Real control, at any rate in theory, lay with Rupert as Lieutenant General. He appeared at last to have gained complete command of the Royalist war effort, yet almost unrelieved disaster would follow. Many contemporaries blamed the prince, but modern writers tend to shift responsibility to Goring, Digby and the 'courtier' faction, as well as to Charles himself.

Prospects for 1645 were bleak, with Parliament increasingly free to concentrate against the remaining Royalist heartlands of war-weary Wales and the south-west. Despite the loss of the north and the major advantage for Parliament which this represented, the king and many of his advisers, including Digby, remained satisfied with the outcome of the 1644 campaign. Rupert did not share this rosy viewpoint. He realized the implications of the loss of the north, and, although he made its recovery, and avenging Marston Moor, a major plank of his proposed strategy, he appears only to have hoped to gain a compromise peace as a result.

Yet even such a limited aim required the same kind of root-and-branch military reforms which the Parliamentarians were currently embarking upon with their creation of the New Model Army. Rupert was aware of the need, and to some extent attempted to implement it. But it never progressed very far, and even basic problems were never addressed. Recalcitrant commanders such as Goring proved unwilling to accept Rupert's authority, and the prince's position, in the case for example of Goring, was undermined by the king's lack of consistent support.

Nor was there any fundamental shake-up of the Royalist command structure. Rupert's known supporters – Bernard de Gomme as Quartermaster General, Will Legge as Governor of Oxford – took over a few posts, but other changes were few. Rupert was undoubtedly limited in his reforms by his youth and foreign birth, and the relatively rigid social structure which sometimes hindered promotion by merit. Yet the prince's sensitivity towards criticism also played a part. For instance he failed to make full use of the undoubted talents of that outstanding but independent cavalry commander, Sir Charles Lucas, or infantry officers such as George Lisle, while he also attempted to undermine Goring, seen as a threat to his favour with the king.

Rupert spent most of the critical opening months of 1645, as the New Model Army was taking shape at Windsor, in ceaseless journeys around Royalist territory, attempting to deal with a succession of crises. In March and April, at a time when decisions for the coming campaign were urgently needed, he was on the Welsh Border, bolstering Prince Maurice's flagging operations and continuing his vendetta against Digby in bitter letters to Legge: 'if the king will follow the wise Counsel, and not hear the soldier and Rupert (according to his promise to me at Bristol, which he may remember) Rupert must leave off all.'[28]

Nevertheless, after travelling some 300 miles in sixteen days, Rupert had checked the raids of Edward Massey out of Gloucester and suppressed the first serious 'Clubman' uprising in Herefordshire. He had raised at least 2,000 new Welsh recruits, and stabilized the situation sufficiently, once Cromwell's incursion around Oxford had been dealt with, for the king to join him for the spring campaign.

Naseby

The fateful Council of War at Stow followed, in which Rupert, despite being supported only by Sir Marmaduke Langdale, gained his wish for the main objective to be firstly the relief of Chester followed by the recovery of the north, rather than turning immediately against the New Model Army. But the same meeting saw a dubious 'deal' between Rupert and Goring, whereby the latter went back to the west to counter the New Model. This had been mooted earlier in the spring, but Clarendon believed that Rupert's main concern was to remove a dangerous potential rival from the proximity of the king, regardless of the serious weakening of the Royalist army resulting from the departure of almost 3,000 veteran horse.

The campaign which followed represented a frustrating balancing act for Rupert. On the diminished Council of War he was consistently opposed by Digby and John Ashburnham, who, particularly after Oxford came under threat from the New Model Army, wished to turn back to deal with it. Only Langdale, for reasons of his own, was a dependable supporter of the prince, so that he had to rely on the ultimate backing of the king, by no means a foregone conclusion.

The result was ultimately fatal hesitancy and dissension at several key moments. With Chester relieved, the Royalists chose to postpone the march north and turn eastwards to capture Leicester in order to force the New Model to raise its siege of Oxford. This was successfully accomplished when Leicester was stormed on 28 May, but was followed by over a week of delay, firstly while the Royalists attempted to round up the large numbers of foot who had deserted with booty gained at Leicester, and then while supplies were conveyed to Oxford, now free from attack, and replenishment ammunition brought back in return. In the meantime, bickering continued between Rupert and the 'courtier' faction, with the prince, obviously in paranoid mood, telling Will Legge on 8 June that:

> there was a plot to send the King to Oxford, but it is undone. The Chief of the Council was the fear some men had that the soldiers should take from the influence which they now possess with the King. I would fain come over to you; but I will not ask leave, for fear of the rest of the officers.[29]

The delay cost the Royalists any realistic chance of avoiding battle with Fairfax and the New Model, now heading northwards in pursuit. Charles withdrew to Market Harborough, with Rupert counselling against offering battle, favouring instead continuing his march north and picking up reinforcements from Newark en route. He still hoped to be joined by Goring from the west and Gerard from south Wales, who had been ordered to rendezvous with the Oxford Army in the Midlands, although neither of them was moving quickly – or, in Goring's case, at all. But on the evening of 13 June, when the Royalists halted at Market Harborough, the surprise of one of their outposts in the village of Naseby, five miles to the south, revealed the proximity of Fairfax and the New Model.

Although the difference in size between the opposing armies was probably not as great as sometimes suggested, at a hastily summoned Council of War Rupert favoured attempting to avoid battle by continuing the retreat towards Newark. Whether there was still time to do this is doubtful. It would have involved a difficult rearguard action to hold off the Parliamentarian cavalry. But in any case, Digby and Ashburnham pressed for an immediate engagement, and with the king on their side, carried the day.

Although out-voted, Rupert seems to have attempted to make the best of a difficult situation. He planned an all-out attack by the Royalists, although this involved abandoning a reasonably strong initial defensive position to the south of Market Harborough, and opted himself to lead his cavalry on the Royalist right.

Naseby came within measurable distance of being a Royalist success, though never perhaps so close as has been suggested. Rupert would be censured for leaving the king in command of the reserve, instead of being with them himself, but in reality it is doubtful whether any action by this relatively small force could have changed the course of events.

Decline and fall

The immediate outcome of the crushing Royalist defeat at Naseby, apart from the loss of the king's veteran infantry, was an open breach between Rupert and Digby. Both had reason to fear blame for the disaster, and both made haste to cover themselves. Digby, in a disingenuous letter to Will Legge, indicated that Rupert had moved forward from the defensive position originally adopted by the Royalist army without consulting a Council of War and against the advice of Lord Astley.

Legge rejected this idea, although it is not in fact disproved by any contemporary evidence.

Rupert himself, in a furious epistle to Legge on 18 June, returned to his old themes:

> Pray let me know what is said among you concerning our last defeat. Doubtless the fault of it will be put upon Rupert. Since this business I find Digby hath omitted nothing which might prejudice Rupert and this day hath drawn a letter from the King to Prince Charles, in which he crosses all things that befell here in Rupert's behalf. I have showed this to the King, and in earnest; and if,thereupon, he should go on and send it, I shall be forced to quit generalship, and march towards Prince Charles, where Rupert hath received more kindness than here . . .[30]

The situation was plainly intolerable, and the king as usual was unable to resolve the festering dispute. Rupert's presence with what remained of the Oxford Army was in any case irrelevant, and it was probably with some relief that Charles permitted him to go to Bristol, ostensibly to supervise the defence of the south-west. With Goring's defeat at Langport on 10 July, whatever prospects for success Rupert might have had were dashed, and he concentrated his efforts on preparing to defend Bristol, now the major Royalist munitions manufacturing centre. He had, however, no illusions, and on 24 July warned the Duke of Richmond: 'His Majesty hath no way left to preserve his posterity, kingdom and nobility, but by a treaty. I believe it a more prudent way to retain something than to lose all.' Charles, however, responded that while 'As a mere soldier or statesman I must say there is no probability but of my ruin, yet as a Christian I must tell you that God will not suffer rebels and traitors to prosper.'

The gulf was unbridgeable. Rupert prepared with about 1,500 men to defend Bristol against the full strength of the New Model Army with 12,000 men. When, on 10 September, he faced the Parliamentarian assault, it is difficult to believe that Rupert was doing more than going through the motions. As he no doubt anticipated, after a stiffly contested action the outer defences of Bristol were pierced. Next day, with the unanimous concurrence of his Council of War, Rupert accepted Fairfax's generous terms.

Unfortunately their leniency was enough to convince a furious Charles, incited by Digby, that Rupert had betrayed him. He was stripped of all commands and ordered to leave the country. Rupert reacted by making an incident-filled dash through enemy territory to confront the king at Newark and plead his case. An acrimonious encounter followed, with Rupert being cleared of wrong-doing by a Court Martial. There would eventually be a partial personal reconciliation between Charles and his nephew, but, even if a restoration to command had ever been considered, there was now no army remaining. After the surrender of Oxford in June 1646, Rupert left England.

Aftermath

Rupert was still only 26 years old, and ahead lay many years of action on land and sea, during which he would gain a reputation as a highly competent fighting admiral. But Rupert's part in the war in England was over, and he would never again command an army in the field. It is as a soldier, in his role in the English Civil War, that we must assess him here.

No one ever questioned Rupert's personal courage and powers of leadership in battle. As a cavalry commander he must rank as one of the outstanding figures of the war. His part in turning the raw Royalist troopers of the summer of 1642 into a fighting force which almost won the war for King Charles was Rupert's crowning achievement. If he had remained in this role, his reputation would have been unchallenged.

Rupert's difficulties arose when, partly because of his royal birth, and also through his own inclinations, he became increasingly involved firstly in the power politics of the royal court and then in higher command. For the first, his youth, foreign birth and abrasive personality left him ill-equipped, and fatally damaged his performance in the second. Rupert was undoubtedly deeply read in all aspects of the art of war, an able military administrator, and, as he proved at Newark and the 'York March', a master of bold and fast-moving operations. As a strategist it is more difficult to assess Rupert. Both of his major campaigns as an army commander were reactive in nature; in 1644 he was attempting to counter the Scots invasion and its after-effects, and in the following year to undo the effects of Marston Moor. Both ultimately failed, although again it can be argued that much of the fault lay with individuals and circumstances out of Rupert's control.

But once again Rupert was ill-served both by his youth, relative inexperience, and his defects of character. Perhaps the greatest test of a general lies in his ability to surmount adversity and criticism, and remain focussed on the wider objective despite setbacks. Rupert probably never fully recovered from the effects of his first real experience of defeat, at Marston Moor. He became increasingly withdrawn, suspicious, embittered and blaming others. By the start of the 1645 campaign, Charles had an army commander who had alienated virtually all of those whose support he needed, and who laboured under a legacy of failure. It is doubtful whether any single man could have saved the Royalists from defeat in 1645, but, second only to his uncle, Prince Rupert must carry a major share of the blame for it occurring in the circumstances in which it did.

Chapter Four
Jacob, Lord Astley

The post of Sergeant Major General, more commonly abbreviated to 'Major General', ranked third in the hierarchy of a Civil War army. The Major General commanded the infantry, and was also responsible for drawing up the army in battle formation, usually in accordance with a 'plan' formulated by the senior commanders at the start of a campaign, and altered as necessary on the day of battle.

This role required a man of considerable ability, and military experience. The contemporary military writer Robert Markham stipulated that;

> In his memory he must ever carry framed the forms and proportions of sundry battles, any of which he is to sort or fashion to the ground, according as the necessity of the place requireth.[1]

Virtually all writers, contemporary and modern, are in agreement that Jacob Astley possessed all the necessary qualities of a Major General of Foot. Clarendon said:

> Sir Jacob Astley was an honest, brave, plain man, and as fit for the office he exercised, of Major General of Foot, as Christendom yielded; and was so generally esteemed; very discerning and prompt in giving orders, as the occasions required, and most cheerful and present in any action. In Council he used few, but very pertinent words; and was not at all pleased with the long speeches usually made there; and which rather confounded, than informed his understanding. So that he rather collected the ends of the debates, and what he was himself to do, than enlarged them by his own discourse, though he forbore not to deliver his own mind.[2]

Astley is perhaps best known for his prayer before the Battle of Edgehill, and for his pithy comments after the last battle of the war, at Stow-on-the-Wold. Peter Young and Richard Holmes sum up the general view when they comment that 'his solid, unpretentious professionalism was a useful antidote to the heady air of the king's headquarters.'[3]

But there was more to this little man, whose sharp grey-haired features thrust out from his portraits like those of an eager little terrier, than a mere 'safe pair of hands'. Of modern writers, only Ronald Hutton has paid tribute to Astley's abilities both as an administrator, and, as displayed in his Stow-on-the-Wold campaign in 1646, as an independent commander.[4] He is an under-rated general who deserves closer examination.

Early life

Jacob Astley was born in 1579, a younger son of Isaac Astley of Melton Constable, Norfolk. Without hopes of inheriting, Astley became a professional soldier. He served widely with the Protestant forces in Europe, fighting in Sir Horace Vere's English volunteers in the Palatinate, and with the Danes, the Swedes and the Dutch. For some years he made his home in the Netherlands, marrying a Dutch lady, Agnes Impel, and becoming a favourite of the exiled Queen Elizabeth of Bohemia. In May 1630, in a letter which hints at the charm with which Elizabeth captivated half of Europe, she wrote to Astley:

> Honest Little Jacob,
>   This is to assure you, that I was very glad to know by your letter, that you had so good fortune in getting your suit of the King, my brother; I hope shortly to see you here, for the Prince [Maurice of Nassau] means very suddenly to be in the field, and means all shall be cashiered who are not at the rendezvous. Therefore, like a little ape, skip over quickly! Your Colonel swears cruelly, that the Prince will not give him leave now to go to my uncle. His daughter is here, I do not find her changed; I end with this, that I desire you to believe me ever,
>   Your most assured friend,
>   Elizabeth.[5]

Soon afterwards, Elizabeth employed Astley as military tutor to the young Prince Rupert, and the two dissimilar characters seem to have enjoyed each other's respect henceforward.

Like many of his fellow professionals, Astley was drawn back to England by prospects of military employment as tensions mounted, and probably by his loyalty to Elizabeth as sister to Charles I. In 1638 he was employed inspecting the Trained Bands, magazines and fortifications in the West Country. In May and June of the same year he was back in the Netherlands, using his contacts there to purchase munitions for the king's forces in the First Scots War. Appointed Major General of Foot in the army being raised, in November Astley was in London, consulting with the king and the Earl of Essex, and a month later headed north to Hull and York, to supervise efforts to place the Yorkshire Trained Bands on a war footing.

The next few months saw Astley active throughout the north-east of England.

At Newcastle-upon-Tyne he began the organization of supply depots, and gave orders for the repair of its neglected fortifications, and also the inadequate defences of off-shore Holy Island. In March 1639, learning that the Scots were preparing to move against Berwick-on-Tweed, Astley hurried there and established a 2,00-strong garrison, anticipating the Scots by only a few hours.

Astley had proved himself indispensable to the king's military efforts, and when the Second Scots War broke out in 1640, he was again at the forefront of preparations. He found the experience highly frustrating. Astley complained that lack of money was costing the king vital opportunities, and resulting in ill-equipped, unpaid, mutinous troops. Throughout the summer of 1640 Astley struggled to discipline his disorderly levies, sometimes hanging mutineers. He explained his frustrations in one of his rare surviving letters, concerning his attempts to deal with some Dorsetshire levies who had murdered one of their officers, and quoted here in its original spelling:

> The dorsettsher men when they came to Selby they thought to do as they were wont but for disobedienties to their officere in the field as they were Musteringe I was fayne to tuck out one of them, and by the Common Vott of the Counsell of War we Harquebussed him the view of the Rest.[6]

Raising the Royalist Foot

Sir Jacob Astley was the obvious choice to be King Charles's Major General of Foot in the summer of 1642. He faced many difficulties. All his foot regiments had to be raised from scratch, sometimes based around existing Trained Band units, drawn from wherever the king's marches took him that summer, and also from cadres of 'volunteers' mustered by loyalist gentry and grandees.

The quality of these troops varied widely, and the great majority had no previous military experience. There was also a severe lack of arms, which lasted throughout 1642 and into the following spring. Clarendon wrote of the Royalist foot on the eve of the first great battle of the war, at Edgehill (23 October):

> The foot (all but three or four hundred who marched without any weapon but a cudgel) were armed with muskets, and bags for their powder, and pikes; but in the whole body there was not one pikeman had a corselet, and very few musketeers who had swords.[7]

It is interesting to compare this with the Royalist *Military Orders and Articles* of 1642, which laid down the following provisions for infantry equipment:

> The Arms of a Pikeman are Gorget, Cuirass, Head-piece, Sword, Girdle and Hanger. The Arms of a Musketeer are Musket, a Rest, Bandolier, Head-Piece, Sword, Girdle and Hanger.[8]

Some of these items, such as full body armour for the pikemen, and head-pieces for the musketeers, were probably rarely issued in the Oxford Army, but certainly the typical Royalist foot soldier in October 1642 bore little resemblance to the ideal.

When the King raised his standard at Nottingham in August 1642, Astley was so short of infantry that he warned Charles 'he could not give any assurance against his Majesty being taken out of his bed if the rebels should make a brisk attempt.'[9] It is tribute to Astley's ability that within two months, mainly during the king's stay at Shrewsbury, where recruits came in from Wales and its borders, he had produced a respectable fighting force. By October 1642 the Royalist Army included at least 19 regiments of foot, totalling about 10,000 men. This meant that most were no more than about half the regulation strength of 1,200 and there remained a critical shortage of experienced officers. Astley was however able to appoint four seasoned tertia (brigade) commanders. Sir Nicholas Byron was a professional soldier, Charles Gerard had served in the Low Countries and the Scots Wars, Henry Wentworth had been a colonel in the Scots Wars, and Richard Fielding had served on the Continent. Only one, John Belasyse, seems to have had no previous experience.

Astley, responsible for drawing up the army in battle formation, was no doubt caught up in the controversy which preceded Edgehill. The then Lord General, the Earl of Lyndsey, favoured the Dutch style of deployment as being better for poorly trained troops. Prince Rupert preferred the more complicated Swedish formations. As discussed elsewhere, Rupert got his way, and Lord Forth took over as Lord General.[10] As a veteran of the Dutch service, Astley might have been expected to have shared Lyndsey's opinion, but John Belasyse said that the army was drawn up:

> . . . in the order which had formerly been designed by General Ruthven [Forth], Sir Arthur Aston and Sir Jacob Astley, which was into several brigades, after the Swedish fashion.[11]

The incident at Edgehill for which Astley is best-known is the short prayer he made at the head of his troops at the start of the battle: 'O Lord! Thou knowest how busy I must be this day, If I forget Thee, do not Thou forget me. March on, boys!'[12]

It is tempting to suppose that the old veteran had used the same prayer in similar situations.

The Royalist foot were noted as advancing 'with a slow steady pace, and a very daring resolution.' The fighting which followed proved a sharp introduction to the realities of battle for the raw recruits. With most of their horse absent pursuing fleeing Parliamentarian cavalry, Astley's men found themselves not only in sustained combat with the Earl of Essex's foot, but also under attack by Sir William Balfour and those Parliamentarian horse not carried away in the rout.

> The foot of both sides stood their ground with great courage, and though many of the King's soldiers were unarmed and had only cudgels, they kept

their ranks, and took up the arms their slaughtered neighbours left to them; and the execution was great on both sides.[13]

The Parliamentarian horse broke at least two of Astley's tertias, but Sir Jacob himself, according to one account wounded, fought on with the remainder until nightfall and the returning Royalist horse enforced a stalemate.

Edgehill had been a sharp blooding for the Royalist foot, some of whom gained revenge for their rough handling a couple of weeks later in the storm of Brentford.

The Oxford Army

The end of the 1642 campaign gave Astley breathing space to continue recruiting and training the Oxford Army foot. As spring approached, further recruits and new units arrived, and had to be equipped, housed, fed and instructed in the basics of military tactics. However, shortages of powder and arms continued to plague the Oxford Army foot until well into the spring, with most regiments still only armed with equal numbers of muskets and pikes, instead of the two to one ratio in favour of the former recommended by military theorists.

This weakness crippled the Oxford Army for much of the spring, and was a factor in their failure to relieve Reading in May. By July, however, the arrival of large convoys of munitions from the north eased the worst of the shortages, and the Oxford Army was ready to take the field, firstly in the capture of Bristol and then the siege of Gloucester.

We know little of Astley's own part in these operations. He was always a man of few words, and probably put pen to paper only when essential. At any rate, few of his letters have survived. In a rare miscalculation, Astley was apparently one of the professional soldiers who advised King Charles that Gloucester would fall within ten days. During the siege he commanded a detachment of the besiegers based at the village of Barton to the east of Gloucester.

Like other senior commanders, Astley took his turn in the trenches, and had at least one narrow escape, reported by Royalist Captain John Gwynne:

I, having guard by the riverside, and standing by Sir Jacob Astley, a bearded arrow stuck into the ground between his legs. He plucked it out with both hands, and said, 'You rogues, you missed your aim.'[14]

The Parliamentarians apparently claimed to have killed Astley, for on 2 September the Royalist newspaper, *Mercurius Aulicus*, commented:

That Sir Jacob Astley and some other commanders were lately slain at Gloucester (were they slain with a musket or a cannon bullet?) Sir Jacob himself desires to know.[15]

The unsuccessful siege of Gloucester, followed by a rapid pursuit of the Earl of Essex's army towards Newbury, took a heavy toll in casualties and stragglers of the Royalist foot. This was one of the factors, together with the terrain and the piecemeal nature of the Royalist attacks, in the less than adequate showing at the First Battle of Newbury (20 September). Once again we have no record of Astley's part in the fighting. Given the disorganized nature of the battle, he can have done little more than fight alongside some of his troops.

The only comfort for the Royalists at the end of a frustrating campaign was their re-occupation of Reading. With winter and the end of active operations approaching, Astley was made Governor of this key front-line garrison. In November, in a brief flurry of activity, he co-operated with Hopton in his relief of Basing House, but otherwise seems to have passed the winter fairly quietly, attempting, with little success, to rebuild the weak regiments of the tertia of veteran Royalist foot who were stationed at Reading.

Gosford Bridge

Astley was aware of the difficulty of defending Reading against any determined enemy attack, and in the spring, like the majority of the Royalist Council of War, seems to have favoured its evacuation. When this was done on 18 May 1644, Astley and his 3,000 men were added to the Oxford Army.

He quickly found himself in action again. The evacuation of Reading and Abingdon enabled the armies of the Earl of Essex and Sir William Waller, for the moment working in uneasy co-operation, to begin closing in on Oxford. By 29 May Essex was at Islip, six miles to the north-east of Oxford. His aim now was to force a crossing of the River Cherwell and attack the Royalist capital from the north. On 30 and 31 May he made two determined efforts to force a passage of the river at Gosford Bridge.

Sir Jacob Astley had taken personal command of the defence of this vital point, as the account in *Mercurius Aulicus* describes:

> This day His Majesty gave order for 2 field pieces of six pound bullet with certain companies of foot to be drawn out for the securing of Gosworth [sic] Bridge (at which the rebels had intended to pass over the Cherwell) under the command of Sir Jacob Astley, who omitting no part of a valiant and expert commander, raised a breastwork and a redoubt for the defence of his men. From whence he did so gall the rebels, and played upon them with such advantage, that though they had 4 pieces of Ordnance on the other side, which made many a shot (the noise of thunder of which was heard to Oxford) yet they did little or no hurt to his Majesty's forces; themselves being shamefully repulsed from their undertaking.[16]

The Royalists claimed to have killed some 100 of their opponents, while the Parliamentarians admitted to the loss of 40.

However, within days Waller's troops had forced a crossing of the Thames to the south of Oxford, and Charles made a bold decision to break out to the west.

He took with him many of his most experienced officers, including Astley, who commanded the detachment of 2,500 musketeers which accompanied the king on his march across the Cotswolds to the relative safety of Worcester.

Thanks to the decision of Essex and Waller to divide their forces, Waller being left to deal with the king while Essex marched west, Charles was unexpectedly able to turn the tables on his opponents, and, after mauling Waller at Cropredy Bridge (29 June), turned west in pursuit of Essex.

Once again, although contemporary accounts make few direct references to him, Astley commanded the 5–6,000 foot of the Oxford Army with efficiency and skill. He played, for example, a major role in the preliminary operations around Lostwithiel designed to tighten the noose around the Earl of Essex and his army. On 14 August, on the eastern bank of the River Fowey, he seized Lord Mohun's house at Bodinnick Ferry and the little port of Polruan at the mouth of the river, thus helping to seal Essex off from relief by land from Plymouth or by sea through the port of Fowey.[17]

Astley's role in the hard-fought Second Battle of Newbury (20 October) is again obscure. Most probably he was with the two Oxford Army tertias commanded by his son, Bernard Astley, and by that other fine infantry commander, George Lisle, in their spirited defence of Shaw House and its environs against the army of the Earl of Manchester.

At the end of the campaign Sir Jacob was raised to the peerage with the title of Baron Astley of Reading.

Astley was now 66 years old, perhaps a little elderly for the rigours of field command. It may be that Prince Rupert, now in command of the Royalist armies, would have considered replacing his old tutor as Major General of Foot by a younger man, such as the well-respected military theoretician Henry Tillier, who had served Rupert in the same role during the Marston Moor campaign. However, Tillier had been captured in the latter battle, and remained a prisoner. In the circumstances, Astley was indispensable. A soldier of his known ability and experience was urgently needed in view of the increasingly heavy odds which the Royalists faced as the campaigning season of 1645 began.

KEY ACTION: NASEBY, 14 JUNE 1645

Astley had to rebuild the Royalist foot, badly depleted in the prolonged campaigning of the previous year. Hitherto Wales had been a major source of recruits, but not only were its manpower resources becoming exhausted, but communications between North and Central Wales and Oxford had been severely disrupted by the loss of Shrewsbury in February. The relief of Chester by Prince Rupert at the end of March enabled the Royalists to conscript at least 1,000 recruits in north and mid-Wales, and despatch them to join Astley, now at Hereford, where he could incorporate them into his existing units. A Parliamentarian account described the desperate efforts which were being made to build up the strength of the Royalist foot:

The princes' army is the main rest of the King's affairs which they strengthen daily, by impressing the country, taking lesser brigades, and draining the garrisons.[18]

Astley was with Rupert at his victory over Edward Massey at Ledbury on 22 April, which may have provided a useful 'blooding' for some of his new recruits. On 9 May Astley, with 3,000 foot, joined King Charles at Evesham for the start of the spring campaign, bringing his total infantry strength to about 6,000 men. It was about the same number with which the Oxford Army had opened its campaign in the previous year, and there were hopes of obtaining further reinforcements from Royalist garrisons as the army marched northwards.

On 14 May the Royalists laid siege to Hawksley House, a small Parliamentarian garrison in Worcestershire. Astley's foot played the main role, and:

in a short time they carry their Lines close by the Moatside (for it was moated close about) and by trenches draws away the Water, which the besieged perceiving after we had made a shot or two, they call for a parley; and at last were fain to yield the house, their arms, and themselves prisoners without any great loss either of men or time.[19]

On 31 May Astley's foot stormed Leicester, though with fierce fighting that cost the Royalists some 500 casualties. Equally serious were the losses resulting from the large numbers of Royalist foot who then deserted with their booty. Although some were rounded up, valuable time was lost.

In the debates which followed the capture of Leicester, Astley probably sided with Rupert and Langdale in pressing for a continued march north, while Digby and his supporters urged that the Royalist army turn south, and engage Fairfax and the New Model Army. The compromise eventually reached, whereby the Royalists would remain in the vicinity of Daventry until Oxford had been re-provisioned, gave Fairfax the time he needed to close in on the King and his army.

On news of Fairfax's approach, King Charles called a hasty Council of War at Market Harborough in the early hours of 14 June. In the recriminations which followed later, Digby would claim that Rupert had chosen to attack the enemy against the advice of Astley. This claim, while demonstrating the value placed on Astley's experience, is impossible to verify. It was denied by Rupert's supporter, Will Legge, and Astley did not record his version of events.

If Astley did oppose the decision to attack, it was probably because of concerns regarding the strength of his infantry. Estimates of the total strength of the Royalist army at Naseby vary widely between 7,500, given by Bernard De Gomme, and John Belasyse's figure of 12,000.[20] The latter figure is probably nearer the truth. We are equally unclear about the strength of the Royalist foot on the day. Astley probably had about 7,000 foot in all, compared with about 8,500 in the New Model.[21] Both included a core of veterans, but also a large number of new recruits, while the Royalists, who still retained a number of weak units brigaded together,

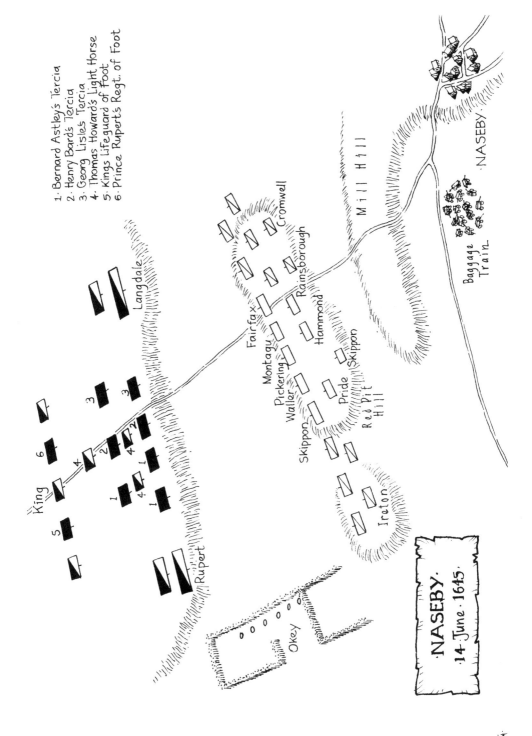

1. Bernard Astley's Tercia
2. Henry Bard's Tercia
3. Georg Lisle's Tercia
4. Thomas Howard's Light Horse
5. Kings Lifeguard of Foot
6. Prince Rupert's Regt. of Foot

King

Langdale

Rupert

Okey

Cromwell

Fairfax

Rainsborough

Montagu
Pickering
Waller

Hammond

Skippon

Pride
Skippon

Red Pit Hill

Ireton

Mill Hill

NASEBY

Baggage Train

NASEBY.
·14·June·1645·

had over a thousand supernumerary officers in their ranks. Astley may have had a slight qualitative edge over his opponents, though by no means as great as sometimes suggested.

The battlefield of Naseby consisted of open fields with a few hedges and patches of gorse. To the north was the rising ground of Dust Hill, where the Royalists eventually drew up, and, on the southern side of Naseby Field, a ridge known as Mill Hill. The Parliamentarians began drawing up to the north of Mill Hill on a long escarpment, but Fairfax soon pulled his men back about 480 feet from the scarp, enabling them, probably for morale reasons, to deploy out of sight of the enemy. His Major General of Foot, Philip Skippon, 'obeyed the Orders for doing it only because he could not get them altered.' Presumably Skippon felt that his original position was more favourable for receiving the Royalist attack, the Parliamentarians having decided to stand on the defensive. In their new position the Parliamentarian foot were separated from the level ground by a gentle slope. The New Model foot formed three brigades, Skippon's, Pickering's, and Fairfax's, each of three regiments, in three lines, with six regiments in the first and three in the second and third lines. Discounting the baggage guard and a 'forlorn hope' of musketeers forming a forward skirmish line, Skippon probably had about 6,600 men in his main body.

After detaching bodies of musketeers to support the Royalist horse, and presumably a guard for the baggage, Astley may have had some 6,000 foot available. These were formed into nine bodies or divisions, each totalling about 500 men. Each division was formed six deep, and deployed in 'chequer board' fashion, so that units in the second line could move up in support through gaps in the first line.

Between 10–11am the Royalist advance began. As they sighted each other, the opposing troops 'with mighty shouts expressed a hearty desire of fighting'. If, as is likely, the Royalists also had a forlorn hope of musketeers forward, then these will have initially engaged their Parliamentarian counterparts in a fire fight before the latter fell back on their main body. As they did so the Parliamentarian foot in the first line probably doubled their files from six to three ready to fire a concentrated musket volley known as a 'salvee'.

As the Royalist foot began to ascend the slope from the plain, their right flank was engaged by Henry Ireton's Regiment of Horse. This had avoided being caught up in the on-going cavalry engagement with Prince Rupert, and Ireton now attacked the flank of Astley's right-hand tertia, commanded by Astley's son, Bernard. The attack was beaten off, possibly with the aid of Thomas Howard''s brigade of horse, which was supporting Astley's foot. Ireton had 'his horse shot under him, and himself run through the thigh with a Pike, and into the face with a Halbert [and] was taken prisoner by the enemy.'[22]

As the bodies of opposing infantry closed, the pairs of light guns stationed in the intervals between the divisions in Skippon's front line may have fired a few ineffectual shots, then the Parliamentarian first line advanced to the brow of the hill and fired their 'salvee'. This mostly passed harmlessly over the heads of the Royalists.

Before the Parliamentarians could fire again, the Royalists were on them. The Royalist musketeers may not have paused to fire at all, but 'the Foot charged not each other until they were within twelve paces one of another, and could not charge above twice, but were at push of Pike.'[23]

Each division of foot had a block of up to 200 pikes, six deep, at its centre, and as these moved forward into the kind of pushing, stamping 'rugby scrum' known as 'push of pike', the musketeers prepared to engage each other with clubbed muskets. Hand-to-hand fighting began on the crest of the ridge, and some on both sides 'gave a little back'. There were probably few casualties at this stage, and the Parliamentarians may have had an initial advantage in the encounter.

However, the Royalists, with their second line moving up in support, and possibly pushed on by Howard's horse, came on again, some of the pikemen perhaps dropping their pikes and engaging the enemy with their swords. To Sir Edward Walker, watching the encounter with the king and his reserve a few hundred yards to the rear, things seemed to be going well. He could see that the Royalist foot:

Falling in with Sword and butt-end of Musket did notable Execution; so much as I saw their Colours fall, and their Foot in great disorder.[24]

However, owing to Skippon's longer frontage and slightly larger numbers, Astley was not able to engage the Parliamentarian foot along its entire line. Sir Thomas Fairfax's Regiment on the far right of Skippon's first line was apparently not engaged at all in this first action. Astley, who had initially been significantly outnumbered, now began to push Skippon back, but his own left flank was vulnerable to attack from Fairfax's strong regiment. To prevent this, Astley evidently ordered forward from the reserve the King's and Prince Rupert's Regiments of Foot.

Meanwhile, Skippon's first line was being steadily forced back in a heaving, pushing press of struggling men. Some of the second line of Prince Rupert's horse under the Earl of Northampton also perhaps moved up to threaten Skippon's left flank. Part of the Parliamentarian first line, Pickering's, Montagu's and possibly Waller's Regiments, were pushed back behind their second line regiments. Fairfax's Regiment probably remained in place, still unengaged, while the brunt of the Royalist attack now fell on Skippon's own exposed Regiment, attacked in front and perhaps on both flanks as well. With 130 men seriously wounded, about one in six of its strength, Skippon's unit suffered almost half of the overall total of wounded in the Parliamentarian foot.[25] Skippon, a vulnerable figure on horseback, received a musket shot below the ribs. Though seriously wounded, he refused to quit the field.

Pickering's and Montagu's Regiments also suffered significant losses, while those of the second line units were much lighter, suggesting that the impetus of the Royalist attack had begun to slow before they were engaged.

The infantry battle line began to swing in an easterly direction, with the Parliamentarian right pivoting on Fairfax's Regiment. Patterns of shot which have been uncovered suggest that the Parliamentarians were not actually pushed back very far, certainly not off the plateau of higher ground known as Red Pit Hill.[26]

With the momentum of Astley's attack lost, the customary pause now took place as the opposing foot engaged in a fire fight, the Parliamentarian second line fighting for time for their disorganized first line to reform behind them, and Astley hoping for the intervention of the King's and Rupert's foot regiments from the reserve. The musketeers were now firing successively by file, as explained in detail by the contemporary military writer, William Barriffe:

> advancing of two ranks to fire, ten paces before the Front, is commonly used, when one or both Battles march against each other, the Musketeers being led forth by two ranks together ten or twenty paces before the front of the body: that so they may come near enough to do certain execution. A Sergeant from each flank, leading up the two foremost ranks, (according as they shall have ordered the first rank of each file) is to present, and give fire, wheeling either all off to the right, or to the right and left and so successively, the rest of the ranks advancing, firing and wheeling off this way they may give fire, once or oftener over, as the enemy doth advance. All this while if there be no fear of the enemy's horse, then the Pikes may move Shouldered and close forward to their Order; by that means saving their Pikes from being shattered and broken by the bullets that fly at random.[27]

The main problem now facing Astley was a lack of reserves with which to renew his attack. The King's Lifeguard of Foot and Rupert's Bluecoats, which had been intended to fulfill this role, were now facing problems of their own. Deployed to Astley's left rear to watch Fairfax's Regiment, they found themselves under threat from Oliver Cromwell's victorious cavalry, who had just largely seen off Langdale's Northern Horse on the Royalist left. Cromwell now turned part of his horse against Astley's foot.

They seem first to have fallen on Rupert's men, who formed the customary 'hedgehog' formation designed to meet cavalry attacks, with the pikemen in the centre, their pikes thrusting outwards, and the musketeers crouched firing from beneath their shelter. A Parliamentarian account described how:

> then the right wing of our Horse (wherein the General [Fairfax] was in person) charged in the flank of the blue regiment of the enemie's foot, who stood to it, till the last man, abundance of them slain, and all the rest surrounded, wounded and taken.[28]

Another Parliamentarian report may refer to the same action:

> the Blue regiment of the King stood to it very stoutly, and stirred not, like a wall of brass, though encompassed by our Forces, so that our men were forced to knock them down with the butt end of their Muskets. It is conceived that a great part of them were Irish, and chose rather to die in the field than be hanged.'[29]

Probably at around the same time Nathaniel Fiennes's Regiment of Cromwell's horse engaged the King's Lifeguard of Foot, and broke them after a fierce resistance, taking 15 colours. The Parliamentarians admitted that the Royalist foot 'did as gallantly as ever men on earth could do'[30], but 'were at last overpowered with numbers, and forced to retreat.'[31]

While Cromwell's horse began their attack on the reserve of Royalist foot, Astley's main assault had bogged down. Once Cromwell's horse began their assault, Astley, to judge from the interpretation of shot patterns uncovered by investigators, seems to have begun pulling his main body of foot back in what became an increasingly disorderly retreat, but not a rout. Fighting a series of rearguard actions, Astley's foot, probably still with some of Thomas Howard's horse in support, fell back for more than a mile across the Sibertoft Plateau to the north of Dust Hill.

As the retreat went on the Royalists came under further pressure as Colonel Okey's New Model regiment of dragoons mounted up and joined in the attack. The general direction of the Royalist retreat was towards their baggage train, where another stand appears to have been made. At about this point Astley's hard-fighting foot began to break ranks and attempt to flee, with a final stand probably taking place on Moot and Wadborough Hills.

By no later than 1pm, most of the fighting was over. Astley's foot had been effectively destroyed, John Rushworth claiming that 'the General [Fairfax] hath so broken the Enemy's Foot, that he could not hear or see that they brought off a hundred.'[32] Although the mounted Royalist officers on the whole made their escape, Astley himself reportedly had a close shave: 'Sir Jacob Astley was near taking, we got the cap off his head.'[33]

In all over 4,000 Royalist foot were captured, plus about 450 officers, while many of the estimated 1,000 Royalist dead must have been from among the infantry.

Astley's foot had fought their last battle. The infantry action at Naseby was among the hardest-fought actions of its kind in the entire war. It had been a ferocious encounter between Astley and Philip Skippon, arguably the best two infantry commanders of the war, and the result could easily have gone either way. Astley seems to have handled his men with consummate skill, and only the intervention of Cromwell's horse saved the day for the New Model Army.

Astley accompanied the king and his surviving cavalry on their retreat to Hereford, where, on 23 June, the Council of War resolved to raise another 10,300 foot in Wales and the Marches, as well as attempting to obtain the release by exchange of some of the veteran foot of the King's Lifeguard. They had little success. News of the defeat of the Western Royalists on 10 July at Langport led to large-scale desertions among such levies as had actually been raised, while Parliament took steps to ensure that the foot captured at Naseby, if they did not either enter foreign service or enlist with the New Model, were kept captive. The devastating losses among officers and NCOs in any case made any attempt to rebuild the Oxford Army foot a virtually impossible task.

The last battle

It was not, however, the end of Jacob Astley's part in the war. He briefly replaced the unpopular Charles Gerard in command in South Wales, until the fall of Bristol in September fatally undermined Royalist control in the area. Astley then accompanied the king on his march north and eventually back to Oxford.

One last task remained for him. On 6 December the King appointed Astley as Lieutenant General of Worcestershire, Staffordshire, Herefordshire and Shropshire, with the capable Sir Charles Lucas as Lieutenant General of Horse. Clarendon explains the virtually impossible mission with which they were entrusted:

> There were yet some garrisons which remained in his [the king's] obedi-
> ence, and which were like, during the winter season, to be preserved from
> any attempt of the enemy; but upon the approach of the spring, if the King
> should be without an army in the field, the fate of those few places was easy
> to be discerned. And which way an army could possibly be brought
> together, or where it should be raised, was not within the compass of the
> wisest man's comprehension. However, the more difficult it was, the more
> vigour was to be applied to the attempt.[34]

Apart from parts of the south-west of England, the southern Marches of Wales centred on Worcester were the last major area still under Royalist control, containing a number of garrisons and the last remaining veteran troops. Astley inherited a chaotic situation, with mutinous troops and a discontented and rebellious local civilian population. The fall of Hereford on 16 December worsened the Royalist position still further.

Astley's other pressing task was to try to relieve hard-pressed Chester, which with insufficient forces proved to be impossible. After Chester fell on 3 February Astley shifted his efforts to his main mission; preparing a field army for the spring. As a first step he attempted to regain civilian co-operation by clamping down on undisciplined soldiers. A tough professional soldier, Henry Washington, was made Governor of Worcester, with the equally competent Sir Thomas Tyldesley at Lichfield. Sir Charles Lucas began efforts to clamp down on the depredations of the disorderly Royalist horse.

Despite only lukewarm support from the civil authorities, by early spring Astley had succeeded in restoring a modicum of order to his command, and began calling in detachments from his garrisons to create a field force.

As the Royalist situation steadily deteriorated:

> his Majesty resolved to join himself with the Lord Astley, and either
> endeavour to relieve Banbury, or to retire to Worcester and there take new
> Resolutions. To this end Lord Astley had Order to march with all his Horse
> and Foot out of Worcestershire and over Avon to come to Stow, and so to

Chipping Norton; where his Majesty with about 1,500 Horse and Foot drawn out of Oxford and other Garrisons intended to meet him.[35]

By the middle of March Astley had mustered at Worcester about 700 horse and 2,300 foot, including many 'reformadoes' (officers without commands) and the remnants of a number of veteran units. However, intercepted letters had disclosed Royalist plans to their opponents; Sir William Brereton was preparing to detach troops from the siege of Lichfield to pursue Astley, while forces from Gloucester and Hereford under Colonel John Birch and Major General Thomas Morgan were on alert to intercept the Royalists.

With the usual crossing point at Evesham in enemy hands, Astley had to find means to get across the River Avon, after which he would have to defeat or evade Birch and Morgan, with Brereton heading south with 1,000 horse.

Morgan and Birch rendezvoused at Gloucester on 15 March, then marched to Evesham, where, reinforced from its garrison, they were able to place 2,300 men at Broadway, across Astley's likely line of march to join the king. The old Royalist general reacted skillfully. Leaving Worcester on 19 March, he first feinted towards Evesham using Lucas and the horse, himself with the main body of foot marching northwards along the Droitwich road, as if bound for the relief of Lichfield. Unclear whether the Royalist objective was Lichfield or Oxford, Brereton abandoned his march south and turned back towards Birmingham.

His first aim achieved, early on 20 March, in a night march, Astley swung across country in a south-easterly direction. Using a pontoon bridge he had brought with him, Astley crossed the Avon at Bidford, and then marched on up into the Cotswolds via Honeybourne and Chipping Campden, slipping past the flank of Birch and Morgan at Broadway. By late afternoon the Royalists were marching across the great open downs of the Cotswolds towards Stow-on-the-Wold. Birch and Morgan were unwilling to bring on a major engagement until they were reinforced by Brereton, and skirmished with Astley's rearguard in an attempt to slow him down.

They broke off contact at dusk. By now Astley, though aware of the need for haste, also knew that his men were exhausted after a march of 25 miles. As night fell, he halted around the village of Donnington, about two miles short of Stow. He might have been better to have pushed on and fortified the town, although the hill slopes around Donnington also offered good defensive possibilities.

At about 2am on 21 March Brereton, with 800 horse, joined Morgan and Birch. Astley knew that he could no longer avoid battle. As dawn broke, he deployed the last Royalist army of the First Civil War on the hillside about a quarter of a mile west of Donnington, his foot in the centre and horse on the wings.

Fighting began at about 6am. It was a closely contested action, with at least two Parliamentarian assaults thrown back. But once Brereton's excellent cavalry had routed the opposing horse under Sir William Vaughan, the Royalist foot came under attack from three sides. Astley tried to pull back into Stow in order to make a last stand in the marketplace, but was captured there by an enemy trooper. He ordered his men to surrender, and 'being somewhat wearied from the fight, was given a drum to sit on, remarking: 'You have done your work, boys, and may go play, unless you fall out among yourselves.'[36]

Astley's forecast was of course correct. For the Royalists the war was indeed almost at an end. Astley spent its remaining few months a prisoner at Warwick Castle, and was then released to go home to Norfolk. Although briefly imprisoned during the Second Civil War of 1648, the old soldier had drawn sword for the last time, and died peacefully at home in 1652.

Jacob Astley, unsung professional soldier of few words, was one of the most competent Royalist commanders. Out of unpromising and inadequate materials he created in the Royalist foot one of the finest fighting forces of the war, handled by him with unfailing ability. None other than their eventual vanquisher, Sir Thomas Fairfax, paid tribute to them when he said later that Astley's veteran infantry who had enlisted with them were among the best troops in the New Model Army.

Chapter Five
Prince Maurice

Prince Maurice has always been overshadowed by his elder brother, Prince Rupert. His reputation was fixed in a typically vivid pen portrait by the Earl of Clarendon:

> The prince had never sacrificed to the Graces, nor conversed amongst men of quality, but had most used the company of ordinary and inferior men, with whom he loved to be very familiar. He was not qualified with parts of nature, and less with any acquired; and towards men of the best condition, with whom he might very well have justified a familiarity, he maintained at least the full state of his birth, and understood very little more of the war than to fight very stoutly when there was occasion.[1]

In the nineteenth century, Eliot Warburton, in his ground-breaking *Memoirs of Prince Rupert and the Cavaliers,* (1849), accepted and underlined Clarendon's view of the prince, and more recent writers, though praising Maurice for his loyalty to his brother, on the whole do little to question this image. Alfred Burne and Peter Young commented that Maurice's 'achievements at Ripple Field, Lansdown and perhaps Roundway Down seem to belie this [Clarendon's] judgement.'[2] More recently, Ronald Hutton has shown that Maurice's skills as an administrator have been underestimated.[3]

Early life

In his portraits Maurice has the same darkly handsome looks as his brother, though perhaps without some of the arrogant self-confidence of Rupert. Born in Brandenburg in 1621, one of the numerous offspring of the exiled Frederick, Elector Palatine, and his wife, Elizabeth of Bohemia, it was obvious, particularly in the family's straightened circumstances, that Maurice's destiny was as a soldier. Elizabeth admitted as much when she named the baby after his renowned relative Maurice, Prince of Orange, 'Because he will have to be a fighter.'

Clarendon's assessment of Maurice was supported by incidents of his youth.

He was one of a group of aristocratic rowdies who roamed the streets of the Hague at night, annoying respectable citizens. Within two years Maurice had begun his military career. In 1637, along with Rupert, Maurice, aged 17, served with the Dutch forces at the celebrated Siege of Breda, where both of the young men speedily made a name for themselves. They:

> put themselves upon the perdu [forlorn hope]; and crept up so close to the enemy's works, that they could hear the soldiers discourse on the other side, and made discovery of their design to issue out, waiting till they were just upon the point of a sally. Whereupon the Princes immediately returned, and gave the besiegers so seasonable notice of it, that they were presently ready for them, and beat them in again with loss.[4]

After killing a man in a duel, Maurice was despatched by his mother to the University of Paris, in a foredoomed bid to smooth some of his rougher edges. Within two years he was ready for military action again. Maurice had visited England with his brother and won the favour of his uncle, King Charles, and Queen Henrietta Maria. In January 1639 Lord Leicester recommended to the king that Maurice, back in the Hague from Paris and in need of occupying, should take service in the largely Swedish army of Bernard of Saxe-Weimar: 'for . . . besides that he has a body well-made, strong, and able to endure hardships, he hath a mind that will not let it be idle if he can have employment. He is very temperate, of a grave and settled disposition, but would very fain be in action . . . If Duke Bernhard should die, the army, in all likelihood, would obey Maurice.'

King Charles was evidently impressed with the reports he received concerning his nephew, or at least saw the need to keep him out of trouble, for, late in 1640, Maurice's elder brother, Charles Louis, now Elector Palatine, wrote to his mother that the king 'would seek to get money for Maurice, and then he may go to what army he pleases.' In the event the prince served with the Swedish forces under Marshal Baner, at the Siege of Amberg in January 1641, without Rupert, who was a prisoner of the Imperialists following his capture at Lemgo.

On Rupert's release, the brothers were re-united, and remained closely associated for the remainder of Maurice's life. In August 1642 they arrived in England to offer their services to King Charles in the war against Parliament. Despite his youth, Maurice had a solid body of military experience, and was given one of the earliest commissions to raise a regiment of horse. With the first troop raised, Maurice charged into action at Powick Bridge, on 21 September, and received the first of his many wounds. It was evidently a slight one, for the prince and his regiment, now consisting of four troops, were again in action in the victorious charge of Prince Rupert's wing of horse at Edgehill (23 October).

KEY ACTION: RIPPLE FIELD, 13 APRIL 1643

Maurice was with his brother at the capture of Cirencester in February 1643. His birth and evident military competence, as well, no doubt, as the favour in which he was held by King Charles, led to more senior command. On 2 March 1643 Maurice was given an independent commission with the task of defending Royalist territory in the southern Welsh Marches against the incursions of Parliamentarian forces under Sir William Waller.

Some indecisive manoeuvring followed. Maurice found difficulty in bringing the elusive Waller to bay. In April Waller decided to exploit the victory which he had recently won over Lord Herbert's raw 'mushroom army' of Welsh levies at Highnam near Gloucester by subduing Monmouthshire. On 4 April he marched through Monmouth itself without opposition and, via Usk, reached Chepstow. Two days later he learnt that Lord Herbert, with a scratch force mustered from local Royalist garrisons, was moving towards him from the west, while Prince Maurice had joined other forces under Lord Grandison at Tewkesbury, giving him about 2,000 horse and dragoons.

Maurice attempted to cut off Waller's retreat by securing the crossings of the River Severn in the vicinity of Gloucester. Sir William reacted by returning to the Gloucester area on 10 April with the intention of beating up some of Maurice's scattered outposts. However, he moved too slowly to surprise Maurice's main quarters at Little Dean in a night attack, as he had intended, and only approached after daylight.

Maurice had two regiments of horse and one each of dragoons and foot, the latter consisting of 'commanded' musketeers from a number of units. He drew up his foot on the south side of the village of Little Dean, with the horse stationed on a hill to the north. As Waller approached, the Royalist foot fired a volley and then fell back through the village, followed by Parliamentarian dragoons. On the far side of Little Dean the Parliamentarians took up position behind some stone walls at the foot of the hill on which the Royalist horse were drawn up. Waller's horse formed up behind their dragoons, and an uneasy stand-off followed for the next three hours.

The Royalists were very dubious about attacking, for, as Captain Richard Atkyns of Maurice's Regiment of Horse explained:

> The charge was seemingly as desperate as any I was ever in, it being to beat the enemy from a wall which was a strong breastwork, with a gate in the middle, possessed by above 200 musketeers, besides horse. We were to charge down a steep hill of above 2 score yards in length, as good a mark as they could wish. Our party consisting of between two and three hundred horse, not a man of them would follow us, so the officers, about 10 or 12 of us, agreed to gallop down in as good order as we could and make a desperate charge upon them.[5]

River Severn

CHEPSTOW

MONMOUTH

HEREFORD

ROSS

R. Wye

BRISTOL

COLEFORD

LITTLE DEAN

WORCESTER

UPTON
Ripple Field
TEWKESBURY

GLOUCESTER

EVESHAM

STOW ON-THE-WOLD

BROADWAY

CHIPPING NORTON

R. Avon

·THE·SEVERN·VALLEY·
·CAMPAIGN·
·1643·

·RIPPLE·FIELD·
·13 April·1643·

Maurice

Ordnance Hill

Waller
2nd Position

Waller
1st Position

RIPPLE

Ripple Brook

Fortunately, the Parliamentarians, not relishing the prospect of battle, had already begun to withdraw towards Gloucester. The Royalists charged Waller's rear-guard and a confused action followed in the main street of Little Dean. Atkyns remembered how:

> they [the Royalists] were so wedged together that they routed themselves, so that there was no passage for a long time. All this while the enemy were upon me, cutting my coat upon my armour in several places, and discharging pistols as they got up to me, being the outermost man . . . but when they pursued us to the town, Major Leighton [of the King's Lifeguard of Foot] had made good a stone house, and so prepared for them with musketeers that one volley of shot made them retreat. They were so near to me that a musket ball from one of my own men took off one of the bars of the cap I charged with, and went through my hair and did me no hurt.[6]

Prince Maurice had not particularly distinguished himself in his first action of note in independent command, and the Royalists now decided to return to the eastern bank of the Severn. Waller, back in Gloucester, hoped to isolate Maurice on the west bank. So he sent a detachment of troops under the Governor of Gloucester, Edward Massey, upstream by boat to occupy Tewkesbury and break the pontoon bridge which the Royalists had constructed over the Severn at Upton.

Maurice, however, moving quickly, arrived at Upton in time to frustrate the plan, and drove the enemy bridge-breaking party back across the river. On 13 April, at Ripple, about three and a half miles north of Tewkesbury, the retreating Parliamentarians met up with Waller and about 1,500 men, mostly horse, who were coming to their support. The Parliamentarian commander decided to make a stand near Ripple Field, on the north side of the village. He advanced through Ripple itself, and occupied a ridge known as the Bank, or 'Old Nan's' (Ordnance) Hill which ran from east to west between the village of Uckinghall and the Ripple Brook. To the north lay the wide flat plain of Ripple Field, where Maurice was drawn up with about 2,000 horse. There may have been one or two small hedged enclosures between the field and the foot of the hill.

Waller seems initially to have intended to make a stand, and brought up several light guns, but they proved useless because of 'having neither shot prepared nor cannoniers that understood the business'. Waller also realized that Maurice was outflanking his position on the hill with parties of musketeers who were infiltrating through the hedgerows of the enclosures at its foot. He decide to fall back to Ripple itself.

His route lay along a sunken lane, lined with hedgerows, where Sir William hoped to ambush the pursuing Royalists. After musketeers lining the hedges had thrown the Royalist vanguard into confusion, Waller planned to counter-charge them with his horse as they attempted to deploy out of the lane into a field at its further end.

However, as Waller began his pull-back, Maurice struck aggressively, hitting the Parliamentarians in front and on both flanks before they could reach the lane.

The Royalist cavalry on the right swung out towards Uckinghall village and then back up the gentler slope of Old Nan's Hill. The Cavaliers were aided by having the sun behind them, causing visibility problems for their opponents.

As they crowded back into the narrow entrance of the lane leading to Ripple, the Parliamentarians panicked. They retreated in increasing disorder; the dragoons who were supposed to be acting as a rearguard broke and ran into their own musketeers who were attempting to set up an ambuscade. Waller led about 70 men of Sir Arthur Haselrige's troop of 'Lobsters' (fully armoured cuirassiers) in a counter-attack, but was overwhelmed by superior numbers. The Royalists claimed to have accounted for at least fifty of their opponents, and went in hot pursuit down the lane.

They were temporarily halted by a quick-thinking Parliamentarian trooper, who took a gate off its hinges and used it to try to block the lane. Massey and Waller managed to partially re-form their men on the open ground on the other side of Ripple village, but broke again before another charge, although the Royalist pursuit was checked by the arrival of Parliamentarian reinforcements from Tewkesbury.

Maurice, returning in triumph to Oxford, claimed eighty Parliamentarians killed in action and eighty more drowned in the River Severn for the loss of only two of his men. Enemy losses were almost certainly fewer, but Ripple Field had been a notable success for Prince Maurice, and demonstrated a high degree of ability as a cavalry commander, albeit rather less as a strategist.

Command in the west

Ripple Field convinced the king of Maurice's suitability for more senior command, and he was now appointed Lieutenant General of Horse to the Earl of Hertford, the Royalist commander in the West. They did not have a happy relationship. Hertford, though a devoted Royalist, was no real soldier, and found the brusque and forceful young prince, who tended to treat him with scarcely-veiled contempt, difficult to work with. Atkyns hinted at Maurice's view of Hertford: 'Prince Maurice had such an entire affection to the King, that (not regarding his own dignity, he took a commission under the Marquis, rather than the King's cause should fail.'[7]

Maurice left Oxford on 15 May, with four regiments of horse and one of foot, and on 4 June he and Hertford linked up with Sir Ralph Hopton and the Cornish army at Chard in Somerset. An already difficult command situation was now still more complex, but in practice Hertford and Maurice seem to have uneasily shared senior command, with Hopton acting as 'Field Marshal General', technically second-in-command of the united forces. As would soon be demonstrated, it was far from ideal.

The combined Royalist army, totalling about 2,000 horse, 300 dragoons, 4,000 foot and sixteen guns now advanced on Taunton, which fell without resistance. Probably to the relief of all concerned, Hertford remained at Taunton to organize its defence, leaving Maurice to lead the pursuit of the local Parliamentarian forces. Several small cavalry actions took place in the vicinity of Glastonbury and the Mendip Hills, as the Parliamentarians, under Colonel Edward Popham, formed a rearguard to hold off Maurice while their foot and baggage withdrew.

By now Maurice's old adversary, Sir William Waller, had reached Bath, and on 8 June he reinforced Popham with eight troops of horse and one of dragoons. They arrived soon after dawn, as Royalist horse led by the Earl of Carnarvon fell on Popham's rearguard just outside the village of Chewton Mendip, and scattered it. Waller's reinforcements counter-attacked, and drove the Royalists back through the village until they encountered Maurice and his own Regiment of Horse. The prince led a charge which scattered half of the Parliamentarian horse while they were still forming up, but he got too far ahead of his men, and the remainder of the enemy closed in around him. In the mêlée which followed, Maurice received 'two hurts on his head with a sword and was beaten off his horse'. Possibly because he was dazed, the Parliamentarians remained ignorant of the identity of their prisoner, and within a few hours, Carnarvon, now in command of the Royalist horse, mounted a rescue bid.

The Royalist horse attacked strongly, and, Atkyns recalls:

> The dragoons on both sides, seeing us so mixed with their men that they could not fire on us, but they might kill their own men as well as ours: took horse and away they run also. In this charge, I gave one Captain Kitely quarter, twice, and at the last he was killed, the Lord Arundell of Wardour, also took a dragoon's colours . . . But all of us overran the Prince, being prisoner in that party, for he was on foot, and had a hurt on his head, and I suppose not known to be the Prince. My groom coming after us, espied the Prince, and all being in confusion, he alighted from his horse, and gave him to the Prince, who carried him off.[8]

Maurice was evidently not much hurt, and showing the concern for his men which Clarendon had noted:

> The next morning I [Atkyns] waited upon Prince Maurice, and presented him with a case of pistols, which my uncle Sandys brought newly out of France, the neatest that I ever saw, which he then wanted, but as yet he knew not the man who mounted him, nor whose horse it was; when I saw the horse I knew him, and the man that rid him that day; who was the groom aforesaid; the Prince told me he would not part with the horse, till he saw the man that horsed him, if he were alive, and commanded me to send him to him: which I did that day, and when he came to the Prince, he knew him, and gave him ten broad pieces and told him withall, that he should have any preferment he was capable of.[9]

With the customary ingratitude of the Civil War soldier, the man shortly afterwards deserted.

Maurice seems to have enjoyed the company of his officers. At about this time, after killing a buck while hunting, he invited them to dine on it with him. The somewhat Puritanical Atkyns refused, but on another occasion, Maurice demonstrated to Atkyns his grasp of the priorities of a cavalry officer when he asked 'whether I had quartered the horse well, and I told him I had; he bid me to say no more but to sit down to supper.'[10]

It is not entirely clear what role Maurice had in events leading up to the bloody battle of Lansdown (5 July). He seems to have been in effective command of the Royalists during the preliminary operations, but deteriorating relations between the Oxford horse and the Cornish foot did nothing to make matters run smoothly. Maurice was never noted as a disciplinarian, and his failure to check some of the worst excesses of his cavalry angered the Cornish, who may also have resented the natural advantages of a horseman over a foot soldier when it came to looting. As a result, fleeting opportunities to inflict significant damage to Waller were lost.

Maurice apparently had no part in the decision to launch a frontal attack on Waller's strong position at Lansdown, which evidently was either made unilaterally by Hopton, or was the result of unauthorized action by the Cornish foot. The mauled Royalists made a difficult march to Devizes and, faced with imminent siege by Waller, considered their next move. It was agreed that Maurice and the horse, accompanied by Hertford, should break out and head for Oxford to obtain assistance.[11]

Maurice rode as a volunteer with the relief force which returned on 13 July and inflicted a crushing defeat on Waller on Roundway Down. Although credit is usually given to Lord Wilmot, it seems that, until commissions were compared, Maurice felt that he was the senior officer present, thinking that he deserved more praise for the victory than he is generally given.

Maurice was present with the Western forces at the capture of Bristol (26 July), and afterwards became involved in a potentially serious dispute. Clarendon claimed that:

> There was not from the beginning that conformity of humour and inclinations between the two princes and the Marquis of Hertford, as had been to be wished between all persons of honour who were engaged in a quarrel that could never prosper but by the union of the undertakers. Prince Maurice, and on his behalf, or rather the other by his impulsion), Prince Rupert, taking to heart, that a nephew of the king's should be lieutenant-general to the marquis, who had neither been exercised in the profession of a soldier, nor even now punctually studied the office of a general: on the other hand, the marquis, who was of the most gentle nature to the gentle, and as rough and resolute to the imperious, it may be, liked not the prince's assuming to himself more than became a lieutenant-general, and sometimes crossing acts of his with relation to the governing and disposing the affairs of the country, in which he knew himself better versed than the prince. . .[12]

The upshot was that in an attempt to exert his own authority, Hertford appointed Sir Ralph Hopton as Governor of Bristol, apparently ignorant that Rupert had requested the post for himself. A potentially explosive situation was defused by the personal intervention of the king, who reached a compromise by which Hopton served as deputy, and to all practical purposes actual, Governor of Bristol under Rupert's nominal command.

Nonetheless the affair was an example of the problems which the two princes could cause among the Royalist generals, and the need to find some useful and fitting employment for Maurice, preferably away from the main field army, was one of the considerations influencing Royalist decision-making after the capture of Bristol. Among the reasons against the Oxford Army and the Western forces being united was 'that if both armies had been kneaded into one, prince Maurice could have been but a private colonel.'[13]

Much of the west, including Dorchester, Exeter, Plymouth and a number of other towns, were still in Parliamentarian hands, and a separate Western army was required to subdue them. So the king ordered firstly the Earl of Carnarvon to march against Dorchester with the Western horse and dragoons, and Prince Maurice next day to follow with the foot and guns. Hertford, though still nominally General, was taken with the king to Oxford, in the honourable position of a member of his council.

The decision in Clarendon's view was a mistake; never fond of Maurice, he felt that if Hertford and Hopton had been given command in the West instead of the prince, 'a greater tide of good fortune had attended that expedition.'[14]

However, operations in the west opened favourably, when, on 2 August, Dorchester surrendered to the Earl of Carnarvon, and he also granted lenient terms to the defenders of Weymouth and Portland. Unfortunately, on Maurice's arrival, the agreements made by Carnarvon were partially ignored, and Carnarvon, angered by this and the looting carried out by the prince's forces, resigned his command and returned to the king. According to Clarendon, fears of retribution by Maurice's men caused the defenders of the small port of Lyme to reject the prince's summons to surrender. Leaving Lyme defiant, Maurice marched into Devon, and turned his attention to Exeter.

He believed that the appearance of a substantial Royalist army would result in the speedy submission of the Devon Parliamentarians. Exeter had been under ineffective Royalist blockade since the early summer, but the defences had been steadily strengthened by the garrison under the command of the Earl of Stamford. By early August a Royalist force of about 3,000 men had cut communications on the northern and western approaches to Exeter. The Parliamentarians hoped to hold on until relief could be organized from their other garrisons in the area, and from the sea by the Earl of Warwick's fleet.

But Royalist control of the mouth of the River Exe dashed the latter hope, and Maurice, adopting tactics suggesting that he had learnt from Carnarvon in Dorset, offered easy terms to the outlying Parliamentarian garrisons. On 27 August the townspeople of Barnstaple accepted a free pardon, and surrendered, and they were quickly followed by Bideford and Appledore.

At the same time Maurice's small-scale attacks had begun to eat away at the perimeter of Exeter's defences. By 4 September the Royalists were in a position to begin a bombardment of the city itself. This, together with the news of the surrender of the north Devon towns, broke the will of the citizens to resist. Offered Maurice's now customary easy conditions (on this occasion not fully adhered to), Exeter surrendered on 7 September.

Sending a detachment under Colonel John Digby to blockade Plymouth, Maurice moved against Dartmouth. With hindsight, he might have been better to have concentrated on Plymouth, where, after the fall of Exeter, morale among the townsfolk was at a low ebb. On 19 September Maurice, with 1,000 men, reached Totnes. His force was too weak to storm Dartmouth, if, as proved to be the case, its defenders were defiant. Forced to resort to a regular blockade, the Royalists' operations were frustrated by very wet weather, which hindered digging and caused widespread sickness among the attackers. It was not until 4 October that Maurice was able to bring up sufficient artillery to subdue Dartmouth Castle and begin to break down the outer defences of the town. Next day Dartmouth, granted generous terms, joined Maurice's list of conquests.

But his best chance of taking Plymouth had arguably now gone, and Maurice was struck down by a serious illness. Its nature is uncertain; both typhoid and the 'new disease', influenza, have been suggested. Certainly it was serious enough to be considered life-threatening. The king despatched his own personal physician, William Harvey, to assist Maurice's doctor. By mid-October they were able to send a favourable report to Prince Rupert; the illness, they said, was 'the ordinary raging disease of the army, a slow fever with great dejection of strength'. The doctors 'concluding the disease to be venomous, they do resolve to give very little physic, only a regular diet, and cordial antidotes.'[15]

Possibly because of the doctors' forbearance, Maurice made a gradual recovery, although when his forces moved against Plymouth in the middle of October, he was still probably far from fit. This may have been a factor in the failure of the siege which followed. Like other Royalist commanders before and after him, Maurice set up a string of outposts around the landward perimeter of Plymouth, and attempted to harass shipping in the Sound by means of gun batteries. This had no decisive effect, and although Maurice carried out several bombardments of Plymouth's outworks, and attempted on more than one occasion to mount limited assaults, these had no more success than attempts to gain the town by means of treachery.

On 22 December, still apparently unwell, Maurice ordered his forces to pull back into winter quarters around Tavistock and Plympton. He had suffered his first serious military reverse, though in justice to Maurice, it has to be said that no other Royalist commander had any more success at Plymouth.

One of the problems which had hindered Maurice's operations ever since he came to the West was the numerical weakness of his army. Early in 1644, in an attempt to remedy this, a Royalist Association of Devon and Cornwall was formed to recruit and provide supplies for Maurice's Western Army.

Siege of Lyme

With the arrival of spring the prince switched his attention back to unfinished business in Dorset, where Lyme remained in Parliamentarian hands. It not only provided a base for raids into Royalist territory, but its capture would complete a chain of garrisons, including Bridgwater and Taunton, running from coast to coast across the neck of the Western peninsula. Early in April, stripping the Devon garrisons of troops to augment his army, Maurice moved eastwards. On 19 April he established his headquarters at Axminster, and next day his army of about 4,500 men began closing in on Lyme, with the Royalists anticipating an easy success.

Lyme was contemptuously dismissed as 'a little vile fishing town defended by a small dry ditch'. Certainly its defences, the usual earth mounts or forts with connecting breastworks, were fairly weak. The town itself was small, with thatched houses vulnerable to incendiary attack, though the small fields and enclosures which surrounded its landward sides provided good defensive terrain. However, the Royalists had the advantage of holding the high ground which overlooked Lyme.

The defenders consisted originally of the ten companies of Colonel Sir Thomas Sealey's town regiment of foot, and a few horse, and though reinforced from time to time by sea, never totalled more than 1,500. Sir Thomas Sealey was nominal Governor of Lyme, but the real inspiration of the defence was the redoubtable Lieutenant Colonel Robert Blake. He did what he could to strengthen the outer defences, which eventually consisted of a trench, known as the 'Town Line', with a six-foot rampart and four 'mounts'. The line was probably about a mile in length, and the limited number of defenders had to be concentrated in the mounts. Keystones were the two central mounts, Davie's and Gatcher's or Middle Fort. The latter commanded any approach along the valley of the River Lim, while Marshall's or the West Fort covered the road into Lyme from the west.

The defenders rejected Maurice's summons, promising in return no quarter to any Cornish or Irish who fell into their hands. Deploying his forces, Maurice placed his four Cornish regiments, the remnants of those who had fought under Hopton in the previous year, but greatly reduced in numbers and morale, in the centre of his line to the north of the town. His two 'Irish' regiments, who seem to have included a number of 'native' Irish, were stationed to the left of the Cornish, their positions running down to the sea. On Maurice's right were his Devon troops and Lord Paulett's Regiment of Foot, occupying the line of cliffs overlooking Lyme's quay, known as the Cobb.

Their summons rejected, the Royalists launched their first assault next day, trying to seize some outlying cottages on the western side of the town. These were fired by the defenders, and the Royalists tried to take advantage of the cover of their smoke to approach nearer to the town. Nathan Drake, the diarist of the siege, reported that they:

> came down into the smoke into the closes from hedge to hedge, brandishing their swords, and so crept into ditches and lay very boldly shooting at us

every hour the same day with very great courage within very near pistol shot of our lane and the Western fort.[16]

This action would prove typical of the fighting around Lyme, with both sides taking advantage of the thick natural cover around the town to make attacks and sorties. On 22 April the Royalists established their first artillery battery to the north-west of the town in order to open fire on the West Fort. The Parliamentarians made a sally the next day, taking the battery and thirty-five prisoners, though they were then pushed back by Cornish troops.

This set the pattern for much of the action during the siege. The Royalists would set up gun batteries to fire at the defence works, and these would be subjected to vigorous sallies by the defenders. The result was that Royalist guns made little impression on the earthworks. On 28 April, in a change of tactics, the Royalists made their first attempt to storm Lyme. They do not seem to have pressed the assault very hard, as Drake said that the Royalist horse were employed to drive on their unenthusiastic foot, a common tactic. Those attackers who came near the mounts were repulsed by case shot. The Royalists also made use of fire arrows in an attempt to ignite the thatched roofs of the closely-packed houses, but these were generally quickly extinguished. More injurious were the effects on morale of the continuous bombardments and growing food shortages within Lyme.

On the evening of 6 May, under the cover of a thick fog, the Royalists mounted another major assault, timed to strike when most of the defenders were likely to be at supper. They attempted to storm the defences at three points, calling 'Fall on, fall on, the Town is ours, the day is ours!' One party of attackers managed to reach the centre of Lyme before being driven out. The Royalists were thought to have lost about 100 men, together with a set of colours said to be of Maurice's own regiment.

Whatever the actual tally of losses, there would be no further assault on Lyme for the next fortnight.

The besiegers now concentrated their gunfire against the Cobb in an attempt to prevent supplies from being disembarked. Although they could not reach Warwick's ships anchored out in Lyme Bay, the gunners could hit the small vessels used to ferry supplies to the Cobb. On 22 May there was intense action. Royalist guns sank one small ship, and later in the day a party, throwing 'wild fire' (probably incendiary grenades) broke through to the Cobb, and burnt several vessels. The Parliamentarians retaliated with a sortie which spiked one gun of a battery of whole and demi-cannon which had been established opposite the West Fort, but were themselves driven back by Cornish foot.

Over the next few days Maurice maintained his pressure on the Cobb. The townsfolk were by now desperately short of food, ammunition and even clothing, though some of the latter deficiencies were made up by a collection among Warwick's seamen.

On 25 May the Royalists brought up more guns to the cliffs overlooking the

Cobb, so that supplies could now only be brought in under cover of darkness. Three days later a steady build-up of Royalist troops convinced Warwick that a renewed assault was imminent. He reinforced the garrison with 300 of his seamen. At about noon on 29 May a force of about 1,000 Royalists began their expected onslaught. Carrying scaling ladders, they attacked the outworks 'even to the setting of the sun very hotly'. After eight hours of frequently fierce fighting, in which the women of Lyme took part, the assault died down.

Royalist losses are uncertain, but it proved to be the last such attempt on Lyme. Over the next few days the besiegers resumed their efforts to set fire to houses in the town by means of incendiary attacks, but with limited success.

On 15 June, with the news of the approach of the Earl of Essex and his army, Maurice raised the siege.

The prince's failure to take Lyme was the greatest setback of his military career. He had faced the usual difficulties experienced by other Royalist commanders in attempting to capture a coastal garrison, which thanks to Parliamentarian naval supremacy could be kept supplied by sea. His own troops, particularly his foot, were very variable in quality and morale, though many of the Cornish were veterans. Nevertheless, Maurice may be faulted for his frequent shifting of objectives. A concentration of his efforts on preventing the Parliamentarians from making use of the plainly vulnerable Cobb might have given the Royalists Lyme fairly quickly and at a lower price than the 2,000 or so men the unsuccessful siege may actually have cost them.

Later campaigns

Maurice, his army severely weakened by its losses at Lyme, was in no state to oppose Essex's advance into the West. The prince pulled back towards Exeter. He had only about 4,000 men immediately available, and tried to call in as many troops as could be spared from the neighbouring garrisons, warning Colonel Edward Seymour, the Governor of Dartmouth, to take care so that 'watchfulness may timely prevent their wicked purpose.' He was further distracted by the need to attempt to prevent rebellion in the notoriously pro-Parliamentarian towns of north Devon. In the event, Essex bypassed Exeter in favour of relieving Plymouth and entering Cornwall, and, although Barnstaple was lost, Maurice's immediate worries were eased on 27 July when his army of 5,000 foot and 2,000 horse, including 800 foot from Bristol and 1,000 new Somerset levies, linked up with the king and the Oxford Army.

Maurice, working in close consultation with the king's Lord General, the vastly experienced Earl of Forth, and probably benefiting from his advice, played a prominent part in the operations around Lostwithiel which eventually resulted in the surrender of Essex's foot.

On 27 October at the Second Battle of Newbury, Maurice's army, its numbers halved by desertion, especially among the Cornish infantry, consisted of a brigade of horse and two of foot, mostly very weak regiments merged together, and about nine guns. The Western Army lacked both cohesiveness and perhaps commitment. Tasked with holding Speen village, they were attacked by larger numbers of Essex's foot, under Philip Skippon, anxious to even the score for Lostwithiel. After a stiff action the Royalists were pushed back out of Speen, losing their nine guns.

However Maurice redeemed himself that same night, when, with the wounded Forth, he successfully extricated the Royalist army under cover of darkness.

Rupert, now de facto commander-in-chief of the Royalist forces, seems to have felt that Maurice had served long enough in the West. His record, after a promising start, had been one of failure. It may have been thought that, while Maurice's rank required him to hold some kind of independent command, one more closely under his brother's eye might be more appropriate. In December 1644 he was appointed to part of Rupert's old command on the Welsh Borders, with control of North Wales, Cheshire, Shropshire, Staffordshire, Herefordshire and Worcestershire.

Maurice left Oxford on 14 January, taking with him a force including his own Regiment of Horse, and set up headquarters at Worcester. The situation throughout his new command had deteriorated in the months following Marston Moor, with military reverses and a breakdown in Royalist administration and relations with the local population. Rather surprisingly, given his previous record, Maurice seems to have made a favourable impression, at least on many of the Worcestershire gentry. He tried to address their grievances, and issued a charter intended to clarify the respective roles of the civil and military authorities and also attempted to impose stricter discipline on the local Royalist forces. However Maurice remained fundamentally mistrustful of the local civilian authorities as represented by the Worcestershire Association. On 29 January, in one of his few surviving letters, Maurice wrote to Rupert asking that he be granted the same powers in the area which had been enjoyed by his brother, and added:

> I desire you to be very careful in the business of the Association; which I fear, tends much to the destruction of military power and discipline. For there are some cunning men amongst them. . .[17]

But whatever progress Maurice made in the field of administration was undermined by military reverses. During February his main concern was to ease pressure on Chester, in increasing difficulties as a result of the leaguer by the Parliamentarian forces of Sir William Brereton. Stripping his garrisons to provide a relief force, Maurice moved into north-east Wales, and, with the lukewarm assistance of local Welsh troops, managed partially and briefly to restore the situation around Chester, although, probably fortunately given the condition of his own troops, whose lack of discipline was described as 'barbarous', he failed to bring Brereton to action.

However this limited success was undermined on 14 February, when the key garrison town of Shrewsbury, stripped of troops by Maurice, was surprised and captured by the Parliamentarians. One of his officers, Sir Richard Cave, wrote anxiously to Rupert next day 'I wish your brother had some experienced commanders by him.'[18]

A Parliamentarian report described how, in Worcestershire, following Maurice's military reverses:

> they begin to fall off from him, and that his strength doth rather lessen than increase, especially such as were pressed by him, and forced to serve, many of whom do daily run away and those who are left, have little to subsist with, but plunder, which doth harden the hearts of the Country against them.[19]

The outcome was that Rupert felt compelled to come and assume command in the area himself. He had some success, although the outbreak in Herefordshire in March of the first significant 'Clubman' rising was another indication of the measure of Maurice's failure.

The prince never again enjoyed any significant independent command. He was with the Royalist forces at Naseby on 14 June. It is perhaps indicative of Maurice's limitations that, although he was with the right wing of Royalist horse, Rupert chose to lead them himself, rather than delegate the responsibility to his brother.

Following the defeat Maurice returned to Worcester, though he saw little action, apparently suffering from another bout of illness. When, in September, Rupert was dismissed following his surrender of Bristol, the king wrote to Maurice assuring him of continued confidence and support. But Maurice, inevitably, took the side of his brother, and, with forty men, joined Rupert in his cross-country dash to confront Charles at Newark. In the heated exchanges which followed, Maurice rejected overtures from the king, and chose to share in Rupert's exile from royal favour.

On 8 July 1646 the two princes left England and Maurice stayed for some time with his mother at The Hague.

Aftermath

He was not long to be denied action, however, and two years later, as Vice Admiral, joined the Royalist fleet of which Rupert had taken command. He shared in all the varied fortunes and wanderings at sea of the next few years. But for Maurice the end came in September 1652, when his flagship, *Defiance*, was lost with all hands in a hurricane off Puerto Rico. Rupert was devastated, and for many years refused to accept that his brother was dead. One of those serving in the fleet wrote of Maurice:

> Many had more power, few more merit: he was snatched from us in obscurity, lest, beholding his loss would have prevented some from endeavouring their own safety; so much he lived beloved, and died bewailed.

As a general Maurice had distinct limitations. Though hindered by recurrent ill-health, he failed to demonstrate real ability for higher command, although this might have come with time. While Clarendon's description of him may appear too harsh, for Maurice certainly showed distinct promise as a cavalry commander, fate and circumstance prevented him from providing convincing evidence that his talents extended any further.

Chapter Six
Ralph, Lord Hopton

After Rupert and Montrose, Ralph Hopton is the best known of King Charles' generals. Hopton was fortunate to be judged largely on his own description of his military career as penned in his autobiographical accounts,[1] and it is rare to find any serious criticism of his generalship by later writers. The reverses he suffered are generally put down to ill-luck, overwhelming odds or the mistakes of others. Alfred Burne and Peter Young felt that Hopton 'worked by trial and error. But speedily he found his feet and obtained the confidence and obedience of the Cornishmen, It was as much these qualities as purely military aptitude that brought him to the top and kept him there.'[2] His biographer, F.T.R. Edgar, is, however, more circumspect; while acknowledging that 'as a drillmaster and tactician he was both acute and tireless', he adds that 'Hopton lacked strategic insight and military imagination.'[3]

In his later years Hopton was a close friend of the Earl of Clarendon, but the latter, while admiring his friend's many excellent qualities, said that he was 'a man of great honour, integrity and piety, of great courage and industry, and an excellent officer in an army for any command but the supreme, to which he was not equal.'[4]

The best known portrait of Hopton, clad in black, with heavy and careworn features, was probably painted later in his life, after he had suffered serious injury, and fails to capture the vigour and charisma which he certainly possessed. More helpful is an earlier picture, possibly by Daniel Mytens, in which Hopton, with the dark brown hair, reddish beard and florid complexion remarked on by contemporaries, appears forceful and confident.

Early life

The Hoptons were a long-established Somerset gentry family, who had gained their family seat, Witham Friary, near Frome, after the Reformation. Ralph was born in 1596, and after the customary education of a gentleman, followed many contemporaries by enlisting with the English volunteers of Sir Horace Vere to fight for the Protestant cause in Europe. He assisted in the escape of Elizabeth of

Bohemia and her family from Prague, and continued to serve in Europe until 1625, rising to the rank of Lieutenant Colonel, and numbering among his comrades several later to achieve prominence in the Civil War in England, notably his close friend and eventual greatest opponent, Sir William Waller.

During his time in Europe Hopton gained the reputation of being a capable soldier, and when he returned to England at the end of 1625 he was made a Knight of the Bath. Over the following years he was involved in many aspects of the government of his county, serving as an MP, JP, and as a Deputy Lieutenant, putting his military experience to work in administering the Somerset Trained Band.

Hopton was counted as a moderate reformer. He voted for the impeachment of the Earl of Strafford, and favoured a partial reform of the Church. But the growing influence of the more radical elements among the Parliamentary opposition to Charles caused Hopton to part company with them. In his own beliefs and values Hopton was firmly conservative. He was a devout member of the Anglican Church, supported continued royal control of the militia, and when faced with the stark choice, believed in the institution of the monarchy as a bulwark against chaos. His final decision seems to have come in January 1642, after the king's failure to arrest his five leading opponents in Parliament. Hopton spoke in defence of the royal action, and as a result was imprisoned in the Tower of London for two months by an angry House of Commons.

The war in the west

In the summer of 1642, as scattered outbreaks of violence heralded the onset of civil war, Hopton became principal lieutenant in Somerset to the Marquis of Hertford, the King's Lieutenant General in the West. Hertford had need of a competent military adviser, for, as Clarendon put it, he was 'not fit for much activity and fatigue, and wedded so to his ease that he loved his book above all exercise.'[5]

With such a dilatory commander, and facing a local population predominantly Parliamentarian in sympathy, it was not surprising that Hopton and a few Somerset Royalist gentry made no progress. Despite winning a minor victory in a skirmish at Marshall's Elm (4 August), the Royalists steadily lost ground as Parliamentarian reinforcements under the Earl of Stamford arrived. Defeated in a small encounter at Babylon Hill (7 September), where Hopton was almost captured, Hertford and his officers resolved to cut their losses and pull out of the county. They headed for the port of Minehead, where, against Hopton's advice, Hertford decided to ship his foot and guns across the Bristol Channel to South Wales.

Sir Ralph remained behind, with 110 horse, 50 dragoons, a number of professional officers, and, significantly, the influential Cornish Royalists Sir Henry Killigrew and Sidney Godolphin. Cut off from the east by the Parliamentarians, Hopton had little choice but to turn westwards towards Cornwall.

Cornwall in 1642 was still isolated geographically from the rest of England by poor roads and the barrier of the River Tamar, forming its eastern boundary. This physical remoteness encouraged a strong sense of separate identity among the Cornish people, deeply aware of their Celtic past, with the Cornish language still widely spoken in the western parts of the county. They had an enduring suspicion and dislike of England, a feeling which was strongly reciprocated.

Cornish society remained conservative, with strongly feudal characteristics diluted or absent elsewhere in England. In 1644 the Royalist Sir Edward Walker noted that the Cornish people had 'that obedience to their superiors which the rest hath cast off. For the Gentry of this County retain their old possessions, their old tenants, and expect from them their ancient reverence and obedience.'[6]

If the gentry of Cornwall retained powers less apparent elsewhere, their control, though firm, was generally more patriarchal than tyrannical in nature. As well as the distrust of change characteristic of such a society, Cornish attitudes towards the Civil War were influenced by the fact that the Crown was a major landowner in the Duchy of Cornwall, and had generally proved to be a benevolent landlord.

But, in the summer of 1642, although the Royalists were by far the larger faction among the Cornish gentry, there remained a significant Parliamentarian minority, as well as strong leanings towards neutrality. Cornwall's support for the king was not yet a foregone conclusion.

It was in this finely balanced situation that, on 25 September, Hopton and his little force arrived at Sir Bevil Grenville's home at Morwenstow in the north of Cornwall. Here he learnt that the Parliamentarian faction in Cornwall had called a muster of the county militia for 28 September at Bodmin, to oppose Hopton's entering the county 'in a warlike manner'. It was essential to forestall this, and, joined by a few additional recruits, Hopton marched on Bodmin on 27 September, the Cornish Parliamentarians beating a hasty retreat to Launceston. Appearing before the Michaelmas Quarter Sessions at Truro, Hopton delivered a speech to what was probably a carefully hand-picked jury justifying his actions. He was not only acquitted of hostile intent, but promised full support.

Hopton's first task was to organize an effective fighting force. A muster on 4 October at Moulesbarrow Down, near Lostwithiel, produced only about 3,000 ill-equipped peasants. With these Hopton occupied Launceston, last foothold of the Cornish Parliamentarians, who fled eastwards across the Tamar.

Success was tarnished by an outbreak of looting by Hopton's unruly troops, and none of the Cornish Trained Bands or militia were prepared to leave the county in order to prosecute operations further.

The Cornish Royalist gentry had been endeavouring to whip up support, but even so supposedly popular a figure as Sir Bevil Grenville complained that many of his neighbours had failed to join him. He would, he explained to his wife, attempt to save 'some of the honester sort, yet others shall smart.'[7]

Hopton's solution was to raise from scratch an all-volunteer force, prepared to serve beyond the county boundaries. Also essential was reliable logistical and financial support, including adequate equipment and munitions. The latter would be supplied in part by the proceeds of Cornish tin, sold on the Continent, and by the booty obtained by a growing flotilla of privateers, based in Cornish ports and operating against what was deemed to be 'Parliamentarian' merchant shipping, as well as from the confiscated estates of Cornish Parliamentarians and the contributions of Cornish gentry.

In the absence of the Marquis of Hertford, King Charles appointed a 'triumvirate' of Hopton and two Devon Royalists, John Ashburnham and Sir John Berkeley, to command in the West. Hopton was to be Lieutenant General, Ashburnham Major General, and Berkeley Commissary General. Any two of them could make decisions, though in practice Hopton seems to have acted as senior commander, with the result that a potentially difficult arrangement operated surprisingly smoothly.

As in other cases, the term 'volunteer' when applied to the men enlisted in the Cornish forces is not entirely accurate. The majority were the tenants of the Cornish Royalist gentry, and can have had little or no choice but to follow their landlords' orders.

During the autumn of 1642 a force of five infantry regiments, totalling 5,000 men and 500 horse, with five small guns, was raised. All of the infantry commanders were leading Cornish gentry, including Grenville, Lord Mohun, Sir Nicholas Slanning, John Trevanion, and William Godolphin, of whom Grenville and Slanning were the most influential.

As well as recruiting and training, the Royalists were endeavouring to raise funds, and were not over-scrupulous in their definition of disloyalty when confiscating property, although a Parliamentarian writer in Plymouth admitted: 'I can no ways disparage Sir Ralph Hopton's actions, for he carrieth himself nobly without doing any mischief or great spoil.'[8]

Hopton was eager for action, arguably overly so, and in November, after they had been paid a cash bounty, the Cornish volunteers reluctantly agreed to cross the Tamar into Devon. The expedition, ill-planned and over-ambitious, without realistic strategic aim, reflected little credit on Hopton's generalship. On 21 November the Royalists summoned Exeter to surrender. On its rejection Hopton advised retreat but his Council of War at first refused, until a successful sortie by the defenders forced a Royalist withdrawal to Tavistock. Here Hopton hoped to raise the Devon Royalists and blockade Plymouth. But, as Sir Ralph himself admitted, a muster of the Devon militia on 6 December at Modbury was:

> rather like a great Fair than a Posse, all the Gentlemen of the County being so transported with the jollity of the thing, that no man was capable of the labour and care of discipline.[9]

The Plymouth garrison, in a timely sally, dispersed the unwary militia, and Hopton, who had narrowly escaped capture, on 31 December 'in the bitter season of the year', began pulling back across the Tamar. His Cornish troops, not for the

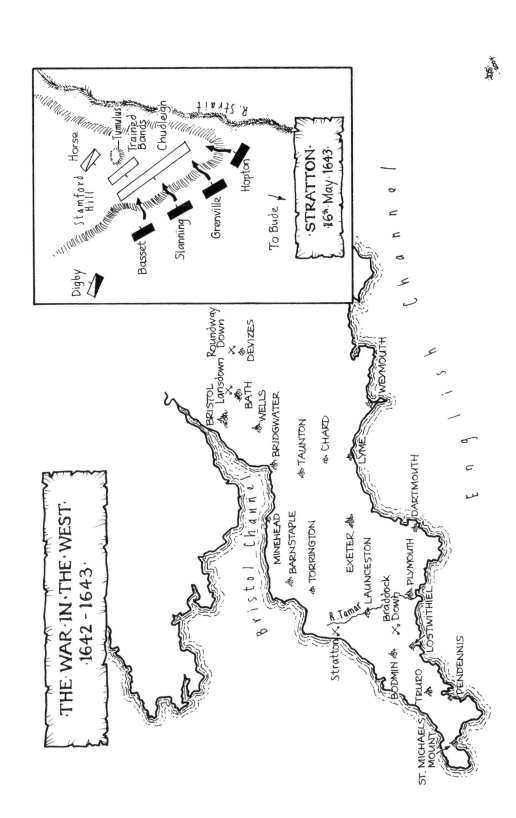

THE·WAR·IN·THE·WEST·
·1642 - 1643·

Bristol Channel

English Channel

STRATTON·
·16th. May·1643·

STRATFORD HILL INSET:
Stamford Hill
Stamford Horse
Tumulus
Trained Bands
Chudleigh
R. Strait
Digby
Basset
Slanning
Grenville
Hopton
To Bude

MAP LOCATIONS:
Bristol
Roundway Down
Lansdown
DEVIZES
BATH
WELLS
BRIDGWATER
TAUNTON
CHARD
MINEHEAD
WEYMOUTH
LYME
BARNSTAPLE
TORRINGTON
EXETER
DARTMOUTH
LAUNCESTON
R. Tamar
Braddock Down
PLYMOUTH
Stratton
BODMIN
LOSTWITHIEL
TRURO
PENDENNIS
ST. MICHAELS MOUNT

last time, were in a discontented mood: 'the whole so disobedient and mutinous, as little service was expected of them if they should be attempted by the Enemy.'[10] However, when some enemy cavalry approached, the Cornish promptly fell in and beat them off.

Hopton is generally credited with being a tough disciplinarian, with a policy of 'pay well, command well, and hang well',[11] who turned the unruly Cornish into a well-trained and obedient force, largely through his own powers of leadership. To an extent this may have been true. The Cornish seem to have had more respect for him than they did for any other 'outsider'. But even so, their first loyalty, and that at times only a conditional one, lay with the Cornish gentry who were the traditional leaders of their society. It was men like Grenville, Slanning and John Trevanion who provided much of the real leadership and inspiration of the Cornish Army. But although the Cornish could be formidable fighters, their obedience could never be taken for granted. A cavalry officer, Richard Atkyns, said of them in 1643:

> the Cornish foot could not well brook our horse (especially, when we were drawn up upon corn) but they would many times let fly at us: these were the very best foot I ever saw, for marching and fighting; but so mutinous withal, that nothing but an alarm could keep them from falling upon their officers.[12]

By 4 January 1643, Hopton's opening campaign had ended in failure. He was back at Launceston, with the Plymouth Parliamentarians, under a Scottish professional soldier, Colonel William Ruthven, moving up in pursuit and Parliamentarian reinforcements led by the Earl of Stamford on the way. Overruling Hopton's desire to make a stand, the Royalist Council of War ordered a withdrawal to Bodmin, where the militia were to be mustered.

Ruthven, anxious to gain the credit for defeating Hopton before Stamford took over, crossed the Tamar on 13 January, and advanced towards Lostwithiel. With no money to pay his dispirited troops, nor ammunition, Hopton was in a fairly desperate situation. Providentially three Parliamentarian ships carrying munitions were driven into Royalist-held Falmouth by bad weather, and at the same time Hopton's Treasurer, Francis Bassett, scraped together £300, sufficient to pay the Cornish their arrears plus two weeks wages in advance.

Reinvigorated, the Royalists met Ruthven on 19 January on Braddock Down. The battle which followed displayed little tactical finesse. After, as was his custom whenever possible, holding prayers at the head of his troops, and resolving 'to leave all to the mercy of God and the valour of his side',[13] Hopton launched a general attack on the Parliamentarians, spearheaded by the pikes of Sir Bevil Grenville, who described the outcome in a letter to his wife:

> I bid my part away, who followed me with such good courage, both down the one hill and up the other, it struck a terror in them, while the second came up gallantly after me, and the wings of the horse charged both sides but their [the enemy] courage failed them, as they stood not our first charge

of foot but fled in great disorder, and we chased them; many were not slain because of their quick disordering.[14]

Cornwall was for the moment secure, although with the Earl of Stamford now at Plymouth the longer-term threat remained. Hopton and his fellow commanders doubted their ability to resume the offensive, and they unsuccessfully attempted to negotiate a local truce with Stamford, by which Devon and Cornwall would nominally be neutralized, although their fortresses would be handed over to the Royalists and the Cornish Army allowed to march to join the king.

Unsurprisingly, Stamford rejected the proposal, which Hopton admitted was only a ploy to gain time to move his forces closer to Plymouth. It is hard to see how he expected his second blockade of Plymouth to meet with any better success than his first attempt, especially as the garrison, under the energetic command of the young Major General James Chudleigh, struck back at every opportunity. By the end of February Hopton was back in Cornwall, and, with apparent stalemate, both sides agreed to a truce which would be extended until 24 April.

As Hopton had expected, as soon as the treaty expired, Chudleigh resumed operations with an attempt to take Launceston, where Hopton himself was with 1,200 men of Grenville's Regiment. The remainder of his forces were stationed to protect various crossings of the Tamar. For most of the daylight hours of 23 April fierce fighting continued for possession of Beacon Hill, outside Launceston. Eventually the arrival of John Trevanion's Regiment enabled Hopton to form his infantry into three bodies, under himself, Berkeley and Francis Bassett, and make a general assault which drove Chudleigh back. However, the Parliamentarian commander conducted a skilful retreat to Okehampton, the Royalist pursuit rendered ineffective by an exploding powder magazine and a mutiny among the Cornish foot, 'according to their usual custom', as Hopton noted sardonically.[15]

On 25 April, with 300 horse, 300 dragoons, 3,000 foot and four guns, joined en route by some Devon volunteers, Hopton launched his third invasion of Devon. He apparently hoped to surprise Chudleigh at Okehampton, but once again his lack of precautions let him down. Next day, with half of his men forming the van of his march, the guns in the middle then the remainder of his troops bringing up the rear, Hopton set off across Sourton Down in column. News of his approach reached Chudleigh at Okehampton at about 9pm, and he prepared an ambush with 1,000 foot and 100 horse.

The Royalist operation was mismanaged from the start. Without apparently sending out any scouts, Hopton's column blundered on through the darkness, 'never as they conceived, in better order, nor in better equipage, nor ever (which had like to have spoiled all) in lesser apprehension of the Enemy.' At 11pm, Hopton and the other Royalist commanders were 'carelessly entertaining themselves' at the head of the column when the Parliamentarian trap was sprung. With cries of 'Charge all, charge all, kill them all which will not lay down arms', Chudleigh's men bore down on them.

The result was an ignominious rout, as the Cornish, their panic heightened by a thunderstorm, fled wildly back across Sourton Down. Only a hastily improvised stand by some of the Cornish officers, together with confusion among the Parliamentarians, saved Hopton from total disaster. Though his casualties were light, he lost 1,000 muskets, five barrels of powder and all of his correspondence, including orders from the king to take the Western army to Somerset to rendezvous with reinforcements from Oxford.

It is difficult to find any mitigating factors for Hopton's performance; he had neglected to adopt the most elementary precautions laid down by military writers for such situations, and had been totally surprised as a result. It was not the last occasion on which over-confidence was to cost him dearly.

KEY ACTION: THE BATTLE OF STRATTON, 16 MAY 1643

The revelation of Royalist strategy contained in Hopton's captured papers reportedly caused the Earl of Stamford, stricken with gout, to 'leap out of his Chair for joy', and he ordered a general rendezvous of his forces at Torrington, to exploit Chudleigh's success. Hopton meanwhile, after falling back to Launceston, made a brief and apparently pointless foray towards Tavistock. Stamford was preparing a new invasion of Cornwall, via the Grenville heartlands of North Cornwall. By the middle of May his advance had begun, heading for Grenville's home near Stratton, four miles into Cornwall.

The Royalists were at their customary low ebb. Although Hopton now had, on paper, seven regiments of foot, only one of these, Grenville's, was at full strength. Hopton's 1,400 horse were thought only to include 150 of any real value. However, this disadvantage was largely removed when Stamford detached 1,200 of his own 1,400 horse in a bid to seize Bodmin and divide the Royalists. With the remainder, and 5,400 foot, he crossed into Cornwall, Grenville and his regiment falling back before them. It seemed that the Parliamentarians were at last poised to win a decisive victory.

Mustering all available troops, Hopton headed north to join Grenville. On 13 May he reached the village of North Pelverton, where he halted for the night, dry biscuits the only available provisions for his men. Next day the Royalists arrived at Week St Mary's, only five miles from Stratton, which had been occupied by Stamford on 13 May. That evening Grenville and his men came in, giving Hopton a total of 2,400 foot and 500 horse. A Council of War decided to strike before Stamford could be rejoined by the rest of his cavalry, and, just before dawn on 16 May, the Cornish army moved out to fight.

The Parliamentarians were positioned on a 200 foot-high plateau, known later as Stamford Hill, located about a mile to the north-west of Stratton. The plateau had steep slopes on its southern and eastern sides, with a more gentle approach to the west, and its summit was crowned by some ancient earthworks. It was apparent to Stamford that the western approach to his position was the most vulnerable, and he positioned his 13 guns and one mortar to cover it.

The attack plan devised by Hopton echoed that employed at Launceston in the previous month. Four columns, under Hopton and Mohun to the south, Berkeley and Grenville on the south-west, Slanning and Trevanion to the west and Godolphin and Basset on the north, would make a converging attack on the Parliamentarian position. Meanwhile Colonel John Digby and the horse were held in reserve to the west ready to counter Stamford's cavalry if they should appear.

The Royalists faced a formidable task. Outnumbered two to one, they were also short of ammunition. With unrecorded intervals, their attacks lasted for about ten hours. The Royalists seem to have formed each of their divisions with a line of musketeers in front and pike blocks behind. While the opposing musketeers exchanged fire in the hedgerows, the pikes moved up in assault columns.

At about 3pm, Hopton was informed that his army was down to its last four barrels of powder. He and his officers decided that the lack 'could only be supplied with courage', and ordered a renewed assault, giving instructions that their men should not fire until they reached the summit of the plateau. As the Royalists advanced, Chudleigh launched a counter-attack against Grenville's column. Grenville was knocked off his feet, and his men began to waver until Berkeley's musketeers on their flank came to their assistance with their musket butts. In a fierce counter-charge Chudleigh was captured and his men began to fall back:

> the enemy gave ground apace, insomuch as the four parties, growing nearer and nearer as they ascended the hill, between three and four of the clock, they all met together upon one ground near the top of the hill, where they embraced with unspeakable joy, each congratulating the others' success, and all acknowledged the wonderful blessing of God, and being there possessed of some of the enemys' cannon, they turned them upon the camp, and advanced together to perfect their victory.[16]

Losing over 300 dead and 1,700 prisoners, as well as a considerable quantity of arms and ammunition, the Parliamentarians had suffered a decisive defeat. The battle had been a tribute to Hopton's skills as a tactician, adopting an already well-tried approach with considerable success. It also demonstrated yet again the qualities of the Cornish foot when fighting on their home ground under officers they knew and trusted.

Lansdown and Roundway Down

Cornwall secure, Hopton headed east in obedience to his orders to link up with troops from Oxford. He could look back on six months of varying fortunes, which had brought him the partial satisfaction of securing Cornwall for the king, though he had failed to make any progress in Devon. More impressive had been the achievement of Hopton and the Cornish Royalist leadership in persuading their men to march so far away from home.

On 4 June, at Chard in Somerset, the Cornish Army linked up with the forces from Oxford under the Marquis of Hertford and Prince Maurice. The result was a re-organization of the command structure. Hertford was, at least nominally, General, with Maurice as Lieutenant General of the Horse (technically second-in-command) and Hopton in the rather ill-defined post of 'Marshal of the Field.' In practice, Maurice and Hopton seem effectively to have shared command. But the consequence was a diminished role for the Cornish commanders, and a gradual deterioration of the conduct and discipline of their men. Mary Coate felt that 'Had Hopton been able to impress on the Royalist forces as a whole his own standards of loyalty, discipline and piety, the fate of the monarchy might have been different.'[17]

The united Western Army totalled about 2,000 horse, 4,000 foot and sixteen guns, but as it moved on through Taunton towards Bridgwater 'began the disorder of the horse visibly to break in upon the prosperity of the public proceedings'.[18] Prince Maurice was never noted as a disciplinarian, and the behaviour of his troops began to infect the Cornish.

However the Royalists were able to push the local Parliamentarians steadily eastwards in a series of rearguard actions, until the Parliamentarians joined reinforcements under Sir William Waller at Bath, while the Royalists halted at Wells.

A pause of almost a fortnight followed, during which Hopton wrote to Waller, possibly hoping to negotiate with his old friend. The latter declined in a moving letter, telling Hopton that:

> That great God, which is the searcher of my heart, knows with what a sad sense I go upon this service, and with what a perfect hatred I detest this war without an enemy, but I look upon it as an *Opus Domine*, which is enough to silence all passion in me . . . We are both upon the stage and must act those parts that are assigned us in this Tragedy: Let us do it in a way of Honour, and without personal animosities, whatsoever the issue be, I shall never willingly relinquish the dear title of,
>   Your most affectionate friend and faithful servant,
>   William Waller.[19]

On 1 July the Royalists resumed their march, and over the next three days a series of manoeuvres and skirmishes brought them close to the commanding height of Lansdown Hill, about five miles north of Bath. In a serious error, a Royalist Council of War held on the evening of 3 July decided against immediately occupying the hill because of the fatigue of their troops. By the following morning Waller had secured the 769-foot summit of Lansdown, erected barricades and emplaced seven light guns. The Royalists, the only approach up the steep northern face of the hill a road exposed to enemy fire, found themselves in an unenviable situation: 'there were very inconvenient ways to retreat, to advance no possibility, and to stay there least of all, for the Enemy's cannon played in to them.'[20]

The Royalists pulled back five miles to the village of Marshfield, their retreat covered by a rearguard under Hopton. Nevertheless it was clear that if the Royalists hoped to press on towards the major prize of Bristol there must be a fight next day. On 5 July they drew out and faced Lansdown again, but the prospect of an attack on Waller's strong position seemed no more enticing than on the previous day. By the early afternoon the Royalist commanders had decided to abandon the attempt and head for Oxford.

But as they began their withdrawal, Waller's cavalry launched an attack, and were beaten back by Maurice's horse. Hopton's part in the events which followed is unclear. According to one Royalist account, the Cornish foot cried out to be allowed to 'fetch those cannon', and a full-scale assault up the northern face of Lansdown began. Hopton fails to make clear whether the attack was spontaneous, or on his orders, but if the latter were the case he seems to have made no attempt to inform Maurice or Hertford of what was happening. The result was one of the bloodiest battles of the war, after which, at the cost of the lives of Sir Bevil Grenville and many of their men, the Royalists ended the day clinging to the edge of the summit of Lansdown.

Waller withdrew into Bath during the night, enabling the Royalists to make an unconvincing claim of victory, but Lansdown had in fact cost them so dearly that it was a near-disaster, for which Hopton must carry a good deal of the responsibility.

A further setback came next day. As the Royalists, too battered to hold their ground, began to withdraw towards Marshfield and Devizes, Captain Richard Atkyns noticed some Parliamentarian prisoners sitting smoking their pipes on an ammunition wagon, with Hopton questioning them:

> I had no sooner turned my Horse, and was gone three Horse-lengths from him, but the Ammunition was blown up, and the Prisoners in the Cart with it, together with the Lord Hopton on Horseback and several others. It made a very great Noise and darkened the Air for a time, and the Hurt men made lamentable screeches. As soon as the Air was clear, I went to see what the matter was; there I found his Lordship miserably burnt, his Horse singed like parched Leather.[21]

Temporarily blinded, and in considerable pain, Hopton was placed in a horse litter, and the Royalists continued their retreat; 'our horse were bad before, but now worse, our foot drooped for the Lord Hopton, whom they lov'd, and that they had no powder left to defend him.'[22] Their rearguard holding off attacks from Waller's horse, the Royalists limped into Devizes, where it was resolved that Hopton and the foot should stand siege while Maurice, Hertford and the horse went to Oxford for help.

Despite being confined to bed, Hopton retained a firm grip. Learning on the morning of 11 July that only 150lb of match remained for his musketeers, he ordered all the bed cord in the town to be requisitioned and boiled, which provided another fifteen hundred weight.

Over the next two days Waller carried out a desultory bombardment of

Devizes, and made an unsuccessful storming attempt. It has been suggested that he hesitated out of concern for his old friend, but it is more likely that he wished to avoid unnecessary casualties among his own troops.

The delay, however, proved fatal. On 13 July, on Roundway Down, relieving Royalist cavalry under Wilmot and Maurice swept away Waller's army in one of the most crushing victories of the war.

The Western forces now took part in the storm of Bristol (26 July), where crippling losses effectively destroyed the old Cornish Army. It is unlikely that Hopton was present. He was probably still recovering in Devizes, but found himself caught up in the aftermath of the capture of Bristol when Hertford proposed him as Governor of the city, a post which Prince Rupert wanted for himself. The affair was eventually settled through the mediation of the king, who appointed Rupert as Governor, with Hopton as his Deputy, and wrote in embarrassed terms to the latter, asking for his support:

> We have been so far from intending you thereby any disrespect, as we now hear, nor imagined that you should have been named to that command, knowing how necessary your continued presence is to our Western army assuring you that we can think no man fitter for that command than yourself (it being by far too little recompense for your great deservings). . .[23]

Hopton, as the king no doubt expected:

> abhorring very much that his Majesty's affairs should be disturbed by any concernment of his, disposed all his endeavours to the composing of the business between the two great Lords, and for himself wholly submitted to his Majesty's pleasure.[24]

With his skills as an administrator, Hopton was an excellent choice as effective Governor of Bristol, which would be a key Royalist arms manufactory, supply and recruitment centre. In harnessing these resources Hopton faced many difficulties, with shortages in all areas, especially money, having to borrow to meet his needs.

Possibly in another sop to ease the king's conscience, on 4 September Sir Ralph was created Baron Hopton of Stratton. He also received a no doubt appreciated gift from the Corporation of Bristol, who, doubtless with their own interests at heart, resolved on 17 August :

> It is thought meet and so agreed that there shall be a present conferred and bestowed upon the lord Hopton the present Governor vizt a Butt of sack two hogsheads of claret one of wine and a cwt of sugar, at a cost of £22.[25]

'Hopeless Employment'

The Royalist failures at Gloucester and the First Battle of Newbury led to a re-think of their strategy. The planned advance of the main field armies on London was to be supplemented by a thrust into Sussex, Surrey and Kent, where an uprising by Royalist supporters was confidently expected. Hopton, partly because of his injuries, and the need to find suitable employment for Prince Maurice, had not resumed his command with the Western forces, and, now that he was sufficiently recovered to take the field, on 29 September he was called to a meeting of the Royalist Council of War in Oriel College, Oxford. Here Hopton was given command of a new army designed to clear Dorset, Wiltshire and Hampshire of their remaining Parliamentarian garrisons before advancing as far as possible towards London.

The initial, and only partially solvable problem, was raising a viable field force. Hopton was able to muster about 1,400 horse and 1,000 foot, drawn from a total of some seventeen regiments, many of them poorly equipped. Though promised £6,000 to equip them, Hopton only received £1,500, and the grandiloquent title of Field Marshal of the Western Army, extended on 27 October to include, Sussex, Surrey and Kent.

In the meantime, Hopton, as he put it, was 'struggling through all exigencies as well as he could'.[26] His army remained a motley collection of badly under-strength veteran and newly-raised units, though he received some encouragement in October when two regiments of English troops from Ireland, under Sir Charles Vavasour and Lord Paulet, joined him. Each was around 500 strong: 'bold, hardy men, and excellently well officered, but the common-men very mutinous and shrewdly infected with the rebellious humour of England.'[27] Thus reinforced, Hopton planned to reduce Wardour Castle and the other Parliamentarian garrisons in Dorset in order to secure his rear before advancing further eastwards.

But before he could do so, Hopton was ordered by the king to support Sir William Ogle, who had just occupied Winchester. Hopton arrived there on 6 November, with Sir William Waller, facing him once more, pulling back east-wards towards Royalist-held Basing House. The regiments from Ireland, which had been left to blockade Wardour Castle, as Hopton had feared, now mutinied. Arriving on the scene early in the morning, with a regiment of horse and some dragoons, Hopton seized the ringleaders of the mutiny; 'And upon that terror, and the execution of two or three of the principal offenders he drew the regiment quickly to Winchester.'[28]

By now Hopton had 'a very handsome little army' of 2,000 horse and 3,000 foot and dragoons, and resumed his advance. Waller abandoned his ineffectual siege of Basing and pulled back to Farnham. But Hopton proved unable to capitalize on his initial success. For the next fortnight the opposing armies skirmished ineffectually, both commanders struggling to supply and pay their troops. Waller retained a healthy respect for Hopton, suspecting that he would resume his offensive: 'my old friend is so violent an enemy.'[29]

Hopton indeed had a plan to break the stalemate, which involved seizing Cowdrey House, about 26 miles to the east of Winchester, and then pushing on into Sussex. However, the Parliamentarians anticipated him, and occupied Cowdrey House first.

In retrospect Hopton saw this setback as a turning point:

> this failure proved to be the beginning of the Lord Hopton's misfortunes, for till that time, it had pleased God to bless him from the beginning of the war with reasonable good success, without any considerable disaster. But, by this failure, he was prevented in the most important part of his design, which was, by fortifying the pass at Midhurst, to have had that winter a fair entrance through Sussex into Kent.[30]

It is arguable whether, given the limited resources at his disposal, Hopton could ever have carried out his grand design. His advance had stalled, and it was probably too late in the year to have revived it.

Early in December Hopton went into winter quarters. He made the serious error of splitting his forces into four widely separated quarters, each about ten miles apart, in a triangle around Winchester. One of Hopton's officers, Colonel Joseph Bampfield, would claim later that he had warned that the quarters were so far apart that they were individually vulnerable to attack, but that his fears had been dismissed.

In a final fling that year, the Royalists seized Arundel Castle, on the Sussex coast, which Hopton optimistically thought might act as forward base for a spring offensive, though in fact it would prove to be an isolated liability. The reality was that Hopton's campaign had ended in failure. Not all of this was his fault. He had insufficient troops to realize over-ambitious objectives, and he had suffered unhelpful interference from the king at Oxford. But he had also displayed a lack of drive during the campaign, and the lack of clarity in strategic planning which he had shown previously in the West.

Hopton's feelings were expressed, somewhat incoherently, in a letter of 12 December to Prince Rupert:

> the truth is, the duty of the service here were unsupportable, were it not in this cause, where there is so great a necessity either of prevailing through all difficulties, or of suffering them to prevail, which cannot be thought of in good English.[31]

Next day came proof of Hopton's failure, when Waller launched a surprise attack on the Royalist troops quartered at Alton, killed their commander, Colonel Richard Bolles, and took 900 prisoners. For Hopton the disaster, perhaps because he had ignored the earlier warning he had been given, was a major blow. In a letter to Waller, he rather unconvincingly claimed the reverse at Alton to be 'the first evident ill-success I have had.' Waller now moved against the vulnerable Royalist outpost at Arundel, and Hopton, not receiving the reinforcements which he called for, was unable to prevent its surrender on 6 January 1644.

Remaining at Winchester, Hopton was relying on the onset of wintry weather to preserve him from further disaster until spring, by which time he hoped to be reinforced. It seems clear, however, that the Royalist high command in Oxford was losing faith in Hopton. The king's response was to send Hopton's friend, the Lord General, Patrick Ruthven, to join him with about 2,000 reinforcements, and exercise a watching brief. The implication seems to be that Hopton had lost confidence in his own ability, but the arrangement which had been reached was ripe with potential for confusion, as was quickly demonstrated.

On 26 March 1644, Waller began his spring campaign with a march towards Winchester. Hopton and Forth, still operating their strange command arrangement, met him three days later at Cheriton. From the Royalist point of view the battle which followed was hopelessly mismanaged, with Hopton and Forth effectively impeding each other, and a hopeful Royalist beginning degenerating into a series of failed and increasingly uncoordinated attacks.

Blame for the reverse, and credit for successfully extricating the bulk of the Royalist army, lies with both commanders. Cheriton was, however, the end of Hopton's independent command. His troops were absorbed into the main Oxford Army, and Hopton himself returned to Bristol and the administrative and logistical responsibilities for which he was well suited. He accompanied the king on the Lostwithiel campaign in the summer, and on 20 August, following the disgrace of Lord Percy, was named General of the Ordinance, though like his predecessor, Hopton seems to have left most of the work to an able deputy, Sir John Heydon.

End in the west

On 26 January 1645, the fifteen-year-old Charles, Prince of Wales, was made Captain General of the new Western Association, with Hopton as his Lieutenant General. Hopton's actual operational duties were limited to a brief and unsuccessful overseeing of the siege of Taunton. For most of the time, as one of its leading members, he was occupied with the day-to-day routine of the Council of the West.

Hopton proved reluctant to become involved in the squabbles among Royalist military commanders which effectively paralyzed any coherent strategy during the summer of 1645, refusing to exercise command, as suggested by the king, without a clear commission.[32]

It was not until January 1646, the Royalists pushed back almost to the Tamar, and their forces on the verge of collapse, that Hopton resumed active command. With the other generals in the area at each others' throats 'it was absolutely necessary that his highness should constitute one superior officer, from whose these independent officers might receive orders.'[33] Hopton himself had no illusions as to his prospects of success on taking over 'a dissolute, undisciplined, wicked, beaten army.'[34] Taking for the motto on his standard the words 'I will Strive to Serve My Sovereign King', Hopton told the Prince of Wales:

Since his highness thought it necessary to command him, he was ready to obey him with the loss of his honour.[35]

The hopeless task facing Hopton was illustrated by the fact that only 150 of the Cornish Trained Band were now willing to march with him. Hopton found his army to be 'full of necessities, complaints and all kinds of distempers . . . Amongst them were some excellent men, but I cannot say they were exact upon duty.'

In the middle of February Hopton led his force of just over 4,000 men into North Devon in a forlorn attempt to relieve pressure on Exeter, under siege by Sir Thomas Fairfax and the New Model Army. Fairfax did indeed raise the siege, but only to go after Hopton. On 16 February he caught up with the Royalists, who had fortified themselves in the town of Torrington. Outnumbered two to one, Hopton's men fought hard behind the cover of their barricades. Hopton himself was wounded while leading a counter-attack by the Royalist horse. After three charges the Royalist horse were repulsed, and the defence collapsed, the Royalists streaming back through the streets of Torrington and over the bridge out of the town, while eighty barrels of gunpowder stored in the church exploded, taking a number of Royalist prisoners with them.

The battle of Torrington marked the effective end of the war in the West. The disintegrating Royalist army retreated over the Tamar to Launceston, with the Cornish no longer willing to resist the New Model. As remnants continued to retreat further westwards, on 5 March Fairfax sent their commander a letter offering to discuss terms and to mediate for Hopton himself:

whom (for personal worth and many values but especially for your care of, and moderation towards the county) we honour and esteem above any of your party whosoever (supposing you more swayed with principles of Honour and conscience than others) we most pity, and whose happiness (so far as consistent with the public welfare), we should delight in more than in your least suffering.[36]

Hopton, agreeing to open negotiations, declined any special consideration for himself 'rather than in the least point to taint my honour in that particular', and admitted that while 'God hath indeed of late humbled us with many ill successes, which I acknowledge as a very certain evidence of his just judgement against us for our personal crimes: yet give me leave to say, your present prosperity cannot be so certain an evidence of his being altogether pleased with you. . .'[37]

On 10 March Fairfax entered Truro, and, after Hopton had reinforced the garrisons of Pendennis Castle and St Michael's Mount, a cessation of hostilities was observed by both sides until 16 March, when the Royalist Western Army began to disband. In this bleak time, Hopton suffered a personal loss when Elizabeth, the wife to whom he had been married for 23 years, died.

Later life

Hopton made his way to France, remaining an active Royalist. In 1648–9 he commanded a naval flotilla operating off the Cornish coast, and made a brief landing near Pendennis. It was all that came of a proposed Western rising of which Hopton was to have taken command.

Throughout the next few years Lord Hopton was a senior adviser to Charles II in exile. Clarendon commented:

> There was only one man in the Council of whom nobody spoke ill, nor laid anything to his charge; and that was the lord Hopton. But there was then such a combination, by the countenance of Prince Rupert, with all the other lords of the Council . . . Upon former grudges, to under value him, that they had drawn the Prince himself to have a less esteem of him than his singular virtue and fidelity, and his unquestionable courage and industry (all of which his enemies would not deny he excelled in) did desire.[38]

As a result Hopton found himself increasingly excluded from the inner circle around Charles.

In October 1652 Secretary Sir Edward Nicholas informed a correspondent: 'Gallant and virtuous Lord Hopton died on Tuesday senight [8 October] at Bruges of an ague, in whom all honest and well-affected men had a loss, but none so great as the King.'[39]

Peter Young and Richard Holmes rated Hopton the ablest of the Royalist commanders after Rupert himself,[40] but this seems an overgenerous assessment. Even Hopton's own accounts admit to a number of failings. He was undoubtedly a man of integrity and personal courage, an excellent organizer and administrator. But in field command he was much less adept. His early campaigns in the West, and above all his unfortunate independent command during the autumn of 1643 betray a man without strategic vision or clarity of purpose. As a tactician, Hopton may have been adequate, although his early victories owe as much to the Cornish leaders such as Bevil Grenville as to Hopton himself, but his performance at Lansdown may have cost the Cornish Army dearly.

The verdict of Lord Clarendon, who knew Hopton well, was:

> The Lord Hopton was a man superior to any temptation, and abhorred enough the license, and the levities, with which he saw too many corrupted. He had a good understanding, a clear courage, an industry not to be tired, and a generosity that was not to be exhausted; a virtue that none of the rest had: but in debates concerning the war, was longer in resolving, and more apt to change his mind after he had resolved, than is agreeable to the office of a commander in chief: which rendered him rather fit for the second, than the supreme command in an army.[41]

Chapter Seven
George, Lord Goring

Few generals of the English Civil Wars are more controversial than George Goring. To Victorian writers, Goring was 'the worst of the bad men who brought reproach on the name of Cavalier'[1] This opinion was shared by many of Goring's contemporaries; the Earl of Clarendon, who was able to observe Goring closely in the West Country, felt that he:

> Would have passed through . . . pleasantries, and would without hesitation have broken any trust, or done any act of treachery, to have satisfied an ordinary passion or appetite, and in truth, wanted nothing but industry (for he had wit and courage and understanding and ambition uncontrolled by any fear of God or man) to have been as eminent and successful in the highest attempt in wickedness of any man in the age he lived in or before.[2]

Yet even Clarendon conceded Goring's outstanding leadership skills and charm:

> A person very winning and graceful in all his motions . . . He had a civility which shed itself over all his countenance, and gathered all the eyes and applications in view; his courage was notorious and confessed; his wit equal to the best and in the most universal conceptions, and his language and expression natural, sharp and flowing, adorned with a wonderful seeming modesty, and with such a constant and perpetual sprightfulness and pleasantness of humour, that no person had reason to be ashamed of being disposed to love him, or indeed of being deceived by him.[3]

Sir Richard Bulstrode, who served as Goring's Brigade Major in the West Country in 1645, while admitting that his commander 'Strangely loved the bottle' went on to say that:

> He was a Person of extraordinary Abilities, as well as Courage, and was, without any Dispute, as good an Officer as any served the King, and the most dextrous in any sudden Emergency, that I have ever seen, and could

extricate himself with the least Concern, of which I was a particular Eye-witness upon Several Occasions. . .[4]

Given the difficulties of his contemporaries in making up their minds about Goring, it is not surprising that later writers have been equally ambivalent. On one hand he was a dissolute unprincipled rake, a self-seeking intriguer. Yet he was also the brilliant cavalry commander who smashed Sir Thomas Fairfax at Marston Moor, and in the later stages of the war, when Royalist cavalry superiority was a thing of the past, repeatedly bested Cromwell's 'Ironsides'. To Peter Young and Wilf Embleton, he was 'an engaging ruffian who could charm birds out of a tree'.[5] Young and Richard Holmes felt that Goring's 'fondness for the bottle, pride and hot temper cannot conceal his very real talent.'[6]

Mark Bence-Jones characterizes George Goring as 'Brave, brilliant and charming [but] he was also frivolous and irresponsible.'[7] Pointing out the undoubted ability of one who could, for example, dictate several letters simultaneously, he plausibly proposes that much of Goring's behaviour may be attributable to his being an alcoholic.

Goring's portraits do little to resolve the mystery of his personality. Fair-haired and conventionally good-looking, he has a look of restless energy, and a hint of that charm which could make him 'blush like a girl'. But ultimately his features retain the enigma which lay at the heart of Goring.

Early life

Born in 1608, Goring was the eldest son of George Goring of Hurstpierpoint, Sussex, courtier and diplomat to Charles I and his father, King James. His father's influence and Goring's own considerable charm and wit assured him entry to Court circles, where Goring quickly gained a reputation for extravagance and high living. He was soon, despite his father's assistance, heavily in debt. Marriage in 1629 to Lettuce Boyle, daughter of the Earl of Cork, brought Goring a dowry of £10,000, but this was quickly spent, and, with his father-in-law reluctant to pay his debts indefinitely, Goring adopted the time-honoured expedient of young men of his background with financial difficulties, and sought military service abroad.

Thanks to the support of Lord Wentworth (later Earl of Strafford) who praised Goring's 'frank and sweet generous disposition', the Earl of Cork was prevailed upon to put up the money to buy George a commission with the English forces in the Low Countries. Goring proved to be a natural soldier, and was soon in command of a troop of horse and twenty-two companies of foot.

He first came to prominence in 1637, at that great proving ground for commanders in the Civil War, the Siege of Breda. Fighting alongside other later Royalist stalwarts such as Rupert, Maurice, Wilmot and Sir Charles Lucas, Goring's gallantry made him the hero of contemporary English writers. When the advanced siege works came under heavy fire from Breda's defenders, Goring rallied the English troops, offering to reward any who agreed to serve in the trenches with him. More than 20 men were shot around him, but Goring continued working under enemy fire until he received a shot in the ankle which permanently lamed him. It has been suggested that it was constant pain from this injury which lay behind Goring's well-known drinking habits, though this may be an unduly charitable explanation.

Goring returned to England a popular hero. Favoured by Queen Henrietta Maria, in 1639 Goring was appointed Governor of Portsmouth, and then saw service in the Scots Wars, which gave him little opportunity for distinction, other than as the subject of verses by the Cavalier poet Richard Lovelace, who in 1639 wrote a tongue-in-cheek sonnet entitled 'To General Goring, after the pacification at Berwick'. Its opening stanza ran:

> Now the Peace is made at the Foe's rate,
> While men of Arms to Kettles their old Helmets translate,
> And drink in Casks of Honourable Plate,
> In every Hand a Cup be found,
> That from all Hearts a health may sound
> To Goring! To Goring! See't go round.[8]

As the tensions between king and parliament mounted, Goring appeared to be firmly in the royal camp. In 1641 he assured the queen that his garrison of Portsmouth could provide her with a refuge in time of need, while he was initially deeply involved with the so-called 'Army Plot', in which a group of pro-Royalist officers proposed to use the army raised against the Scots to suppress the king's English opponents. It seems that Goring had hoped to be appointed Lieutenant General of the army, and when he learnt that there was opposition to this, said that 'if he had not a condition worthy of him, he would have nothing to do with the matter.' It also appears that Goring doubted the feasibility of the enterprise, and it was probably out of a sense of self-preservation that he chose to reveal its details to the House of Commons.

Portsmouth

Opinions differ as to Goring's true allegiance at this time, but he had so gained the confidence of Parliament that they confirmed him as Governor of Portsmouth, a key naval base and important entry point for supplies from the Continent, and promised him £3,000 for work on improving its fortifications.

However, suspicions arose that the money was being misappropriated. Clarendon said later that the funds had been spent 'in good fellowship or lost ... at play, the temptation of either of which vices he never could resist.'[9] The accusation is given added weight by an account of an exploit of Goring in 1639, when was visited by Goring's friend Lord Portland and his brother Nicholas. They:

drank and shot, shot and drank, till they were scarce *compos mentis*. Then they all came to the island [Isle of Wight] where they did the like. I may truly say that in the space of six days there was never so much powder fired except against an enemy. [At Sandown Castle] at every health tearing at one another's bands and shirts, insomuch as linen was very hard to be found amongst them. [At Newport] they got a ladder and drank healths at the top of the cage [jail] and there Goring made a recantation speech for his former disorders and wished the people, of which they had a store about them, to take example by him how they came to that place . . . The powder that was shot here and at Portsmouth in the space of eight days was better worth than £300.[10]

In November 1641, Parliament summoned Goring to London to give an account of himself. He did so, 'with that undauntedness that all clouds of distrust immediately vanished.' At the end of his explanation, Goring 'received an applause, that, not without some little apology for troubling him, they desired him again to repair to his government, and to finish those works which were necessary for the safety of the place.'[11]

By now Goring was assuring both king and parliament of his loyalty and receiving payments from both. While nothing with regard to Goring's motives can ever be entirely certain, it seems that his true allegiance, so far as that extended beyond his own self-interest, lay with the king, whose servants his family had for so long been. However, as the queen, now on the Continent raising men and munitions, hoped to use Portsmouth as a landing place, Goring had to conceal his true intentions for as long as possible.

It was not until the end of July 1642, with violence already breaking out across the country, that Goring finally showed his hand and declared for the king. Neither the townspeople nor most of the garrison of Portsmouth shared his sympathies, and by the middle of August Parliamentarian forces under Sir William Waller commanded the approaches to Portsmouth by land, while the Parliamentarian fleet dominated the English Channel. Goring had only about 300 semi-mutinous soldiers with whom to man the defences of Portsmouth. Although the garrison made a number of sorties, at least one led by Goring himself, they were quickly confined within the town. In one of their last raids, Goring's men were pursued with such enthusiasm by a Scots soldier serving with the Parliamentarians that he found himself trapped within the town after the gates were closed. He fought on, only surrendering after being almost blinded by three sword cuts to the head. Appreciating a brave action, Goring had the man's wounds dressed, gave him three gold pieces, and arranged for his exchange.

By early September Goring was faced with large-scale desertion by his men and an increasingly effective bombardment from Parliamentarian artillery. With only a few score of his troops remaining loyal, on Wednesday 7 September Goring surrendered on generous terms. He took ship for Holland, reportedly throwing the town key into Portsmouth harbour as he left.

Goring was generally condemned for his actions at Portsmouth. Clarendon commented that ' he cared not to lose what he did not care to keep.'[12] However, with the Parliamentarians in full control of the surrounding district, and blockading Portsmouth from the sea, Goring never had any chance of success.

War in the north

Joining the queen in Holland, Goring rapidly gained her favour. Opportunity for more active employment was not long in coming. In December 1642 the Northern Royalist forces of the Earl of Newcastle had failed to destroy the Yorkshire Parliamentarians under Lord Fairfax at Tadcaster. This had been blamed by some on the incompetence or worse of Newcastle's Lieutenant General of Horse, the Earl of Newport, and Newcastle had urgent need of a replacement. The queen was despatching a number of professional soldiers to his assistance, and Goring, promised the post of Newcastle's General of Horse, went with them.

The Northern Royalist cavalry, many of them descendants of the reivers who had plagued the Anglo-Scottish border in the previous century, were noted for their independence and indiscipline, as well as their fine fighting qualities. It is a tribute to his skills of leadership and personal charm that, as an outsider, Goring was able to win their confidence and loyalty.

Goring landed at Newcastle in late January, and marched south to join the Royalist forces with General King and a convoy of munitions. Parliamentarian troops from Scarborough attempted to intercept him at the crossing of the River Tees at Yarm, but were virtually wiped out, allowing Goring to reach York safely.

During the next few weeks Goring's cavalry raided deep into enemy territory. By late March, their position weakened by the defection to the king of Sir Hugh Cholmley, Governor of Scarborough, and the equivocal attitude of the Hothams, father and son, in Hull, Lord Fairfax and his son, Sir Thomas, decided to pull back from their forward outpost at Selby to their West Riding heartland around Leeds. While Lord Fairfax and his main body made their retreat, Sir Thomas with a covering detachment moved forward to Tadcaster, as if contemplating an advance on York. The Earl of Newcastle sent Goring with a force of horse to block his path.

Having given his father the time he needed, on 29 March Sir Thomas began to pull back. He had three troops of horse and a number of raw newly recruited foot. Goring shadowed the Parliamentarians with twenty troops of horse. Once he had crossed Bramham Moor, Fairfax had only 12 miles to cover before he reached the safety of Leeds. Having successfully completed the first stage of his retreat, Sir Thomas ordered his foot to continue across the open Moor while he and the horse acted as a rearguard, making a staged withdrawal.

To his horror, on reaching the edge of the Moor, Fairfax found his infantry halted, waiting for him, with five miles of open ground still to cross. Making the best of things, Sir Thomas formed his foot into two divisions, and with his horse in the rear, resumed his march, Goring and his cavalry following at about two musket shots distance, awaiting their opportunity. The spring day was unseasonably hot, and when they reached the hamlet of Polerton Beck, Fairfax's infantry broke ranks in order to get something to drink. Fairfax managed to get most of them back into rough order, and resumed his march, but as he began the descent from Whin Moor towards the village of Seacroft, Goring launched an attack on his rear and right flank. The Parliamentarians broke in total rout, as the inexperienced countrymen who comprised most of Fairfax's foot threw down their weapons and fled. Sir Thomas himself escaped with difficulty to Leeds, but, according to the Royalists, lost 200 dead, and seven colours captured with 800 prisoners.[13]

Seacroft Moor had been a notable success for Goring, and an excellent demonstration of the disciplined use of cavalry. Goring's reputation was riding high, and on 22 April he wrote cheerfully to an old drinking companion, Lord Henry Percy, recently gone south to join the king:

> My Partner,
>   Though the last messenger called not for this enclosed, which only presented my due to you, my love and service, yet send it I must, to let you see I was not unmindful, though unuseful, which being bred in the bone will never come out in the flesh. Her Majesty will best tell you her own resolutions, while I shall our desires, and those are, that she stir not southward till things are better prepared for her conveyance, which will not be long a doing, after some few days that we fall a sweeping away the rubbish crowded in two or three holes of the country, that only obstruct, no way endanger us. Within a few days I shall send you somewhat of more importance to this; but in the interim, the 'Nonsuch', the 'Flying Horse' and the 'Bull' must not be forgotten; and so goodnight, my dear partner, from yours as your own,
>   George Goring
>   York, April 22 1643, late[14]

Goring's father, well aware of his son's failings, was less enthusiastic, writing to him on 17 April regarding the plans for the Queen and her convoy of munitions to march south to join the king at Oxford:

> I pray you think seriously hereof, and once in your life follow the advice of your best friend and dearly loving Father.[15]

The elder Goring's forebodings were soon justified, if not in quite the manner he had expected. In May Newcastle launched an offensive to gain control of South Yorkshire. To guard against the Fairfaxes at Leeds, he stationed Goring and his Major General of Foot, Sir Francis Mackworth, at Wakefield with a force of seven troops of horse and almost 3,000 foot.

Sir Thomas Fairfax was being pressed by the families of those captured at Seacroft Moor to obtain some Royalist prisoners to exchange for them, and believing Wakefield to be held by only 8–900 troops decided to make a surprise attack. He gathered a force of about eight troops of horse, 1,000 foot and three light guns, under the command of himself, Sir Henry Fowlis and Major General Gifford at a rendezvous at Howley House on 20 May.

By nightfall the Parliamentarians were approaching Wakefield. There was no sign of the enemy being aware of their approach. Indeed Goring, never at his best when inactive, had allegedly allowed his usual temptations to overcome him:

> There was a meeting at Heath Hall upon the Saturday at a bowling; and most of the officers and the Governor were there, and had spent the afternoon in drinking, and were most drunk when the town was alarmed.[16]

At about 2am, Fairfax's men surprised a Royalist outpost on the approaches to Wakefield, but two hours later, as they neared the town itself, discovered that the Royalists were partially alerted, and engaged a party of horse and some musketeers in the hedges. Sir Thomas realized that he was facing a larger enemy force than he had expected, but decided to continue with his attack. The Parliamentarian assault was made at two points at the ends of Northgate and Warrengate. Fairfax himself, with General Gifford, attacked along Warrengate. Sir Thomas described how:

> After two hours dispute the foot forced open a Barricado where I entered with my own Troop. Colonel Alured's and Captain Baynes followed with theirs. The Street which we entered was full of their Foot which [we] charged through, and routed, leaving them to the Foot which followed close behind us. And presently we were charged again with Horse led by Gen. Goring, where, after a hot encounter, some were slain, and himself taken prisoner by Captain Alured.[17]

The Royalist foot, including some of Sir William Lambton's Regiment of 'Whitecoats', staged a 'last stand' in the marketplace, but were broken by cannon fire and a cavalry charge, and about 1,500 of them captured.

The Royalist newspaper *Mercurius Aulicus* gave its own version of Goring's capture, naturally without any suggestion of his being inebriated. It claimed that the Royalist commanders had been on the alert all night, but that the attackers had exploited a weak point in the defences in order to enter the town:

> The noise whereof coming to Colonel Goring, then sick of a Fever in his bed, he got on horse-back, and flew amongst the Rebels, with some few followers, courageously making good the entries, till being over-pressed by the numbers of the Rebels, and not well-seconded by his own men, none but the Troops of Captain Carnaby and Captain Lambton coming in to help him, he was taken.[18]

The Parliamentarians were understandably jubilant at the capture of such an arch-enemy, and Goring was incarcerated in the Tower of London. The Royalists began attempts to arrange his exchange immediately, but his captors proved reluctant to let their prisoner free. Goring remained in prison for almost a year, no doubt impatiently chafing at his lost opportunities to gain further renown, until in April 1644 he was at last exchanged for the Scottish Earl of Lothian.

Marston Moor

On 10 April Goring was ordered north to resume his old post as General of Horse to the Earl (now Marquis) of Newcastle. With the intervention of the Scots on Parliament's side, the war in the north had turned against the Royalists, and before Goring could join him, Newcastle was forced to fall back to York. He sent his horse, under their Lieutenant General, Sir Charles Lucas, south into the Midlands, where, on 26 April, Goring assumed command.

Goring marched via Leicestershire into Derbyshire where he was recruiting when ordered to join Prince Rupert in Lancashire. He headed north-westwards, the Derbyshire Parliamentarian commander, Sir John Gell, reporting that 'Goring's horse are extreme barbarous and plunder all but Papists.'[19] Goring's men were rounding up large numbers of sheep and cattle to sustain both themselves and Rupert's forces.

Goring linked up with Rupert near Bury in Lancashire on 4 June. By now he was reported to have about 5,000 horse and 800 foot, 'not so well appointed as expected', and urged the prince to move quickly to the relief of York.

Rupert needed little encouragement, and in the march across the Pennines Goring and his horse were in the vanguard, reaching Skipton on 25 June ahead of the other Royalist forces.[20]

It was Goring, as General of the Northern cavalry, whom Rupert sent into York on the night of 1 July to give his orders to Newcastle. There is no evidence that Goring had any part in the attempts made by some of the Northern officers to fan Newcastle's resentment towards the prince, and Goring was back with Rupert next morning, as the opposing armies formed up on Marston Moor.

Goring's horse, totalling at least 2,100 men, supported by 500 musketeers, formed the Royalist left wing, and were deployed behind a hedge and ditch with a drop of about six feet onto the Moor beyond. It may have been the difficulties which this caused the attacking Parliamentarian horse under Sir Thomas Fairfax that prevented Goring from being taken at the same disadvantage as Royalist troops elsewhere when the unexpected Allied assault began, or perhaps his well-attested presence of mind in an emergency once again stood him in good stead.

Goring's men were able to give Fairfax's troopers a devastating reception. Met by a storm of musket fire as they attempted to deploy out of Atterwith Lane, the only feasible approach to Goring's position, the bulk of Fairfax's men were swept from the field by a well-delivered counter-charge. While Goring, with his first line, pursued Fairfax's broken horse up Marston Ridge through the Allied baggage train, his second line, led by Sir Charles Lucas, struck savagely at the exposed right flank of the Allied foot.

For a short while, it seemed that Goring might retrieve the day for the Royalists.

But then more Allied foot moved up, and Lucas was unhorsed and captured while leading another attack on a Scottish infantry 'hedgehog'. Their impetus lost, his disorganized troopers pulled back. Cromwell and the Eastern Association horse, victorious against Rupert's horse on the Allied left, now moved across the field to fill the position which had been occupied at the start of the battle by Goring's horse.

Goring was trying to reform his own scattered troopers, some of them busily engaged in looting the Allied baggage train. The Royalist Sir Hugh Cholmley would later criticism Goring's handling of the situation:

> Goring was possessed of many of their Ordnance, and if his men had been kept close together, as did Cromwell and not dispersed themselves in pursuit, in all probability it had come to a drawn battle at worst . . . but Goring's men were much scattered and dispersed in pursuit before they could know of the defeat of the Prince's right wing.[21]

Goring did rally some of his men, but they had the same disadvantages which had faced Fairfax's men at the start of the battle, and were possibly outnumbered by as much as three to one. Nevertheless, Goring attempted to make a stand, as a Parliamentarian officer with Cromwell, Lionel Watson, related:

> the enemy seeing us come on in such a gallant posture . . . left all thoughts of pursuit, and began to think that they must fight again for that victory which they thought had been already got. They marching down the Hill upon us, from our Carriages, so that they fought upon the same ground, and with the same Front that our right wing had before stood to receive our charge.[22]

After a fight of uncertain duration, Goring's men were beaten, though their withdrawal in the direction of York may have been assisted by the onset of darkness and the weariness of Cromwell's troopers.

It is hard to find any major fault with Goring's conduct at Marston Moor. Given the situation, it was inevitable that he should lose control of some of his troopers, and the comparison with Cromwell's conduct is in some ways misleading. Cromwell had at least half as many horse again as Goring, nor did he have to divert a large proportion to shore up his own foot. Given the unfavourable circumstances in which the battle had been fought, Goring had reason to be pleased with his performance at Marston Moor.

General of Horse

Goring's days in the north were drawing to a close. Even before Marston Moor, the king had been planning to replace Lord Wilmot as Lieutenant General of Horse of the Oxford Army with Goring. The Marston Moor campaign temporarily postponed this move, but Goring's part in the battle boosted his reputation.

On 17 July, the king's Secretary of State, Lord George Digby, an accomplished intriguer who perhaps already saw Goring as a useful counterbalance to Prince Rupert, wrote to him in flattering terms:

> Noble General. As we owe you all the good of the day in the Northern battle, so we owe you all the good of the news from thence.[23]

On 27 July Digby informed Prince Rupert:

> We are very glad here to understand that Goring is come so near as Bath the business he came for, shall be gone through with, the superseding of Wilmot, but till we have spoken with him, I cannot certainly tell your Highness in what particular manner.[24]

The Royalist forces were currently engaged against the Earl of Essex around Lostwithiel in Cornwall. Goring arrived at Liskeard, and presumably met with the king, on 7 August. Next morning Wilmot was arrested at the head of his troops, who were told by the king that the action was at the request of Prince Rupert. Rupert, who at the same time resigned as General of Horse, was replaced by Goring, with Lord Wentworth acting as his second-in-command as Major-General.

Despite later bitterness between them, there is nothing to suggest that Goring's appointment met with anything but Rupert's full approval. Soon after taking up his command with the Oxford Army, Goring wrote to the Prince in fulsome terms:

> Your Highness will receive an account of your business from the King. This army is now so far from your hests, and so much engaged that the [business] which I solicited for, will be deferred for a time; but I am confident that neither the distractions of this army can be settled, nor we get any great advantage upon the Rebels, until Rupert command us. And I am happy to find, by the King, that he desires and intends nothing more than that, after his controversy with Essex is decided in these parts. In the meantime, nothing in this world troubles me more than the distance I am from your Highness's immediate command. And I am very confident I am taken from a place where I would have rendered some service to his Majesty and to your Highness, and put into another where I am so much a stranger, that I shall not be very useful until Rupert be with us. And, in effect, this is the most mutinous army that ever I saw; not only horse, but foot, though I believe it is rather their poverty and fear than any general dislike of the remove of officers. Sir, I most humbly beseech you to continue the honour to me of preserving a place in your immediate service for me, when this crisis is past, there being nothing in this earth I more passionately desire than to sacrifice my life in your service, and near your person, being by all manner of ties,
>
> Your Highness's most humble faithful servant,
> George Goring.[25]

For the moment, Goring had to bend his well-known charms and leadership skills to winning the confidence of the Oxford Army horse, initially bitterly resentful at the manner of Wilmot's removal. On 23 August, Goring, with 2,000 horse and 2,000 foot, was sent west towards St Blazey and Par in order to hinder Parliamentarian foraging.[26] A week later, on 30 August, the king received word from two Parliamentarian deserters that Essex's horse, under Sir William Balfour, were planning to break out eastwards that night. Clarendon blamed Goring for the debacle which followed, saying that he was:

> in one of his jovial excesses when the order to pursue reached him, and he continued his delight till all the enemy's horse were passed through his quarters nor did then pursue them in any time.[27]

On this occasion, though, the allegations are unfair. Goring, still at St Blazey, was some four or five miles from Balfour's escape route. Furthermore, he only received news of the breakout next morning. Goring seems to have joined the king in the fighting around Castle Dor by about 10am, too late for him to have intercepted Balfour, and according to Richard Symonds, an officer of the King's Lifeguard of Horse, and an eyewitness, Goring was heavily involved with the current fighting. At about 6pm:

> General Goring met with us and told him [Lord Bernard Stuart, commanding the Lifeguard] that the room was too little for [his] horse and our troopers to charge too, and advised he would be pleased to face a little and draw off to the king.[28]

He adds that it was not until 7am on 1 September (next morning) that 'General Goring was sent with the horse to pursue the enemy's horse, who as the King was informed were gotten into Saltash.'[29]

Although Goring must share the blame for Balfour later extricating his cavalry from Plymouth, the principal charge lodged against him by Clarendon is clearly unjust.

Key Action: Newbury, 27 October 1644

Following the surrender of Essex's foot, the combined Oxford and Western Armies moved slowly eastwards, reaching Salisbury on 15 October. For the moment their principal opponents were separated and seemingly vulnerable. One force, under Sir William Waller, lay at Andover; the Army of the Eastern Association, under the Earl of Manchester, was at Reading, awaiting reinforcements from the London Trained Bands, while the Earl of Essex, still re-organizing and re-equipping his battered infantry, was at Portsmouth.

Goring urged the king to strike at Waller's 3,000 men at Andover. It was a good plan, provided that the Royalists moved quickly enough. But, according to Sir

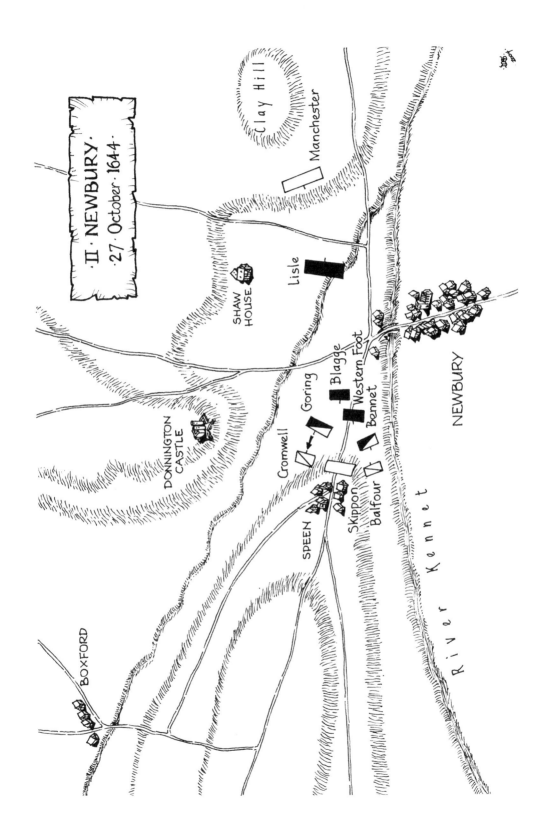

·II·NEWBURY·
·27·October·1644·

Clay Hill

Manchester

Lisle

SHAW HOUSE

DONNINGTON CASTLE

Goring

Blagge

Western Foot

Bennet

Cromwell

SPEEN

Skippon

Balfour

NEWBURY

River Kennet

BOXFORD

Edward Walker, the operation, timed for 18 October, was mismanaged from the outset. The Western infantry of Prince Maurice, supposed to reach the rendezvous outside Salisbury at 7am, did not appear until four hours later. It was about 3pm when the Royalists approached Andover, and, claimed Walker, 'If upon the first advance we had but sent 500 horse over the Pass below the Town, they could not possibly have escaped us.'[30]

As it was, Waller hastily pulled back towards Basingstoke, leaving a rearguard to hold off pursuit. Goring was in the forefront of such fighting as occurred:

> General Goring raised a forlorn of horse, consisting of about 200 gentlemen, who were spare commanders of horse, beat them out of Andover. Took about 80 prisoners, followed the chase of them two miles, who all ran in great confusion. Had not night come so soon, it might have made an end of Waller's army for our intention was to engage them, but they disappointed our hopes by their heels.[31]

On 22 October the Royalists advanced to Newbury, from whence 1,500 horse under the Earl of Northampton were despatched to relieve Banbury, the remainder of the Royalist army of about 9,000 men, including 4,000 horse, remaining at Newbury to await the arrival of reinforcements under Prince Rupert from Bristol.

However, on 27 October the united Parliamentarian armies of Waller, Essex and Manchester launched a complex operation designed to assault the Royalists, who were in defensive positions around Newbury, from two sides.

Fortunately for the Royalists, the enemy intention to attack simultaneously on the east and west failed. The bulk of Astley's foot were deployed to the north-east of Newbury, around Shaw House, while Prince Maurice and his forces held the village of Speen to the west. The king, with Goring and most of the horse, were in reserve in the centre, drawn up in the fields to the east of Speen.

A Parliamentarian force led by Waller, including Skippon's foot of Essex's army, his horse under Sir William Balfour, and Waller's own cavalry, together with Oliver Cromwell and the Eastern Association horse, made a long detour to the north of Newbury in order to attack Speen from the west.

When the attack began, at about 3pm, Balfour's horse were on the right, Cromwell's on the left and Skippon's foot in the centre. The latter, burning for revenge for their humiliation at Lostwithiel, and significantly outnumbering their opponents, drove Maurice's Western foot back out of Speen after a sharp fight, taking at least nine guns. Maurice's men fell back on the main body of horse in the fields between Speen and Newbury.

The Parliamentarian horse advanced in pursuit. On the south side of Speen Balfour's men drove back Sir Humphrey Bennet's brigade of Oxford Army horse, while to the north of the village Cromwell clashed with the Earl of Cleveland's brigade. At one point the king himself was in danger of being captured in the confused fighting south of Speen. He was rescued by a counter-charge mounted by his Lifeguard of Horse, while the Western foot rallied along the hedges of Speenhamland Field, and drove Balfour back with musket fire.

To the north of Speen Cromwell's attack was in progress. According to the Royalist version in *Mercurius Aulicus*:

> those on the east [north] side were more confident of success; so having settled three Bodies of Foot in certain Enclosures and ditches, advanced over a ditch with a good Body of Horse, hoping thereby to break in through his His Majesty's guards. But this was as soon discerned and prevented by General Goring, who instantly drew up the Earl of Cleveland's Brigade, put himself in the head of it, together with the Valiant Earl himself and the other Colonels of his Brigade (Colonel Thornhill, Colonel Hamilton, Colonel Culpeper and Colonel Stuart). The General then told them 'They must now charge home' and thereupon suddenly advanced to the gap where about four score of the Rebels were already come over (the rest hasting after) these he soon fell upon, and forced them back again in much confusion; As soon as he had got part of the Brigade over the ditch, he halted to order them as fast as they came over, but the eager Rebels would not grant him so much leisure, and therefore a new Body came to second the former, whom the General received with those few horse he had already over the ditch, and then charged so home, that he made them quickly scatter and shift for themselves, many whereof were killed in the place, others so wounded as not able to fly, among whom was Major Urrey (Colonel Urrey's nephew) who was mortally hurt in the head by Captain Ellys of Colonel Thornhill's Regiment, whose prisoner Urrey was; though he died within an hour after he was taken. In this charge the most Valiant Earl of Cleveland engaged his Person among the thickest of the Rebels, where his Horse was shot under him, which gave the Rebels opportunity to take him Prisoner . . . This charge was the more gallant, because this Brigade of Horse not only went over the ditch to meet the Rebels, but passed by three Bodies of the Rebels' Foot, who were placed in the ditches and enclosures, two of which Bodies shot at His Majesty's Horse both as they pursued the Rebels, and as they came back.[32]

The Parliamentarians claimed that Cromwell and his horse played little part in the engagement, but it seems clear that Goring had defeated some at least of the redoubtable 'Ironsides'.

Together with the dogged resistance of Astley's foot around Shaw House, Goring's charge had saved the day for the Royalists, and under cover of darkness the king's forces regained the safety of Wallingford and Oxford.

Disputes with Rupert

On 1 November Rupert replaced Forth as Lieutenant General of the Royalist forces. Goring found being back under the prince's command not to his taste.

Rupert had been furious that the king had fought at Newbury against his advice, and probably blamed Goring along with Digby for this decision. So, far from receiving the praise which he anticipated, Goring probably found himself the objective of Rupert's criticism, no doubt expressed in customary un-compromising fashion. The prince also resented Goring's favour with the king.

Clarendon gives a vivid portrait of Goring at this time, comparing him with his predecessor, Lord Wilmot:

> Goring, who was now General of the Horse, was no more gracious to prince Rupert than Wilmot had been; and had all the other's faults, and wanted his regularity and preserving his respect with the officers. Wilmot loved debauchery, but shut it out from his business, and never neglected that, and rarely miscarried in it. Goring had a much better understanding and a sharper wit, (except in the very exercise of debauchery, and then the other was inspired), a much keener courage, and presentness of mind in danger; Wilmot discerned it further off, and because he could not behave himself so well in it, commonly prevented or warily declined it, and never drank when he was within distance of an enemy. Goring was not able to resist the temp-tation when he was in the middle of them, nor would decline it to obtain a victory, . . . and the most signal misfortunes of his life in war had their rise from that uncontrollable license. Neither of them valued their promises, professions or friendships, but Wilmot violated them the less willingly, and never but for some great benefit or convenience to himself; Goring without scruple, out of humour, or for wit sake, and loved no man so well, but that he would cozen him, and then expose him to public mirth for having been cozened, and therefore he had always fewer friends than the other, but more company, for no man had a wit that pleased the company better. The ambitions of both were unlimited, and so equally incapable of being contented; and both unrestrained by any respect to good nature or justice from pursuing the satisfaction thereof. Yet Wilmot had more scruples from religion to startle him, and would not have attained his end by any gross or foul act of wickedness. Goring could have passed through those pleasantly, and would without hesitation have broken any trust, or done any act of wickedness, to have satisfied an ordinary passion or appetite. . .[33]

In December, now Lord George Goring following his father's elevation to the peerage as Earl of Norwich, Goring was made Lieutenant General of Hampshire, Sussex, Surrey and Kent. According to Richard Bulstrode, many were surprised at Goring's rapid rise, which was put down to the queen's intercession. He had about 3,000 of the Oxford Army horse, and 1,500 foot, and launched a number of raids towards Farnham, briefly occupying the town in January 1645. But, short of supplies, and pay for his men, Goring could get no further, and his mood was rapidly darkening.

Tensions had risen between him and Rupert at the end of December, when Goring had declined to sign a petition asking that the prince should have a place in the abortive negotiations taking place at Uxbridge, saying that 'if the King does intend to put you in it, it would be needless to send a petition with so many hands to obtain that which is already granted.'[34]

In a more far-reaching breach, Goring now took his complaints directly to the king, bypassing Rupert. On 9 January he told Charles:

> I esteem myself very unhappy to be diverted from the pursuit of a distracted enemy, by that which, of itself, is a greater misfortune, a want of arms, disorder in the train, and a universal deadness and backwardness in the officers of foot to undertake any action without refreshment. I was necessitated to call a council of war, rather to please some of them than to hear them, and I find so many difficulties and objections raised in all things I propose of action, that I shall esteem it a great advancement to your Majesty's service hereafter, if I have the honour to receive your Majesty's positive orders with your own hand to them, and advise with these of nothing but the way to obey them . . . I do most humbly beg a positive order from your Majesty for my undertakings to dispose the officers more cheerfully to conduct them. . .[35]

This may not have been intended as insubordination to Rupert, but the latter certainly interpreted it as such, evidently rebuking Goring, who responded angrily:

> Your Highness is pleased to think yourself disobliged by me, for desiring my orders under the King's hand. As I remember, sir, the reason I gave his Majesty for it, was the having more authority by that to guide the Council of this army to his obedience: and one reason I kept to myself, which was, I found all my requests denied by your hand, and therefore desired my orders from another. As for having made means, under-hand, to get an independent commission from his Majesty, I assure you, sir, I never did. And if I find myself so unhappy, as, for want of your favour, to be disenabled to serve his Majesty in this charge, I shall think it easier to resign my command than to lessen yours. And sir, whereas I hear your Highness accused me for desiring your orders at the same time I did the King's, truly sir, I did not think them inconsistent, and though I begged that honour from the King, yet till it were granted, I remained under the same obligation I was formerly, which was to address myself to your Highness for orders, and being in the same condition at this present, I shall beseech your Highness not to attribute the applications I make to you, to a mean courtship, but to my obedience to the King, and respect to his Nephew and my Superior Officers.[36]

In any event, Goring's offensive had collapsed. His disorderly forces gradually retired westwards, and by March were at Exeter, where, according to Clarendon:

> the lord Goring himself and most of his principal officers taking the opportunity to refresh themselves . . . where they stayed three or four days in most

scandalous disorder, a great part of his horse living upon free quarter and plundering to the gates of Exeter.[37]

Goring versus Waller

Goring and his troops, part of the Oxford Army, were now within the area of command of the newly-established Council of the West, nominally headed by the Prince of Wales. By referring to them for instructions and advice, Goring was able to distance himself from the direct control of Prince Rupert. On 31 March, Rupert wrote to his confidante Will Legge: '[The Council of the West] already sends orders to Goring, and are well received. Pray desire to know of the King if he have given them power so to do.'[38]

Parliament had meanwhile mustered an expedition to deal with Goring. On 15 January 1645, Waller had been appointed commander-in-chief of a force with an establishment of 6,000 horse and dragoons, though in reality only about two-thirds that number. At the end of February Waller was joined by Cromwell with about 2,000 Eastern Association horse. Throughout March, the Parliamentarians and Goring skirmished indecisively on the borders of Wiltshire and Somerset, both claiming to be hindered by the lack of foot which they deemed essential in the enclosed countryside. With the support of the Council of the West, Goring saw his main task as being to prevent the Parliamentarians from raising the in-effectual Royalist siege of Taunton. In justice to Goring, he was handicapped by the refusal of some of the Western Royalist commanders, notably Sir Richard Grenville, to cooperate with him.

The opposing cavalry engaged in raid and counter-raid in the Mendips. On 25 March Goring took command against 200 Parliamentarian horse at Pitminster, two miles from Taunton; 'For which purpose his Lordship took his own troop and Lord Percy's regiment of Horse (the Army being two miles behind) and presently fell in amongst the Rebels, took 50 horse, 34 prisoners and 200 pistols and Colours.'[39]

Goring was now styling himself 'general of his Majesty's force of Horse that are or shall be raised in the Kingdom of England and dominion of Wales. And commander in chief of all the forces of the West for the present expedition [against Waller and Cromwell]'. None of this clarified Goring's exact authority, though Clarendon claimed that he resented instructions from the Council of the West so much that he spent several critical days sulking at Bath. Goring, however, claimed his inaction was due to ill health.

Perhaps the most objective assessment of Goring at this time is that of his Brigade Major, Sir Richard Bulstrode:

But after all that can be said in General Goring's Behalf, he had likewise his blind Side, for he strangely loved the Bottle, was much given to his Pleasures, and a great Debauchee, and the great Misfortune was, when he commanded in chief in the West of England, his Excellency had two

Companions who commanded next under him [Lord Wentworth
and Commissary-General George Porter, Goring's brother-in-law], who
fed his wild Humour and Debauch, and one of them, if not both, wasted his
great and natural Courage. These two Commanders, the one [Wentworth]
being Lieutenant-General, made the General turn his Wantoness into Riot,
and his Riot into Madness; So that if the King had been truly informed of
their continued strange Debauches his Majesty would either have removed
them from him, or all Three from future Trust and Employment.[40]

Rumours of Goring's behaviour had reached Oxford; on 29 March, his ally, Lord
George Digby, warned: 'Dear General, I have nothing to add but to conjure
you to beware of debauchees, there fly hither reports of the liberty you give yourself, much to your disadvantage, and you have enemies who are apt to make use
of it.'[41]

However, with typical ineffectiveness, the king did nothing to remove or discipline Goring. On his good days, Goring was still a highly effective cavalry
commander. On 30 March he claimed another victory over Cromwell's Eastern
Association horse, reinforced by a detachment which had broken out of Taunton:

As soon as I heard of the forces of Taunton and Cromwell drawing towards
Sir Grenville I marched next day with some of the foot to Yeovil and the rest
to Stonebridge where I had notice that Cromwell with all the forces of
Taunton and some foot from Weymouth being in all some 4,000 were
quartered in Dorchester and the Villages thereabouts and conceiving that
they were not joined with Waller I intended to march towards them next
day with horse, foot and cannon, and that night to fall into some of their
quarters with a thousand horse but most of those horse missing the
Rendezvous we failed of a very great advantage of them as it appears. For
next morning at seven of the clock having notice that the enemy were still in
their quarters and knew nothing of our coming I advanced towards them
with above 1,500 horse giving order to the foot and the rest of the horse to
follow for our retreat and the Enemy by coincident were drawn out of their
quarters half an hour before almost four mile from Dorchester, were there
already assembled about eight hundred Horse. Which seeing our horse
come forwards defended a pass upon a little river. But some of our men
forcing them from thence and others getting behind them upon another pass
they quitted the [first] pass and our men had the pursuing of them almost
to the town of Dorchester. In which our men killed and took many of them,
took three colours of horse and great store of Carbines and pistols. What
prisoners yet we have I know not for they are not all brought in, but our men
were much greedier of their horses and arms than taking prisoners. . .[42]

Mercurius Aulicus claimed that the Parliamentarians lost forty dead, 'many more'
wounded and eighty prisoners, with 300 horses.[43]

Following up the slowly retreating Parliamentarians, Goring established his headquarters at Bruton in Somerset, and continued almost nightly raids on Waller's quarters. Although their effects were certainly exaggerated by Goring, they caused Waller to send him a rueful letter, proposing an exchange of prisoners:

> Noble Lord, God's Blessing be on your Heart, you are the jolliest Neighbour I have ever met with. I wish for nothing more but an Opportunity to let you Know I would not be behind in this kind of Courtesy.[44]

Both sides seem to have enjoyed the negotiations which followed, Bulstrode noting that:

> The country folk, believing we were appointed to make a peace, flocked in great numbers to Shaftesbury, where we stayed fifteen days to release all prisoners of quality on both sides from Lands End in the West to Portsmouth. Sir William Waller sent us a great present of wines, which came from London, believing we could have none such elsewhere.[45]

Waller, and, temporarily, Cromwell, a few days later laid down their commands under the terms of Parliament's Self-Denying Ordnance and their troops were dispersed elsewhere.

Naseby

Although Goring had had the best of the campaign, he had missed, apparently through carelessness, several opportunities of inflicting severe damage on his opponents. He was, furthermore, in an increasingly discontented frame of mind. In early April he was complaining about orders from the Prince's Council. He was temporarily brought to a better mood by a cajoling letter from one of its members, Lord Culpeper, urging him: 'For God's sake, let us not fall into ill humours, which may cost us dear. Get good thoughts about you, and let us hear speedily from you a better tune. . .'[46]

Clarendon gave a number of reasons for Goring's discontent. He alleged that Goring had been planning to obtain overall command in the West since the beginning of the year, 'and I fear had some other encouragement for it than was then avowed.'[47] He quoted an alleged conversation between Goring and Colonel William Ashburnham at the time of Goring's dispute with Rupert, in which Goring complained, 'with very contemptuous language of the King and Queen' of the poor treatment which his father and himself had received from them and, that he himself 'was only courted here for his interest in the soldier, and because the king could not be without him, but swore, as soon as he had put himself into such a posture as, he doubted not, he should be shortly in, he would make them do his father and himself justice, or they should repent it.'[48] These sound suspiciously like the complaints of a man when drunk, but Goring retained ambitions for a command independent from Prince Rupert. The latter, on a flying visit to the West in April, seems to have attempted to sow discord between Goring and the Council of the West. At the end of April, Goring was recalled to Oxford, with 2,000 horse, to counter Cromwell's incursion in the area and to prepare for the spring campaign: 'How unwelcome soever these orders were to the lord Goring, yet there was no remedy but he must obey them.'[49]

His new orders gave Goring the opportunity to score another success over Cromwell's troopers. Cromwell was still in the vicinity of the Royalist garrison of Faringdon, where he had been repulsed, prior to linking up with Sir Thomas Fairfax and the rest of the New Model Army in the neighbourhood of Newbury. On the night of 7 May Parliamentarian scouts took some Royalist prisoners around Hungerford and Marlborough, who informed their captors that Goring planned to beat up Cromwell's quarters that night or early the following morning. Cromwell placed his men on the alert, but early in the morning 'General Goring marched with what speed he could on the West of Faringdon and recovered Radcot Bridge.'

The precise sequence of events which followed differ sharply in the Royalist and Parliamentarian accounts. The official Parliamentarian version says that Cromwell sent a party of horse over the Thames to investigate Goring's movements, and 'Major Bethell (of Cromwell's Regiment) engaging too far in the dark, was taken prisoner, and about four more were lost, and two colours, several wounded.'[50]

The Royalist account suggests a more serious engagement, in which after a preliminary skirmish, some 1,000 Parliamentarian horse met 400 Royalists under Goring and, after some significant fighting, Goring 'broke them all to pieces, though with some difficulty, . . . there were very many of them killed and wounded, Major Bethell himself (who commanded in chief) taken prisoner, two Colours of horse, and divers common soldiers, the rest saved themselves in the dark.'[51]

Clarendon admitted that Goring's success 'gave him a great reputation, and made him extremely welcome' when he joined the king that day.[52] Goring joined the other Royalist commanders on 8 May at Stow-on-the-Wold for the fateful Council of War to decide on strategy for the coming campaign. The majority, including the courtier faction of Digby and John Asburnham, wanted to march to confront the New Model Army, bound for the relief of Taunton. Rupert, supported by Sir Marmaduke Langdale, favoured a campaign aimed at firstly relieving Chester and then recovering the north of England. Goring's own preferences are unclear, but his main objective remained to secure for himself an independent command.

Rupert and Goring found themselves in an unlikely alliance:

> Now the very contrary affections towards each other between prince Rupert and the Lord Goring began to co-operate to one and the same end. The prince found that Goring, as a man of ready wit and an excellent speaker, was like to have the most credit with the King in all debates, and was jealous

that, by his friendship with Lord Digby he would quickly get such an interest with his majesty that his credit would be much eclipsed. Hereupon he did no less desire that Goring should return again to the west than Goring did not to remain where he commanded. This produced a great confidence and friendship between them, and the prince told him all that any of the council [of the West] had spoken freely to him, when his highness abhorred nothing more than that Goring should be near the Prince of Wales, and Goring said all of the council which he believed would most irreconcile him to them; and so they both agreed to do all they could to lessen their [the Council's] credit and authority.[53]

As a result Goring gained 'so much credit' with the king that on 10 May Charles directed that he should not only be admitted to all meetings of the Council of the West, but that the latter would have powers only to advise him, while Goring was 'to put both his commissions of generalissimo and of general of the [Western] Association in execution as he found most convenient.'[54]

The decision to send Goring back to the West was not new. During preliminary strategy discussions in April it had been decided that Goring and his horse should remain there as a counter to the New Model Army. In any event, once the decision was made for the Oxford Army to march north, Fairfax could hardly be left to operate unchecked in the Royalist heartlands. The major error made by the king and Rupert was the enlarged commission which they granted Goring, which left him outside anyone's effective control.

By 12 May Goring had put his commission as Generalissimo in the West into operation, though he assured Rupert that, once joined by the infantry from before Taunton, he would be ready to follow Fairfax if the New Model went after the king: 'I assure your Highness that I will hazard 8,000 lives rather than leave anything undone that I think may conduce to the King's service and to your Highness's satisfaction.'[55]

But by now the situation around Taunton had been complicated by the arrival of Weldon's relief force. On 19 May Goring's forces failed to destroy Weldon's men when they made a sortie from Taunton, in what Goring described to Digby as 'the most fantastical accident that has happened since the war began'.[56]

Weldon's survival suited Goring's own purposes very well. On 19 May Rupert had written curtly to him, ordering him to bring 3,500 horse and all his own and Grenville's foot without delay to a rendezvous with the Oxford Army in the Midlands. In more conciliatory vein, Digby repeated the instructions, saying that the orders were sent:

by the unanimous advice of all here as a thing most absolutely necessary to our preservation, the Rebels setting their whole rest upon encountering and distressing this army, where the king's person is. . . If their aims had been for the West, all things had been laid aside to succour you, and now vice versa you must do the like. For God's sake use diligence and come as strong as you can. In my conscience, it will be the last blow in the business.[57]

Such a direct order placed Goring in a difficult position, particularly as the chances of Grenville's men accompanying him were slim. Whether he ever had any thoughts of obeying is debatable; Clarendon claimed that Goring had already written to the king explaining his inability to do so before he lobbied the Council of the West for their support. The latter were ready enough to back Goring. On 24 May they reported to the king that as there were about 2,000 horse and 3,500 foot in Taunton, the whole West would be threatened if Rupert's orders were obeyed. Only Goring's original force of horse and foot could be spared, and even these would not be despatched until further orders were received from the king.[58]

It was the end of any possibility that Goring would place the greater good of the Royalist cause above his own interests. On the eve of Naseby, Fairfax intercepted a letter from Goring in which he reiterated his inability to leave the west at present, but begged the king not to fight until he arrived.

Lord Goring has been justifiably universally condemned for his inaction in the critical weeks leading up to Naseby. While it is probably true that he could not have brought all the troops Rupert demanded, his own veteran force of 2–3,000 horse could have been spared, and might have turned the tide at Naseby.

Langport

Throughout June Goring and his troops made no progress at Taunton. When, about 25 June, the Western Royalists learnt of the defeat at Naseby, an angry Clarendon informed Sir Edward Nicholas at Oxford:

> The lord Goring hath taken his pleasure of us, I pray God he doth not so too of the king. I had no mind to give him your cipher with me. You know [his] old way of opening letters and I have no mind he should know my secrets . . . If Lord Goring had been so much soldier as we expected that work [Taunton] had been done before this time, but he nothing but drinks and plays.[59]

In fairness to Goring, he was experiencing shortages of ammunition and lack of cooperation from the Cornish forces, and Royalist indiscipline was leading to increasing unrest among the civilian population, characterized by the rise of the 'Clubman' movement. Goring met its leaders, and, with his usual persuasiveness, briefly won their support with promises of improved discipline which he proved unwilling or unable to keep.

Their victory at Naseby had released Fairfax and the New Model to move into the West, where Goring commanded the last major Royalist field army. By 4 July Fairfax was at Beauminster in Dorset, causing Goring to raise the siege of Taunton as he prepared to meet the imminent threat. Linking up with a brigade under Edward Massey, near Chard, Fairfax now had some 14,000 men against Goring's army of about half that number.

On 5 July Fairfax reached Crewkerne. Goring's position was arguably already hopeless, but he planned to hold the line of the River Yeo in order to keep Fairfax back from Bridgwater and the Bristol Channel ports long enough for expected reinforcements from South Wales to arrive.

Against the New Model's superior numbers the plan had few prospects of success. Parliamentarian troops under Colonels Thomas Fleetwood and Edward Montagu secured a bridgehead over the Parret at Petherton Bridge. On 7 July Fairfax's main force began its advance from Crewkerne, and secured a crossing of the Yeo at Yeovil, left unguarded by the Royalists because of a misunderstanding.

His strategy in ruins, Goring pulled back, abandoning the other crossings of the Yeo at Long Load and Ilchester. His last chance now lay in dividing the Parliamentarians. If he could cause Fairfax and Massey to separate their forces, he might be able to engage one of them with a slim prospect of success. On 8 May he sent George Porter with most of his horse in a feint towards Taunton. As Goring had hoped, Fairfax detached Massey in pursuit, but Porter on 9 May allowed the latter to catch his troops dismounted and resting on the banks of the River Isle near Isle Moor, and was routed with the loss of over 500 men.

A furious Goring, with the remainder of his troops at Langport, managed to extricate some of the horse, and was slightly wounded in the process. But he admitted that his cavalry were 'very much shattered', and as Fairfax advanced towards Langport that evening, Goring's prospects were bleak. He considered an immediate retreat to Bridgwater, but feared that he would not be able to extricate his foot and guns. He saw his only hope in fighting a delaying action at Langport.

As night fell the Royalist heavy guns began to move off towards Bridgwater, and the remainder of the army prepared to fight that most difficult of actions, an orderly withdrawal under fire. Early on 10 July Goring drew up east of Langport on Ham Down. Fairfax was a mile to the east on corresponding high ground across the shallow valley of the Wagg Rhyne stream. This could only be crossed at a ford from which a narrow hedged lane ran uphill to Goring's position. The hedges were lined with Royalist musketeers and two guns were deployed to cover the ford, while Goring's 2–3,000 horse were drawn up on Ham Down.

Although, thanks to Massey's continued absence, Fairfax could only bring 10,000 men against Goring's 7,000, the Parliamentarian advantage in morale was significant. Fairfax's guns quickly silenced Goring's two pieces, but the Royalist musketeers in the hedgerows put up a stubborn fight, so that it was noon before Fairfax's men got across the Wagg Rhyne. In the decisive move of the battle, Fairfax now sent Major Bethell in a charge up the lane with three troops of horse. Running the gauntlet of enemy musket fire, they engaged the first line of Goring's horse. The struggle lasted 'while you could count three or four hundred', before the Royalists began to fall back.

Bethell almost repeated his mistake at Radcot Bridge by advancing too far, but halted until reinforced by several more troops, then attacked the Royalist centre and right. With the Parliamentarian foot now advancing up the hill in support, panic set in amongst the Royalists, and soon Goring's entire army was in flight through the burning streets of Langport towards Bridgwater.

Goring lost about 300 dead, and 2,000 prisoners, although most of his foot and guns succeeded in reaching Bridgwater. Goring admitted that: 'the consequence of the blow is very much for there is so great a terror and distraction amongst our men that I am confident at this present they could not be brought to fight against half their number.'[60]

Langport marked the effective end of Goring's army and command. Fairfax stormed Bridgwater on 21 July, while Goring remained at Barnstaple, drinking and complaining to the Prince's Council. Only Fairfax's decision to move against Bristol saved Goring from destruction.

But Goring knew that the war was irrevocably lost, and had no further interest in it. After lurking ineffectually around Exeter in his by now usual state of drunkenness, on 20 November he wrote to the Prince of Wales saying that with the enemy now in winter quarters, the campaigning season was effectively over, and desiring two months leave in France to recover his health. Two days later, without waiting for a reply, leaving Lord Wentworth in command of what remained of his army, Goring sailed from Dartmouth, never to return to England.

Aftermath

The remainder of Goring's life was an unhappy epilogue. Although he eventually became a Lieutenant General in the Spanish service, he achieved nothing of note.

He remained chronically short of money and suffered from various illnesses, including ague and gout. In 1657 he was reported to be in Madrid, 'in miserable want' and anxious to serve the Royalist cause again in some capacity.

By the time the story reached the Royalist court in exile, Goring was dead. A persistent story held that he ended his days as a Dominican friar, but this is almost certainly untrue. But he apparently did become a Roman Catholic and possibly a Dominican Tertiary, a lay member of the order who only wore his habit on certain occasions. It would have been a typically calculating act by Goring to cover his options in the hereafter and perhaps obtain some financial support in the present.

Goring is the most enigmatic of Royalist commanders. Peter Young and Alfred Burne suggested that he might have made a great name for himself in a fully independent command, but Goring's irresponsibility was such that it is hard to see him performing well in that role. Indeed his character faults were so great as to render his undoubted talents almost useless to the Royalist cause in any capacity.

Clarendon gave a mixed verdict. He admitted that in the opinion of many 'if [Goring] had been confederate with the enemy, and been corrupted to betray the west, he could not have taken a more effectual way to do it.'[61]

But, despite his detestation of Goring, Clarendon absolved him of treachery. Rather, he believed, Goring's ambition for independent command and reluctance to serve with Prince Rupert had led him to drag out operations in the West for so long that events, in the shape of Naseby and the arrival of the New Model Army, overtook him. He went on:

> All his loose and scandalous speeches [were] imputed to an innate licence he hath always given himself, and his gross and unfortunate oversights to the laziness and inactivity in his nature, which could better pursue, and make advantage upon, good successes, than struggle and contend with difficulties and straits.[62]

In the end, despite all his undoubted brilliance, which might have made Goring the greatest cavalry commander of the war, his character flaws outweighed everything else, leaving George Goring's colourful and wayward life a tragedy of wasted talent.

King Charles I.

Patrick Ruthven.

Seventeenth-century Oxford. Note the castle (centre right) and the Thames and its tributaries which strengthened the town defences.

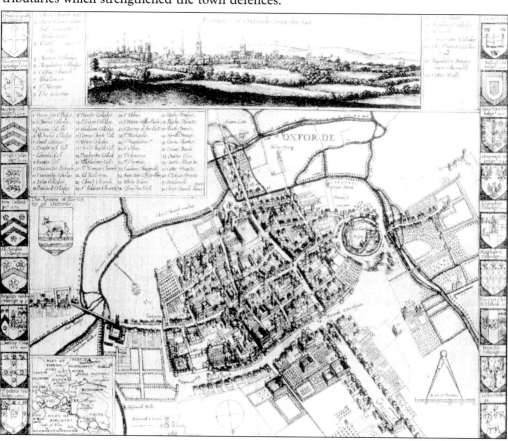

Prince Rupert.

Prince Rupert at Birmingham as depicted in a Parliamentarian newsbook.

Cavalry action from John Vernon, *The Young Horseman,* 1644. Note the ranks firing pistols as the defenders break under attack from front and flank.

Illustration of harquebusiers from John Cruso, *Militarie Instructions for the Cavalerie,* 1635. It was rare for a Royalist trooper to be fully equipped at the start of the war.

Jacob, Lord Astley.

Troops deployed for battle. Note the chequerboard formation (here slightly telescoped) allowing the second line to move up through the gaps in support of the first line.

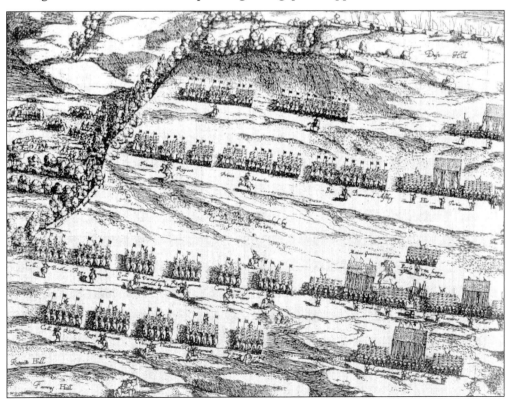

The ideal. A well-equipped Oxford Army musketeer, c. 1643.
(Partizan Press)

The reality. By the end of a campaigning season a soldier was often clad in whatever ragged clothes he could acquire.
(Partizan Press)

Prince Maurice.

Edward Hyde, Earl of
Clarendon.

George, Lord Digby.

Ralph, Lord Hopton.

Sir Horace Vere. Many Civil War commanders gained their earliest experience serving under Vere's command with the English forces in the Low Countries.

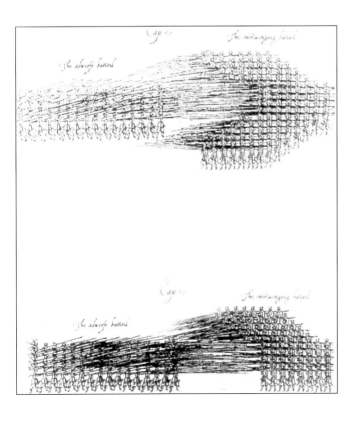

Push of Pike. Depending on the enthusiasm and training of those involved the fighting might range from ineffectual 'fencing' at pike-length to something resembling a modern rugby scrum as the opposing troops tried to push each other over or back.

```
                    Front.
                 E.        C.
S. M M M M D P P. P. P P P P P P D M M M M S
W M M M M   P P P P P P P P       M M M M W
W M M M M   P P P P P P P P       M M M M W
W M M M M   P P P P P P P P       M M M M W
W M M M M   P P P P P P P P       M M M M W
W M M M M   P P P P P P P P       M M M M W
  M M M M   P P P P P P P P       M M M M
S. • • • • D P P P P P P P P P D • • • • S
                    L.
                 Reere
```

```
              Front.
S  M M M M                        M M M M  S
 W                                      W
 W                                      W
 W                    E.   C.           W
S W M M M M D P P P P P P P P. D M M M M S
   M M M M    P P P P P P P P     M M M M
   M M M M    P P P P P P P P     M M M M
   M M M M    P P P P P-P P P     M M M M
   M M M M    P P P P P P P P     M M M M
   M M M M    P P P P P-P P P     M M M M
   • • • • •  P P P P P P P P     • • • •
   • • • • D P P P P P P P P P D • • • •
                    L.
                 Reere.
```

Diagram from contemporary military manual showing the deployment of a company of foot. In the lower diagram musketeers are advancing to fire by file.

George, Lord Goring.

John, Lord Byron.

Contemporary cartoon referring to the looting activities of soldiers in Ireland.

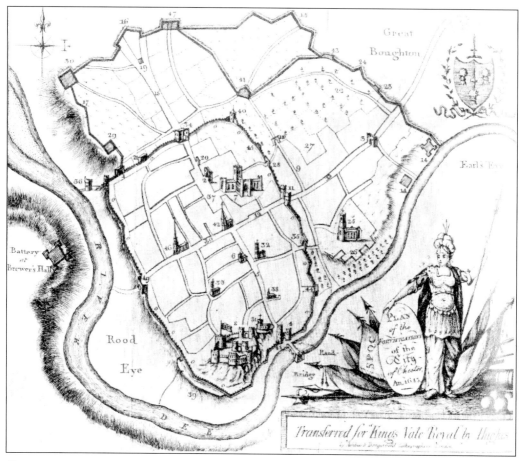

Contemporary plan of the Civil War defences of Chester.

Sir Richard Grenville.

A sconce or mount. Constructed from earth and sometimes surrounded by a moat, the sconce provided a firing platform for artillery and the defending garrison.

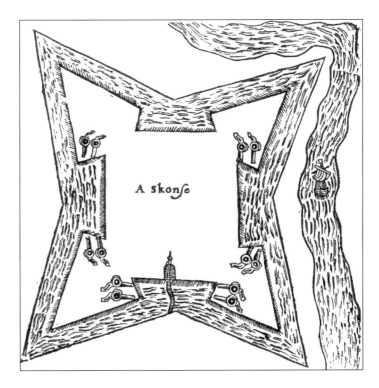

Willliam Cavendish, Marquis of Newcastle.

Queen Henrietta Maria lands at Bridlington under enemy fire.

A Northern trooper
of horse. Many of the
Northern Royalist
troops wore Scottish
blue bonnets.
(Partizan Press)

James Graham, Marquis of Montrose.

Henry, Lord Wilmot.

A musketeer of Montrose's Irish Brigade. The flag, similar to those carried by the Irish troops, combines a declaration of support for King Charles with the Catholic faith of the soldiers.   *(Partizan Press)*

VIVAT
CAROLVS
REX

CR

EXVRGAT DEVS
DISSIPEXTVR INIMICI

Chapter Eight
John, Lord Byron

Early life

John Byron has always attracted considerable criticism. Geoffrey Ridsdell Smith felt that 'no other Royalist officer did more to lose the First Civil War than John Byron.[1] To Brigadier Peter Young he seemed 'Proud, ambitious and heavy handed. . . It may be that he was stupid as well.'[2] R.N. Dore was slightly more favourable, seeing Byron as 'A soldier, and very proud and prickly about it . . . anxious to preserve . . . his own amour propre.'[3]

For Prince Rupert and his associates Byron was the man who lost Marston Moor and the army from Ireland. Only a very few modern historians, notably Stuart Reid, have suggested that the criticism of Byron may be exaggerated.[4]

Byron perhaps laid himself open to censure. There is nothing to suggest that he possessed the wit and disreputable charm of Goring or Wilmot. Although no unlettered soldier, as demonstrated in the terms for the surrender of Chester in 1646 which allowed him to take away his books and documents, Byron evidently lacked charisma. A solid and perhaps unimaginative man, he stares out stiffly from his portrait by William Dobson, his heavily handsome features given deceptive dash by a recent battle scar. Yet closer examination of Byron's career suggests that much of the condemnation is unjustified.

The Byron family were united in their support for the king. No less than seven of them, including John Byron and his five brothers, served in the Royalist forces.

Originally from the Rochdale area of Lancashire, the Byrons had benefited from the Reformation, gaining substantial estates around Newstead Abbey in Nottinghamshire.

John Byron was born around 1600, and was active in local affairs. Little is known of his early life, although his writings would suggest a man who had received an at least adequate education. Knighted in 1624, he was an MP for the county in the Parliaments of James I and Charles I, and served as High Sheriff of Nottinghamshire in 1634.

At some point, following the common practice of young gentlemen of his

119

background, Byron apparently served with the English forces in the Low Countries. Although details of his experience are lacking, on the outbreak of the Scots War of 1640, Byron was given command of a troop of horse in the English forces.

Byron was a firm supporter of Charles I. It appears that he was heavily in debt on the eve of the Civil War, and it may be that he hoped for financial reward from a victorious king,[5] and in the course of the war he would petition to be appointed to a profitable office such as Governor to the Duke of York. It is equally possible that Byron, as a not particularly deep-thinking traditionalist, was simply impelled to support the established order.

As a reliable supporter, with, Clarendon explained, 'as unblemished a reputation as any gentleman of England',[6] Byron was chosen by Charles in December 1641 to replace the unsavoury Thomas Lunsford as Lieutenant of the Tower of London.

Following the failure in December 1641 of the king's attempt to arrest his leading opponents in Parliament, Byron found his position at the Tower increasingly untenable. Summoned before the House of Lords to be questioned regarding the nature of supplies he was said to be gathering, Byron 'gave so full answers to all the questions asked of him, that they could not but dismiss him.'[7]

However, this spirited performance did Byron little good. In the atmosphere of mounting tension, Sir John found himself blockaded in the Tower, and expecting imminent assault, felt his situation to be untenable. He begged the king to release him 'from the vexation and agony of that place', and, after the House of Commons on 27 January also petitioned for Byron's removal, the king reluctantly agreed.

Cavalry commander

In July 1642, when the King began raising troops in the Midlands, the Byron brothers were among to first to rally to him. It was probably Byron's local connections which led to him raising what appears to have been the first regiment of horse to be formed. Byron was aided in his efforts by £5,000 'mounting money' with which to buy horses, donated by the fabulously wealthy Marquis of Worcester.[8]

By early August Byron's Regiment, with three of his brothers among its officers, was about 150 strong, and Byron was ordered to secure the town of Oxford, and the gold and silver plate of the pro-Royalist university.

En route, Byron and his men had the worst of a small skirmish with Parliamentarian supporters near Brackley, and Byron's servant was captured, along with a chest containing Sir John's commission, some clothing and a large sum of money. An angry Byron wrote to the local squire, a Mr Clarke, demanding the return of his property, failing which 'assure yourself I will find a time to repay myself with advantage of your estate.'[9] It was not the last occasion on which Byron, with his prickly sense of honour and correct soldierly behaviour, would find himself at odds with civilians.

Byron arrived in Oxford on 28 August, and found himself in the midst of a confrontation between the predominantly pro-Parliamentarian townspeople and the University authorities. Aided by the scholars, Byron attempted to strengthen the defences of Oxford, but was constantly obstructed by the citizens.

With the approach of Parliamentarian troops from Aylesbury the position of the small Royalist force was untenable. Byron mustered a few recruits from the University, loaded its plate onto wagons, and on 10 September set off across the Cotswolds towards Worcester, with the intention of joining the king on the Welsh Border. The encumbered Royalists, harassed by a hostile local population, averaged only ten miles a day, and Byron was uncomfortably aware that the main Parliamentarian army under the Earl of Essex was approaching from the south-east. He sent urgently for assistance to the king, who was at Shrewsbury, and on 16 September his weary convoy arrived at Worcester.

But the town's poorly maintained medieval defences and hostile inhabitants provided no support, and only the arrival of a cavalry force under Prince Rupert, despatched by the king to Byron's assistance, enabled the Royalists to check the pursuing Parliamentarians at Powick Bridge on 23 September, allowing Byron and his vital convoy to complete their journey to the king.

Byron's first military operation, taken over all, had been a success. The reverse at Brackley had not diverted him from his objective, and while Oxford itself was untenable at this time, the rescue of the University plate had been a highly creditable performance.

A month later at the battle of Edgehill (23 October), Byron led the second line of horse on the Royalist right. His men saw little action and Byron proved no more able than the majority of his fellow commanders to restrain his raw troopers from an uncontrolled pursuit.

Byron, like most Civil War commanders, had little concern for the impact of the war on civilians. In November, during the Royalist advance on London, Byron's regiment was quartered at Fawley Court, home to Parliamentarian Bulstrode Whitlocke. While admitting that Byron and his officers were courteous to his family, Whitlocke wrote scathingly of the behaviour of their men:

> there was no insolence or outrage which such guests commit upon an enemy but these brutish soldiers did it at Fawley Court. There they had their whores, they spent and consumed in one night 100 loads of corn and hay, littered their horses with good wheat sheaves, gave them all sorts of corn, made great fires in the closes . . . Whatsoever they could lay their hands on they carried away or spoiled, and did all that malice and rapine could provoke barbarous mercenaries to commit.[10]

Such behaviour was of course common to troops on both sides throughout the war.

1643 was to prove a year of almost unbroken success for John Byron. His rise was assisted by the launch at the start of the year of the Royalist propaganda news sheet *Mercurius Aulicus*. It editor and principal compiler, John Berkenhead, needed copy for his first issue and this was conveniently provided by a despatch from Sir John Byron, recounting a skirmish which brought Byron to the attention of a wide and influential Royalist audience.

On 30 December 1642 Byron and his regiment had been ordered to escort two wagonloads of ammunition from Oxford to a Royalist force at Stow-on-the-Wold. Next evening Byron quartered at Burford. Byron had ordered his men to be in readiness for action 'at the first sound of the Trumpet' and went off to place his pickets. As he returned to the centre of Burford:

> a musket or two went off, and thereupon the Alarm was given, that the Rebels were entered into the town already. On this Sir John taking the next horse that came to hand, and with his sword only went towards the market place: where meeting his Lieutenant-Colonel, he commanded him to take a competent number of horse, and make good the bridge, lest if the enemy had took it the way might be stopped betwixt him and the Marquis [of Hertford]; the ammunition being sent meantime, with a guard of 30 horse towards Stow . . . By this time it was known for certain both by the fire and by the report of the Muskets that the rebels were about the White Hart, being an inn in the utmost part of the Town, from whence a lane leadeth to the Market Cross. And therefore marching thither with all the speed he could, he found the Lane full of musketeers who were ready to enter the high street, and the guard of horse which had been left there, retreating as well as they could out of danger of the Shot. Sir John considered hereupon, that should the Enemy possess the Cross, and the houses on either side of the street, it was not possible for him to continue there, nor do any service with his horse against them being sheltered and defended: [and] commanded those who were next to follow him, and rushed in upon them, laying about him with his sword, for other weapons had he none. No sooner was he got amongst them, but some of those who were furthest gave fire upon him, which doing no hurt, they presently betook themselves to flight in a great confusion, some crying that they were for the King, and some for Prince Rupert. In this confusion he drove them before him to the further end of the lane, where the Inn stands, into which they ran, and into which he entering pell-mell with them received a blow in the face from a pole-axe or Halberd, wherewith he was in danger to have fallen from his horse. But quickly recovering himself again, he saw the Inn-door full of Musketeers, and himself alone unarmed and naked of defence in the open street, and there-upon retired back to the market cross, where he found his men, who had mistaken his command, conceiving they were to have tarried there to make good that place.[11]

A party under Captain St John stormed the inn from the front at the same time as the enemy made a hasty exit through the back door, and disappeared into the night.

The action at Burford demonstrated Byron's personal courage and resourcefulness in an emergency. Soon afterwards he was portrayed by William Dobson with the scar of the wound to his face clearly visible.

Byron and his regiment saw further action throughout the spring, fighting at Cirencester in February and in a number of minor encounters which confirmed their commander's ability as a cavalry commander.

By July Byron had been given a brigade of horse, and was second-in-command to Lord Wilmot at the sweeping Royalist victory of Roundway Down (13 July). His grasp of the tactics employed by the Royalist horse was displayed in the orders which Byron gave his men as they launched their victorious charge against Waller's cavalry:

> The command I gave my men was, that not a man should discharge his pistol till the enemy had spent all his shot; which was punctually observed, so that first they gave us a volley of their carbines, then of their pistols, and then we fell in with them, and gave them ours in their teeth, yet they would not quit their ground, but stood pushing for it a pretty space. . .[12]

The stiff resistance encountered by Byron at Roundway Down was a sign of the growing professionalism and confidence of the Parliamentarian forces. The Newbury campaign of the autumn provided further testimony of this and Byron's fighting qualities.

In August the Royalist forces, fresh from the capture of Bristol, had laid siege to Gloucester, but had been thwarted by the timely arrival of a relief force under the Earl of Essex. But the Royalist army now lay between Essex and his base at London, and had high hopes of bringing Parliament's principal army to decisive battle.

However, Essex outmanoeuvred his opponents and gained a start of almost 24 hours on the road back to London. The Royalist army went in pursuit, and eventually, on 19 September, blocked Essex's retreat at Newbury. The scene was set for what might be the critical battle of the war.

John Byron wrote his account of the campaign several years later. By then he was in exile, and his bitterness towards Prince Rupert, his one-time patron, is evident. Byron condemned the conduct of the pursuit, blaming Essex's head start on the failure by Rupert to credit intelligence which Byron had provided. He also censured Royalist commanders, again by implication Rupert, for failing to reconnoitre the ground over which the battle would be fought:

> here another error was committed, and that a most gross and absurd one, in not viewing the ground, though we had day enough to have done it, and not possessing ourselves of those hills above the town by which the enemy was necessary to march the next day to Reading.[13]

Essex was able to occupy strong defensive positions on the high ground to the west of Newbury. The key to the Parliamentarian position was a spur of rising ground, known as Round Hill, occupied by small hedged enclosures, thrusting out in a north-easterly direction into the flood plains of the River Enbourne, and overlooking the Royalist forces encamped south of Newbury.

Although the Royalist Council of War had decided to attack Essex's forces, they had hoped that the Parliamentarians might retreat during the night. But at dawn on 20 September Royalist outposts fell back to report that foot of Philip Skippon's brigade were occupying Round Hill in strength and bringing up guns.

The battle which followed was one of the most confused of the war. Byron commented that 'no orders were given out for the manner of our fighting and how the army should be embattled as usually is done on the like occasions.'[14] The Royalist assault basically consisted of apparently un-coordinated attacks by horse and foot at four points along a two-mile front.

Sir John Byron describes his role in the attack on Round Hill.

> The next morning [20 September] my brigade of horse was to have the van, and about 5 in the morning I had orders to march towards a little hill full of enclosures [Round Hill] which the enemy (through the negligence before mentioned) had possessed himself of and had brought up two small field pieces and was bringing up more, whereby they would both have secured their march on Reading (the highway was lying hard by) and withal so annoyed our army which was drawn up in the bottom . . . that it would have been impossible for us to have kept the ground. The hill, as I mentioned, was full of enclosures and extremely difficult for horse service, so that my orders were, only with my own and Sir Thomas Aston's regiment to draw behind the commanded foot led by Lord Wentworth and Colonel George Lisle, and to be ready to second them, in case the enemy's horse should advance towards them: the rest of my brigade was by Prince Rupert commanded to the Heath, where most of the other horse and foot were drawn.[15]

The attack by the Royalist 'commanded musketeers' under Wentworth and Lisle made little progress. So, as Byron relates:

> The commanded foot not being able to make good the place, my uncle [Sir Nicholas] Byron, who commanded the first tertia, instantly came up with part of the regiment of guards and Sir Michael Woodhouse's and my Lord Gerard's regiments of foot, commanded by Lieut. Col. Ned Villiers, but the service grew so hot, that in a very short time, of twelve ensigns that marched up with my Lord Gerard's regiment, eleven were brought off the field hurt, and Ned Villiers shot through the shoulder. Upon this a confusion was heard among the foot, calling horse! horse! Whereupon I advanced with those two regiments I had, and commanded them to halt while I went to view the ground, and to see what way there was to that place where the enemy's foot were drawn up, which I found to be enclosed with a high quick hedge and no passage into it, but by a narrow gap through which but one

horse at a time could go and that not without difficulty. My Lord of Falkland [the king's Secretary of State] did me the honour to ride in my troop this day, and I would needs go along with him, the enemy had beat our foot out of the close, and was drawn up near the hedge; I went to view, and as I was giving orders for making the gap wide enough, my horse was shot in the throat with a musket bullet and his bit broken in his mouth so that I was forced to call for another horse, in the meantime my Lord Falkland (more gallantly than advisedly) spurred his horse through the gap, where he and his horse were immediately killed. The passage then being made somewhat wide, and I not having another horse, drew in my own troop first, giving orders for the rest to follow, and charged the enemy, who entertained us with a great salvo of musket shot, and discharged their two drakes upon us, laden with case shot, which killed some and hurt many of my men, so that we were forced to wheel off and could not meet them at that charge. I rallied my men together again, but not so soon but that the enemy had got away their field-pieces for fear of the worst, seeing us resolved not to give over, so I charged them a second time, Sir Thomas Aston being then come up with his regiment, we then beat them at the end of the close, where they faced us again, having the advantage of a hedge at their backs, and poured in another volley of shot upon us, when Sir Thomas Aston's horse was killed under him, and withal kept us off so with their pikes we could not break them, but were forced to wheel off again, they in the meantime retreating into another little close and making haste to recover a lane which was very near unto it, finding then they could keep the ground, which before they could do, I rallied the horse again and charged them a third time, and then utterly routed them, and had not left a man of them unkilled, but that the hedges were so high the horse could not pursue them, and besides, a great body of their own foot advanced towards the lane to relieve them. Our foot then drew upon the ground from whence we had beaten the enemy, and kept it, and [I] drew the horse back to the former station; for this service I lost near upon a hundred horse and men out of my regiment, whereof out of my own troop twenty-six. The enemy drew up fresh supplies to regain the ground again, but to my uncle's good conduct (who that day did extraordinary good service) was entirely beaten off.[16]

The battle for Round Hill was one of the fiercest engagements between horse and foot of the entire war. The Parliamentarian infantry formed 'hedgehogs', in which the musketeers sheltered under the protection of the pikemen, who formed a bristling barrier to the attacking horsemen. Some of Byron and Aston's troopers were dragged from their mounts and into the centre of the hedgehogs, where they were despatched. That Byron was able to launch no less than three successive attacks, despite the losses suffered, and continue to gain ground, says much for his powers of leadership and the determination of his men in what was a difficult situation for cavalry.

As darkness fell, fighting at Newbury ended in bloody stalemate. Although the

Royalists had gained some ground, they were unable to drive Essex from his position. A Council of War that night received the unwelcome news that the king's forces were now critically short of powder, with insufficient stocks remaining for another day of intense fighting. It was felt that the Oxford Army had no option but to pull back and leave the London road clear for Essex. Byron, again perhaps speaking with hindsight, but undoubtedly bitter that his losses in the fighting had been for nothing, bitterly condemned the decision.

The failure to destroy Essex's army led to furious recriminations among the Royalist commanders at Oxford. King Charles, unable to offer any more tangible rewards, conferred honours on a number of those who had been prominent in the summer's campaigning. Among them was John Byron, who on 24 October 1643 was created First Baron Byron of Rochdale.

Highly regarded by the king and Prince Rupert, Byron was given a new and more responsible task.

An army from Ireland

The failure to achieve a decisive victory in more than a year of war led both king and parliament to seek outside support in an attempt to break the deadlock. While Parliament staked its hopes on an alliance with the Covenanting regime in Scotland, Charles turned his attention to the veteran English troops who, since 1641, had been fighting the rebels in Ireland. He instructed his Deputy there, the Earl of Ormonde, to negotiate a truce, or 'cessation', with the Irish Confederates which would release some of the estimated 20–30,000 English troops who were in Ireland for service with the Royalist forces in England.

Ormonde duly obliged on 15 September. However, the bulk of the English troops were in wretched condition, long unpaid, and clothed in little more than rags. If some at least of their wants could be met, Ormonde felt that the majority of them, by now hard-bitten professional soldiers, would be willing enough to fight for the king. While some units were sent to reinforce Hopton in the south-west, the bulk of the 5–6,000 men eventually despatched in several contingents between November and February made the shorter sea crossing between Dublin and the coast of North Wales and Wirral.[17]

Here they were urgently needed, thanks to a surprise invasion of Royalist-held north-eastern Wales by local Parliamentarian forces which had quickly overrun much of the area. By now the troops from Ireland were 'the daily prayers, and almost the daily bread, of them that love the King and his business.'[18] But concerns regarding their loyalty remained and Ormonde warned that the soldiers:

> will be apt to fall into disorders, and will think themselves delivered from prison, when they come on English ground, and that they make use of their liberty to go whither they will . . . And if the case be such, that plentiful provision cannot be instantly ready, it is absolutely needful that a competent strength of horse and foot, of whose affections you are confident, should be

in readiness by force to keep the common soldier in awe; and whatever provision is made for them, this will not be amiss.[19]

The civil authorities in Chester and throughout North Wales were given the task of collecting clothing for the new arrivals, and raising funds to pay them, while Byron was chosen to command the force of troops recommended by Ormonde.

Byron was later unfairly accused of obtaining command of the troops from Ireland by underhand intrigue. The king had already decided to replace his current commander in the area, Arthur, Lord Capel, who was unpopular and had lost ground to the Parliamentarians. The intention initially was that Ormonde should himself come over to lead the 'Irish' troops, but in the meantime, on 7 November, Lord Byron was commissioned as 'Field Marshal General of North Wales and Those Parts'. This effectively made him second-in-command and deputy to whoever eventually assumed command.

On 18/19 November the first 'wave' of the troops from Ireland, including 1,850 foot, landed at Mostyn in Flintshire. On 21 November Byron set off northwards from Oxford, bringing with him 1,000 foot and 300 horse.

He arrived at Chester to find that the 'Irish' had restored Royalist control of north-eastern Wales, and had been joined by a further contingent of 1,250 foot and 140 horse. There had been considerable debate on how the troops from Ireland should be employed. One suggestion was that they be despatched to reinforce the Marquis of Newcastle in the north-east of England, where he faced imminent invasion by the Scots. Another possibility was that the troops should 'winter' in the Chester area, and then, in the spring, join the king. A third proposal was that they should be employed initially in reducing Parliamentarian garrisons in Lancashire and Cheshire.

It was not particularly desirable to undertake active campaigning in the middle of winter, and Byron's decision to do so has been attributed to his desire to enhance his military reputation before he was superseded. However, he had more pressing reasons. Although the citizens of Chester initially welcomed the troops from Ireland as deliverers, their euphoria quickly wore thin. The new arrivals were hard-bitten soldiers, used to the harsh conditions of the Irish war, and the citizens were shocked by their brawling, drunkenness, thieving and selling the clothing which they had been given in order to obtain money for ale.[20]

Furthermore the demands involved in maintaining indefinitely an army which now totalled over 6,000 men were more than the civil authorities in Chester could bear, and on 2 December the Assembly offered the Royalist commanders £100 of the city plate if they removed their forces from Chester.[21]

So Byron's hand was effectively forced. He was also probably concerned about the impact on the troops of a winter of idleness. On 12 December he marched out of Chester at the head of 1,000 horse and 4,000 foot. His plan was to reduce the Parliamentarian garrisons in Cheshire, principally their headquarters at Nantwich, and then move into Lancashire.

The campaign got off to a good start in the early hours of 13 December, when Royalist firelocks under the bombastic Captain Thomas Sandford surprised the defenders of Beeston Castle, perched on its near-impregnable crag, and captured the fortress without a shot being fired. Over the next few days the exultant Royalists gradually closed in on Nantwich. On 26 December the only significant local Parliamentarian field force, under Sir William Brereton, was mauled by part of the Irish army at Middlewich, and Byron was free to commence operations against Nantwich.

Contemporary Parliamentarian accounts are full of complaints regarding the behaviour of Byron's 'Irish', as they were inaccurately described. A considerable amount of looting took place, but one incident left a lasting stain on Byron's reputation.

On 23 December a Royalist detachment arrived at the village of Bartholmley, south-east of Nantwich. Its church was occupied by a number of armed men, possibly local civilians. Thomas Malbon, a Cheshire Parliamentarian, describes what he alleged then took place:

> The King's party coming to Bartholmley Church, did set upon the same; wherein about 20 Neighbours were gone for their safeguard. But Major Connought [John Connock] Major to Colonel Snead . . . With his forces by welcome entered the Church. The people within got up into the Steeple. But the Enemy burning forms, pews, rushes and the like, did smother them in the Steeple that they were enforced to call for Quarter, and yield themselves; which was granted them by the said Connaught. But when he had them in his power, he caused them all to be stripped stark Naked. And most barbarously and contrary to the Laws of Arms, murdered, stabbed and cut the Throats of 12 of them, and wounded all the rest, leaving many of them for Dead. . .[22]

This version needs to be treated with caution, but is partly confirmed by a letter from Byron's brother, Robert, although he suggested that some in the church were killed after either refusing quarter or firing on the Royalists after surrender terms had been agreed, in a reprisal permitted by the accepted practices of war.[23] Lord Byron himself was not apparently present, and Connock and his men were from a Staffordshire unit, not part of the forces from Ireland. It may be that their action was triggered by now obscure local enmities. The troops from Ireland were involved in at least one similar action in the spring of 1644, at Hopton Castle, where troops under Sir Michael Woodhouse massacred a number of the garrison after its surrender. Other commanders from Ireland, such as Captain Thomas Sandford, were well-known for issuing blood-curdling threats to the enemy, and it is possible that Connock was infected by the attitude of the troops from Ireland, and over-reacted.

Although Byron did not order the 'massacre', he could hardly condemn it publicly without admitting it a crime, and a storm descended on his head when a Parliamentarian newspaper published a letter allegedly written by him to the Marquis of Newcastle, in which Byron described how: 'the rebels possessed themselves of a church at Bartholmley, but we presently beat them forth of it. I put them all to the sword: which I find to be the best way to proceed with these kind of people, for mercy to them is cruelty.'[24]

Henceforward the Royalist commander would be known to his opponents as 'Bloody Braggadocio Byron'. However his alleged comments need to be viewed cautiously. Byron was almost certainly not at Bartholmley to give any orders, nor, despite the wording of the letter, is there evidence that he ever carried out any similar actions. Perhaps the fairest verdict, in respect of Byron's own involvement, is one of 'not proven'.[25]

In early January the Royalists began a regular siege of Nantwich. The town was relatively strongly fortified with earth defences, and had a garrison of about 1,500 men. The Royalists were hindered both by increasingly severe weather and a lack of heavy siege guns. However, Byron was optimistic. A force under Sir Thomas Fairfax, despatched from Lincolnshire to reinforce the local Parliamentarians, received a severe mauling from Byron's horse under Colonel John Marrow at Newcastle-under-Lyme, and reaching Manchester, met with little enthusiasm from the Lancashire Parliamentarian leadership.

On 6 January, as Ormonde could not be spared from his Irish responsibilities, Prince Rupert was named as Captain General of Wales and the Marches. On 14 January Byron wrote to his new commander: 'I hope very shortly to give Your Highness a good account of Nantwich, without which all we have done in this country is nothing.'[26]

On 18 January Byron attempted to take Nantwich by storm, but after bitter fighting he was repulsed with the loss of about 300 men.[27] Byron has been censured, with suggestions that he was attempting to win glory for himself before Rupert arrived. But once again there were sound reasons for his action. Fairfax remained at Manchester, likely in the near future to attempt to relieve Nantwich, while even Byron's seasoned troops will have been suffering from the effects of campaigning in severe winter conditions. Although the assault had failed, Byron, who believed the garrison to be running low on supplies, remained confident. He was, however, concerned by his shortage of ammunition, which had been worsened when a munitions convoy from Shrewsbury was captured.

On 21 January, with the reluctant support of the Lancashire Parliamentarians, Sir Thomas Fairfax set out through the snow for the relief of Nantwich, with an army of about 1,800 horse and 2,500–3,000 foot. In horse he was numerically superior to Byron, though he had slightly fewer foot. Byron was given little information by the generally hostile local population, but he knew of Fairfax's approach no later than 24 January, when patrols clashed in Delamere Forest. Sir Thomas halted that night on Tilstone Heath, eight miles from Nantwich.

Byron was faced with a difficult decision. If he were to prevent the Nantwich garrison from foraging for supplies in his absence, he had to maintain the siege for as long as possible, for he lacked the troops to do this and fight Fairfax at the same time. He also needed to meet the relief force as far away from Nantwich as possible, to minimize the risk of intervention by the garrison. His plan appears to have been to intercept Sir Thomas at Barbridge, about four miles west of the town. However, his army was divided in two, separated by the River Weaver, and linked only by a temporary wooden bridge. Byron himself was apparently with the contingent on the east bank, and planned to unite his forces at Barbridge by the morning of 25 January, in time to meet Fairfax.

However fate, not for the last time, conspired against Lord Byron. As darkness fell, a rapid thaw set in, and the River Weaver, swollen by melting snow, swept away the temporary bridge. This left only about 1,000 foot under Colonel Richard Gibson on the west bank of the Weaver, nearest to Fairfax, while the remainder of the army had to detour about six miles before it could cross the river and rejoin them.

Gibson took up position at Acton Church, about 1.5 miles west of Nantwich. Fortunately for the Royalists, a slow advance by Fairfax enabled Byron and most of his troops to gain contact with Gibson, although they were still deploying when the action began.

The battle of Nantwich was a particularly confused affair, made no clearer by the evasive accounts left by the opposing commanders. Fairfax apparently took the highly risky decision to march across country to link up with the Nantwich garrison, in the process exposing his flank to attack by the Royalists around Acton Church. Byron duly obliged, but his assault was apparently poorly coordinated, partly because of the nature of the terrain, which consisted of a number of small, thickly hedged enclosures, and by the hasty deployment of his troops.

The fighting which followed seems to have devolved into three largely separate actions, as the Royalists attacked Fairfax's front, flank and rear. The battle was fiercely contested, with the Royalists initially gaining ground. After about two hours it was decided in Fairfax's favour by several factors. The Royalist horse, possibly late in arriving, had little impact, while Fairfax's cavalry were well-handled and aggressive. The 'Irish' foot, after a promising start, 'upon an instant unexpected' gave ground. John and Robert Byron claimed that about 60 of Henry Warren's Regiment suddenly changed sides, and opened fire on their comrades, although no Parliamentarian account confirms this. Equally possibly the Royalist foot ran short of ammunition. The decisive event, however, was a sortie by about 800 musketeers from Nantwich, who brushed aside a small Royalist detachment and took Byron's main body of foot in the rear. The result was a rapid and almost total Royalist collapse. Although Byron and the horse, and his brother Robert's strong foot regiment, were able to withdraw to Chester, the remainder of his infantry, some 1,500 in all, were taken prisoner, about a third of them eventually enlisting with their captors.[28]

Not for the last time, Byron was arguably more victim of circumstances beyond his control than author of his own downfall, but he reacted furiously to his first serious defeat. He and Robert blamed treachery by some of the troops from Ireland, and urged that future shipments should be of 'native Irish': 'the English, excepting such as are gentlemen, not being to be trusted in this war.'[29]

Rupert had established his headquarters at Shrewsbury. Byron remained at Chester, receiving a further substantial reinforcement of English troops from Ireland, and, because of his own lack of resources, sent them on to the prince at Shrewsbury. In the meantime he endeavoured to rebuild his own depleted forces, conscripting new recruits in North Wales, attempting to instill some discipline among the remainder by hanging several ill-doers,[30] and restoring confidence by means of some successful small-scale operations in the vicinity of Chester. Following his own advice, Byron also raised a new regiment of foot, including a number of troops recruited in Ireland.

Marston Moor

On the wider scene that spring, the war was turning increasingly against the Royalists. In the north Newcastle was fighting a losing battle to check the invading Scots, while in the Oxford area King Charles was menaced by the combined armies of Essex and Waller. With these considerations weighing heavily, Prince Rupert was forced to move quickly.

Lord Byron joined with Lancashire Cavalier leaders in urging on the prince the need to restore Royalist fortunes in that county, particularly by taking the port of Liverpool. Byron's proposals, as outlined in a letter of 7 April to Rupert, formed the basis of the strategy of the imminent Lancashire campaign:

> upon the importunity of the Lancashire gentlemen, I am forced to renew their humble suite to Your highness that you would be pleased, as soon as you are in a condition to march, to look that way with Your Army before Lathom [House] be lost, which they conceive may run some hazard, if not speedily relieved. . . The constant intelligence from that County is, that if Your highness once appear there, the greatest part of the Rebels' forces will desert them and join with you, and that country being reduced, all this part of England will presently be clear. Upon the relief of Lathom, Your Highness will be sure to have Liverpool, whereby the intercourse betwixt these parts and Ireland will be secured, and the Rebels' ships, for want of a harbour will not be able to continue upon this Coast, and nothing will more daunt the Scots and hinder their designs than to take the support of that country from them.[31]

By early May preparations for the invasion of Lancashire were under way. Byron expressed some prescient concerns to Ormonde:

> this falls out unluckily for the King's affairs in these parts in [that] the army is drawn hence before these counties can be reduced, but if it please God to make us successful against the Northern Rebels, I doubt not but we shall easily prevail against the rest.[32]

Still retaining his position of Field Marshal General, (second in command of the army), Byron rendezvoused with Rupert at Knutsford on 23 May, and served throughout the successful operations in Lancashire. Somewhat surprisingly, Rupert failed to nominate a Lieutenant General to command his cavalry, possibly intending, as at Naseby, to lead them himself in battle. In practice the responsibility rested with Byron, seconded by the Scottish professional soldier, Sir John Hurry.

On 2 July, as the Royalist armies deployed on Marston Moor, following their relief of York, facing the Allied Parliamentarian and Scottish forces, Byron was in command of the horse on the Royalist right. His actions would be held by some, including apparently Rupert, to have cost the Royalists the battle, and perhaps with it the war.

Byron's command consisted of 2,600 horse, deployed in two lines, supported by 500 musketeers. In places the Royalist front line was partially protected by a ditch and hedge, which seems to have presented no serious obstacle.

When the battle began at about 7pm, the Royalist forces, expecting no action that day, had been permitted by Rupert to break ranks in order to eat. As Oliver Cromwell's Eastern Association and Scottish horse, about 4,000 strong, supported by dragoons, advanced in close order down the slope of Bilton Bream towards them, Byron's men were probably mostly dismounted, and hastily formed ranks as best they could to meet the onslaught.

Byron would be bitterly condemned for the action which he now took. Probably deriving his information from Prince Rupert himself, the future King James II wrote:

> The Prince had positioned him [Byron] very advantageously behind a warren and a slough, with a positive command not to quit his ground, but in that posture only to expect and receive the charge of the enemy. The enemy . . . must necessarily be much disordered in passing over to him as having to receive the fire of 700 musketeers in their advance to him, which undoubtedly had been very dangerous, if not ruinous, to them. . .[33]

There is also a brief reference in the document known as Rupert's *Diary*, probably notes prepared by one of his officers: 'Lord Byron then made a charge upon Cromwell's horse. Represent here the Posture the P. put the forces in and how by the improper charge of the Lord Byron much harm was done.'[34]

There are problems with both these accounts. The 'warren' referred to by James, on Bilton Bream, was already held by Cromwell as a result of earlier skirmishing. The 'slough', possibly a ditch or some boggy ground, was evidently not considered a serious enough obstacle by the Parliamentarians to be mentioned in their descriptions of the encounter. It is also worth looking more closely at the nature and purpose of Byron's deployment.

The practice of interspersing parties of 'commanded' musketeers among cavalry was intended to provide additional firepower to disrupt attacking horse. The theory was that after the musketeers had delivered their fire, the defending cavalry would make a counter-charge. The tactic was introduced in Europe by Gustavus Adolphus during the 1620s, and was used by him at the battles of Breitenfeld and Lutzen. It was not, however, referred to by John Cruso in his book *Militarie Instructions for the Cavalerie*, published in 1635, the training manual with which Byron was most likely to have been familiar, nor had the tactic been employed on a large scale in any previous Civil War battle. So, although Rupert had doubtless explained its use to his officers, few of them, and certainly not Byron, though possibly Hurry, will have had any experience of it.

Provided that troops were properly deployed, the combination of firepower and counter-charge could be effective. The problem at Marston Moor was that the Royalist forces were taken partly by surprise. Advancing down the slope of Bilton Bream, Cromwell's first line would have been in contact within moments. It may be that Byron's musketeers were not able to form up and join in the action, a possibility supported by the lack of musket shot uncovered in recent surveys of the locality. With his first line probably still in some disorder, and having to take an instant decision, Byron may have felt that his only option was to make an immediate counter-charge, and, as Parliamentarian sources make clear was the case, engage the enemy immediately after they crossed the ditch in front of him.

The outcome was that Byron's first line, of about 800 men, outnumbered almost two to one by Cromwell's leading formation, was swept from the field almost immediately. Byron himself was probably carried away in the rout; at least we know nothing of his part in the battle. Although he had gained enough time for his second line, under Lord Molyneux, to deploy and make a determined stand, Byron had been comprehensively beaten, on the available evidence more as a result of the surprise achieved by Cromwell's superior numbers than from any failure of his own.

Defeat in the north

The defeat at Marston Moor marked the beginning of a deepening rift between Byron and Prince Rupert. How soon Byron was aware of Rupert's intention to make him a principal scapegoat for the disaster we do not know, especially as, apart from a brief comment in a letter to Ormonde that the defeat was the result of 'such gross errors as I have not patience to describe',[35] no account of Marston Moor by Byron seems to have survived. But the tide of disaster in the north of England which followed swept him along with it.

Rupert entrusted Lord Byron with the already hopeless task of defending Royalist West Lancashire while he attempted to rebuild his own forces at Chester. Byron, critically short of infantry and ammunition, and with his cavalry mounts still exhausted from the Marston Moor campaign, soon found himself at logger-heads with Rupert's protégé, Will Legge, the Governor of Chester.

The Royalists suffered a sharp defeat on 21 August at Ormskirk, which, apart from the garrisons of Lathom House and Liverpool, ended Royalist resistance in Lancashire.

Byron's misfortunes continued in September. His fears that defeat in the north would result in disaster along the Welsh Border proved correct. Climaxing a series of reverses, on 3 September the eccentric Lord Herbert of Chirbury surren-dered Montgomery Castle to the Parliamentarians. Its loss threatened communications between Chester and Shrewsbury, and opened the way for a Parliamentarian thrust into mid-Wales. Byron had no option, though critically short of muskets and ammunition, but to muster the remains of his 'Irish' regiments, battered at Marston Moor, and his still exhausted cavalry, and attempt to retake the castle. On 18 September he encountered a Parliamentarian relief force in an engagement which in some respects resembled the battle of Nantwich. The outcome was also similar. After initial success, the 'Irish' foot were broken by the superior firepower of the Cheshire musketeers, and were routed. Some 1,500 of Byron's foot were captured, and his field army effectively broken.

Byron's defeat provided further ammunition for his opponents. Rupert's agent, Arthur Trevor, launched a vitriolic attack in a letter to Ormonde:

> My Lord Byron is infinitely unfortunate, and hath now finished with your Excellency, that is to say, made an end of all your Lordship's army to a man, without any the least service, and truly, My Lord, people now begin to speak out, and say those forces were trifled away by my Lord Byron, who is here observed never to have prospered since his practice to supplant Capel, who is as prudent and valiant a person as the nation affords.[36]

Much of this was malicious nonsense, as Ormonde, by his continued support for Byron, seems to have recognized.

KEY ACTION: THE DEFENCE OF CHESTER

With his field army largely destroyed, Byron now found himself confined to the Chester area and North Wales, aware that once Liverpool fell, Chester itself would come under attack. His relations with Legge continued to worsen. Byron assumed that he still retained his old command responsibilities, including North Wales, knowing that the defence of that area and Chester were interdependent. It soon became clear, however, that Legge had a different view, and the two men were quickly at loggerheads.

From North Wales, John Williams, Archbishop of York, himself no particular friend to Byron, confirmed the problem in a letter of 30 October to Ormonde:

> the enemy knows too well what little accord there is between Legge and the Prince's creatures with that poor Lord who commands, or should command in chief in these parts. A most worthy man, but unfortunately matched in his Government.[37]

There had been friction between the Governors of Chester and the king's overall commanders in the area since the start of the war. But it became particularly acute while Legge and Byron were at Chester. Rupert seems briefly to have considered recalling Byron to the Oxford Army, but Byron had meanwhile strengthened his connections with the Royalist Cheshire gentry by marrying Eleanor, the young

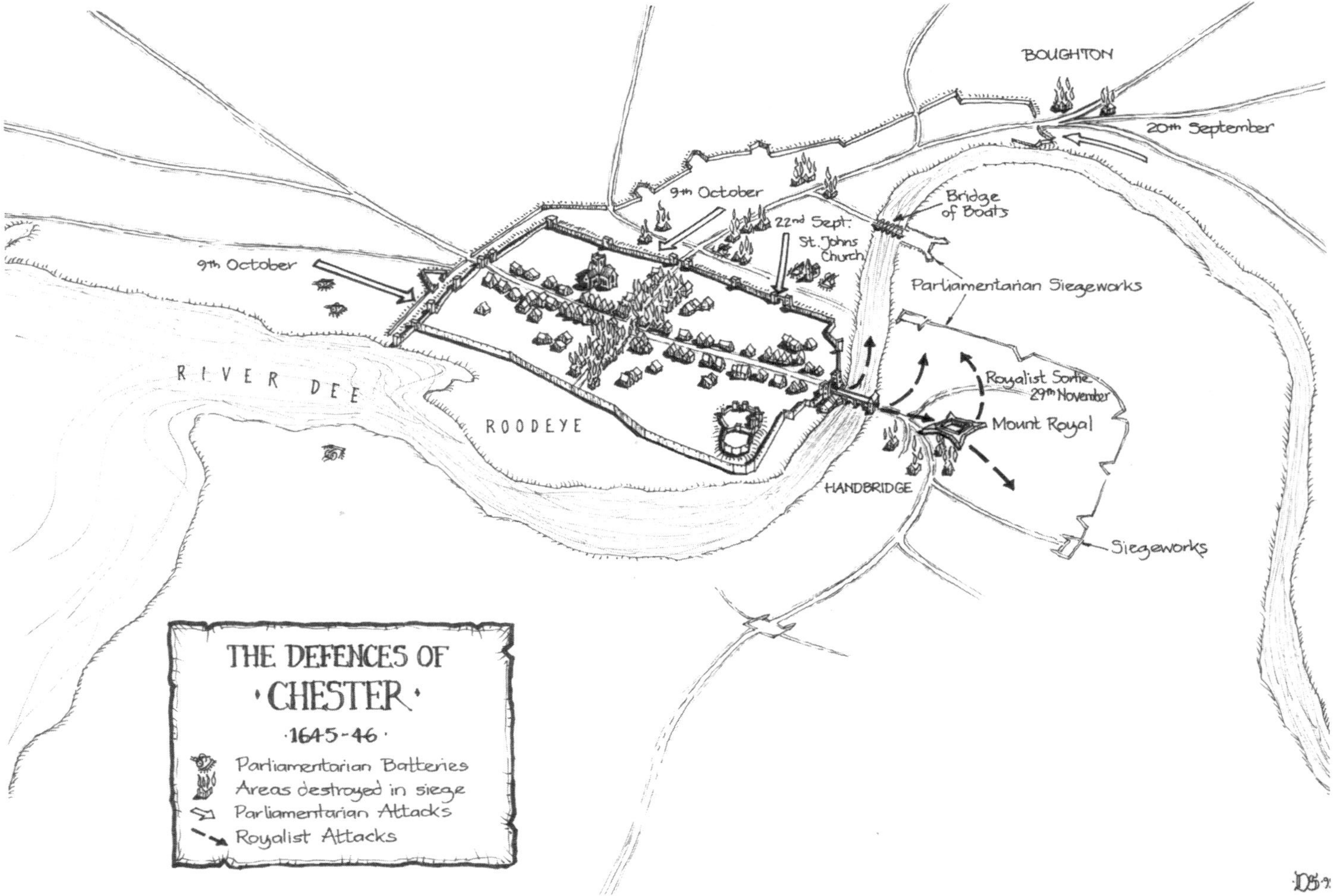

THE DEFENCES OF ·CHESTER·
·1645-46·

Parliamentarian Batteries
Areas destroyed in siege
Parliamentarian Attacks
Royalist Attacks

BOUGHTON

20th September

Bridge of Boats

22nd Sept. St. Johns Church

9th October

Parliamentarian Siegeworks

Royalist Sortie 29th November

Mount Royal

Siegeworks

HANDBRIDGE

9th October

ROODEYE

RIVER DEE

widowed daughter of Lord Kilmorrey. There is no evidence whether this was primarily a political match, but it evidently helped to secure Byron's position at Chester.

In November, after the fall of Liverpool, the Cheshire Parliamentarians under Sir William Brereton established an initially fairly loose blockade of Chester. Since Roman times the city had been of key importance on the routes north and into Wales, and for the Royalists it had added significance as a landing place for any further reinforcements from Ireland. With its man-made defences of medieval walls and earth outworks strengthened by the River Dee and extensive marsh-lands, the capture of Chester was a formidable undertaking.

The defenders struck back in a series of raids, with mixed results, but Byron's own position was clarified in January 1645 when Legge was recalled to be Governor of Oxford. In March Prince Maurice appointed Byron as Governor of Chester.

By then, with Brereton operating on both sides of the River Dee, threatening Chester's communications with North Wales, the garrison was under severe pressure, but was temporarily relieved in the spring by Rupert. The prince withdrew most of the remaining veteran troops in Chester, leaving Byron with only Sir Francis Gamull's City Regiment, his own Irish foot, and Roger Mostyn's Regiment. He sent the latter away, because, he told Lord Digby on 26 April, its:

> officers . . . were ignorant Welsh gentlemen and unwilling to undergo any strict duty . . . I am left in a condition neither to offend others nor defend myself, if pressed by a considerable army . . . for these poor means I have left to maintain the place, you may be assured I shall improve them to the utmost, and how unfortunate soever I may be, you shall have an account of my charge befitting an honest man, and one whom I hope you shall not blush to own. . .[38]

Byron's dislike for most of the Welsh, with the exception of his military deputy there, Sir John Owen, whom he regarded as a capable soldier, was frequently and forcibly expressed. It was an attitude which he shared with most Royalist commanders, and indeed the majority of English people of the time. But in Byron's case it was heightened by his distaste for working with civilians, especially as many of the Welsh leadership placed the interests of their own community above those of the wider Royalist cause.

The safety of Chester had been a key consideration in Royalist strategy, as demonstrated again in May, at the start of the Naseby campaign, when the approach of the Oxford Army once more forced Brereton to abandon the leaguer. But the crushing Royalist defeat at Naseby transformed the situation. Byron knew that once the Parliamentarians resumed the siege prospects of relief would be slim.

During the summer he attempted to prepare for the coming ordeal, repeatedly visiting Wales, 'that land of promises but never of performance' as he sourly described it[39] in an effort to obtain funds to strengthen Chester's defences. In his

absence command rested with the Deputy Governor, Sir Francis Gamul, a prominent Chester citizen whose earlier attempt to be made Governor had been
successfully opposed by Byron.

In the early hours of 20 September, while Byron was again absent in North
Wales, a picked force of Parliamentarian troops made a surprise attack, throwing
Gamul's citizen soldiers into panic and overrunning most of Chester's suburbs,
driving the defenders back into the old city within the circuit of its medieval
walls.[40]

Byron's leadership qualities came to the fore at this time of crisis. Hurrying
back to the city later that day:

> I found all things in such confusion that had the Rebels attempted it, they
> might have carried the City as well as the Suburbs. For though all the City
> were in arms, yet they knew not how to dispose of them or in what place to
> use them to best advantage, but ranged up and down the streets in promis-
> cuous bodies, and would fain have done something, but knew not how to
> go about it.[41]

Byron's first task was to restore order and confidence, and he called a meeting of
his chief officers and city leaders, appointing commanders for various key posts,
and ordering the Mayor, Charles Whalley, to organize the collection of tools and
begin strengthening vulnerable sections of the city walls against bombardment. At
the same time, in the face of opposition from citizens reluctant to see their property
go up in flames, he sent three 'desperate fellows' to burn as much as they could of
the suburbs to deny their cover to the besiegers.

That night, lit by the flames of burning buildings, 'the whole city, big with
expectation of a sudden storm, stood armed for a brave resistance.'[42]

Next day the Parliamentarians began their expected bombardment of the
city's sandstone walls, concentrating their fire on a particularly fragile section
near the New Gate. They quickly opened a breach, which the citizens, under
sniper fire from the steeple of nearby St John's Church, desperately tried to fill
with earth and wool packs. They succeeded in building a barrier within the
town, but 'the battery side towards the enemy was made so flat by reason of the
crumbling of the soft stone, and so wide, that six horses might have marcht up
in rank.'[43]

At about 8pm, aided by gathering darkness, the assault began. The attack on
the 25-foot-wide breach was spearheaded by two companies of firelocks, ironi-
cally consisting of some of those troops from Ireland who had changed sides after
being captured at Nantwich. Byron admitted that they attacked:

> with great boldness, but were received with as much courage by Sergeant-
> Major [Thomas] Thropp's men [Gamull's Regiment] . . . Those in the
> Newgate and the houses adjoining the breach, annoyed the Enemy with
> their Shot, so did the granadoes and the firepikes, which were used by very
> stout men, and placed upon the flanks of the breach. Captain Crosby (who

commanded the Chirk Horse) did good service there, and the Rebels pressed on so resolutely, that I caused more forces to be drawn down to assist Major Thropp's men. Thrice that night the enemy was upon the top of the Wall, but at last beaten quite off. . . [44]

Chester had survived its most dangerous crisis so far, and hopes were raised next day by the arrival of King Charles and his small army. But its defeat on Rowton Heath, outside the city, and subsequent retreat, left Byron to cope as best he could. Although he did not openly admit it, Byron probably knew that the king's departure ended any real chance of outside support, and he could hope only to resist as long as possible. With a garrison of about 1,600 men, half of them citizens, Byron resolved to tie down an opposing army of 3–4,000 troops.

He relied heavily on a small team of professional soldiers, including a somewhat mysterious French mercenary, Lord St Pol. Despite his prejudices, Byron also managed for a long time to work reasonably amicably with the city authorities, headed by the Mayor, and seems to have been energetically seconded by his father-in-law, Lord Kilmorrey. As a result Byron had remarkable success in imbuing the majority within Chester with his own determination to fight on.

On 9 October, preceded by ominous threats of sack and pillage, and a heavy artillery bombardment, which blasted a second breach in Chester's walls, the besiegers prepared a renewed assault. Once more the citizens, including women, strove desperately under fire to repair the breach, Byron and his officers setting an example by working with them. When, that night, the attack began at two points, Byron 'with some Gentlemen with me, rode about the walls, continually, from one guard to another, both to encourage the soldiers, and see such things supplied as were wanting in any place.'[45]

After bitter fighting the attackers were thrown back. It was the last attempt to carry Chester by assault; henceforward the besiegers, with Brereton back in command, would rely on starvation and bombardment to do their work. Making use of a mortar firing incendiary shells, they caused widespread devastation among the timber houses of the old city. Byron organized counter-measures, giving orders:

> that every householder should have a tub of water in readiness at his door, and that provision of raw hides should be made (as the best remedy against any fire that should be occasioned by the granadoes) the City for the most part consisting of wooden buildings. I likewise appointed sentinels to observe where the Granadoes fell, and immediately to give notice of them; and when the mortar pieces began to play (which commonly was about nine or ten o'clock at night and so continued till daylight) I caused the line to be manned, and the reserves to be in readiness, and walked the round myself, commanding that no man should stir from his post, though the Town were all on fire, lest upon the concourse of people . . . either some treachery might be contrived within the Town, or some attempt made by the enemy without. . . [46]

Even more injurious to the morale of the defenders were the effects of hunger. By early December Sir William Brereton was reporting that 'the better sort eat beef and bacon, but little cheese . . . the poorer sort of the city that are not soldiers are ready to starve, but they are compelled to eat horseflesh.'[47] Even Byron's Welsh soldiers, sleeping on straw in a great schoolhouse, were dying of starvation.

Byron knew that the end was approaching, but felt 'it my duty to hold out the town, as long as I could, though at the last I was sure to get the worse conditions, knowing that thereby I engaged an army which (had it been at Liberty) was designed to pursue the King wheresoever he went, and therefore I turned a deaf ear to all notions of a treaty . . .'[48]

But in early January 1646 a survey confirmed that food stocks in Chester were almost exhausted. The citizens, especially the women, were growing increasingly restive and the Welsh soldiers mutinous. In a final bid to prolong resistance, Byron 'took opportunity to invite the Chief of the Malcontents to dine . . . and entertained them with boiled Wheat and gave 'em spring water to wash it down, solemnly assuring them that this and such had been [his] fare for some time past.'[49]

The ruse failed to convince, and by the end of the month, his house besieged by women 'who daily flocked . . . with great clamour, asking whether I intended they should eat their children, they having nothing else left to sustain themselves withal',[50] and with remaining hope of relief, Byron was forced to seek terms.

Byron showed little appreciation for the sacrifices of the citizens of Chester, remarking grudgingly that the terms granted were 'for myself and the Officers with me . . . as good as in such an exigent I could expect, and those for the citizens as ill as I could wish, their folly as well as knavery deserving no better'[51]

Showing characteristic concern for soldiers he felt had served him loyally, Byron strove to have his Irish-born troops, liable to execution by an Ordinance of Parliament, included in the terms. This was not formally agreed, but they were tacitly allowed to depart with Byron and the rest of his men when Chester surrendered on 3 February 1646.

Aftermath

The remainder of Byron's career was an anti-climax. He endeavoured to prolong the resistance of Royalist garrisons in North Wales. But the crumbling medieval castles could not resist Parliamentarian bombardment and blockade, and fell one by one. Byron himself held out at Caernarvon until June 1646, when, short of water and receiving no assistance from Ireland, he surrendered.

Byron chose to go into exile, firstly to Ireland and then to the exiled Royalist court in France. In 1647 he took advantage of a pass from General Fairfax to return to England, and attempted to organize a series of Royalist uprisings in his old command in Wales and its borders. All were thwarted or quickly suppressed by the vigilant Parliamentarians, and Byron was further frustrated by the revival of old enmities between himself and some of the Welsh gentry.[52]

Byron fled once more to Ireland, listed by Parliament among those

permanently exempted from pardon. Writing a moving elegy on the death of
Charles I, he remained in exile until his own death in August 1652, described by
Clarendon as an 'irreparable loss'. Byron died without issue, and his eldest
brother, Richard, who had made a somewhat uneasy peace with the victors,
succeeded to the barony and eventually the family estates. Unlike many Royalists,
Richard, 'a person of narrow soul', did not particularly benefit at the Restoration.
Among his direct descendants, however, would be the famous poet, Lord George
Byron.

In an epilogue which Byron would probably not have appreciated, his young
widow, Lady Eleanor, provided a final service for the Stuart cause by becoming,
according to Samuel Pepys, Charles II's 'seventeenth mistress abroad', and died
in 1664, still attempting to extract a pension from an ungrateful monarch.

John, Lord Byron, was a dedicated servant of the House of Stuart. He was
also among the most capable Royalist cavalry commanders, though lacking the
élan of a Rupert or Goring. In his long defence of Chester, ideally suiting his
qualities of determination and dogged persistence, he arguably proved himself
the greatest of the king's garrison commanders. As a general in the field his performance is more questionable, although any assessment is affected by sustained
character assassination by Rupert's supporters. In the end, perhaps, his failure in
higher command was at least partly due to his lack of that elusive quality which
Napoleon held to be vital in a successful general – luck.

Chapter Nine
Sir Richard Grenville

Few who fought for King Charles in the Civil War have aroused more opprobrium than Sir Richard Grenville, the self-styled 'King's General in the West'. Grenville was understandably hated by the Parliamentarians whose cause he deserted, but their epithets for him of 'Skellum'[1] and 'Red Fox' were mild compared with the condemnation heaped upon him by his fellow Royalists. The pages of Clarendon's *History of the Rebellion* are so filled with denunciations of Grenville that, as R. MacGillivray comments,[2] Sir Richard is portrayed as a greater villain than most of the enemy.

This detestation was shared by many others. Grenville's cruelty was a long-enduring legend in the West Country, and even his descendants, Lord Granville in the eighteenth century and Roger Granville, writing a century later, found difficulty in presenting a favourable picture of Grenville. The latter writer admitted that a major cause of the Royalist defeat in the West was the 'the factious and troublesome pretensions of this particular commander'.[3]

Their views have been echoed by modern writers. His most assiduous biographer, Amos C. Miller, while claiming for his subject 'strong elements of loyalty, devotion to duty and as well as courage',[4] concludes that Grenville was 'a vindictive, brutal and rapacious individual.'[5] Mary Coate, who wrote the classic account of Cornwall in the Civil War, felt 'he was more like the continental soldier of fortune; he had a cruel and malicious temper, a mocking tongue, and an entire want of chivalry to a defeated opponent.'[6] To Peter Young and Wilfred Emberton, 'For an example of greed and treachery there is little to compare with Sir Richard Grenville'[7], while Mark Stoyle, a leading authority on the seventeenth century West Country, concludes that he was 'a brutal careerist, a man who starved prisoners to death, and finally, when the chips were down, sought to bolster his own position through the exploitation of ethnic differences; truly, a villain for our own times'.[8]

Yet virtually all his critics admit Grenville's effectiveness as a soldier and disciplinarian, and his popularity among his troops. Even Clarendon accepted that Grenville was 'a man who did some things well, and was not without some merit in the King's service'.[9] Stoyle wrote that in the later stages of the war few other Royalist commanders could maintain the strength of their forces as successfully as Grenville. Perhaps equally telling was the opinion of Prince Rupert; speaking no doubt of Sir Richard's military skill rather than his personal character, he felt in 1645 that Grenville was 'the only soldier in the West.'[10]

He remains, however, to most eyes a classic villain.

Early life

Benefiting from the acquisition of Church lands at the Reformation, the Grenvilles, their principal seat at Stowe near the village of Kilkhampton, on the rugged northern coast of Cornwall, were the leading family of the area.

Richard's personality reflected the darker facets of the Grenville family character. Born in June 1600, second son of Sir Bernard Grenville, Richard inherited the pride, ferocious single-mindednes, ruthlessness and savage courage of his famous grandfather, Sir Richard Grenville of the *Revenge*, which apparently skipped his own father's generation and were present in more refined form in his older brother Sir Bevil, who was noted for his charm and honesty – 'the most generally loved man in Cornwall.'[11] No one would ever say that of Richard.

A rift seems to have developed between the brothers at an early age. Even in appearance they differed sharply. Bevil was fair-haired and open countenanced. In Richard's portraits his russet hair and sharp suspicious eyes, with their aggressive stare, predominate. Unlike his more conservative brother, Richard was an extrovert, noted for his temper, sardonic humour, his colourful lifestyle, and his often flamboyant dress. His extravagance and debts caused a breach between Richard and his family.

It may have partly been as a result of this estrangement that in 1618 Grenville embarked upon his career as a professional soldier. For two years he served in the Low Countries with the Dutch, then in 1620 he followed in the footsteps of many of his contemporaries by enlisting with the English regiment under Sir Horace Vere in the Palatinate. Though the first expedition in which he was involved proved a failure: 'In that service he was looked upon as a man of courage, and a diligent officer, in the quality of a captain, to which he attained after a few years' service.'[12]

As a major, Grenville took part in the unsuccessful Cadiz expedition of 1625 and, after being knighted at Portsmouth, in the Duke of Buckingham's failed attempt to relieve La Rochelle two years later. On the latter occasion Grenville was slightly wounded, and was appointed as colonel of a regiment of foot, 'with a general approbation, and as an officer who well deserved it.'[13]

Returning to Cornwall, Richard was engaged to train the county militia, and served briefly as an MP. But his debts were becoming more pressing, and Grenville embarked on what appeared to be the best solution – marriage to a wealthy widow.

Mary Howard, who had already buried three husbands, 'had been a lady of extraordinary beauty, which she had not yet outlived'.[14] She was plainly a deter-mined and forceful woman, who took the precaution of placing her estates in a trusteeship which prevented Grenville from gaining control of them. The couple settled at Mary's property of Fitzford in Devon, but the marriage did not prosper. Richard discovered not only that his wife's wealth was largely outside his control, but that it was not so great as he had been led to believe:

> By not being enough pleased with her fortune, he grew less pleased with his wife; who, being a woman of a haughty and imperious nature, and of a wit superior to his, quickly resented the disrespect she received from him, and in no degree studied to make herself easy to him. After some years spent together in these domestic unsociable contestations, in which he indulged to himself all those licenses in her own house which to women are most grievous, she found means to withdraw herself from him, and was with all kindness received into that family in which she had before been married, and was always very much respected.[15]

Richard found that with his wife's departure the rents from her tenants dried up, and were paid instead to her former brother-in-law, the Earl of Suffolk. His response was to institute long and acrimonious legal proceedings. On the courts finding in favour of Mary and Suffolk, Grenville:

> being a man who used to speak bitterly of those he did not love, after all endeavours to have engaged the earl in a personal conflict, he revenged himself upon him in such opprobrious language as the government and justice of that time would not permit to pass unpunished, and the earl applied for reparation to the court of the Star Chamber, where sir Richard was decreed to pay three thousand pounds for damages to him, and was like-wise fined the sum of three thousand pounds to the King, who gave the fine likewise to the earl, so that sir Richard was committed to the prison of the Fleet in execution for the whole six thousand pounds; which at that time was thought by all men to be a very severe and rigorous decree, and drew a general compassion towards the unhappy gentleman.[16]

In October 1633 Grenville was released, on condition that he went abroad and entered Swedish military service in Germany. It was an experience which dark-ened Richard's already bitter and vengeful nature. In 1639 the outbreak of war with the Scots gave Grenville the opportunity to return and offer his services to the king, who needed every experienced soldier he could obtain. In the Second Scots War of the following year Grenville was one of the few English commanders to emerge with any credit from the debacle of Newburn, when with a few officers and his own troop of horse he unsuccessfully contested the Scots' crossing of the River Tyne.

But once again scandal hovered around Grenville. He was accused of cheating his men out of their pay, and using money given him to purchase saddles to buy older ones at a lower price, pocketing the difference.[17]

Ireland

Once again, war proved Grenville's refuge. In November 1641 the outbreak of the rebellion in Ireland created an urgent need for experienced soldiers. Grenville was commissioned as Major in the Earl of Leicester's 400-strong regiment of horse, and arrived in Ireland on 21 February 1642.

Sir Richard was ideally suited to the ruthless and bloody Irish war. In early March, during a cavalry skirmish near Waterford, he captured a rebel leader, and soon afterwards, in an English victory at Kilrush, led a cavalry charge uphill, routing the opposing horse. Later in the month, serving under Sir Charles Coote, Grenville took part in an expedition which captured the town of Trim in Meath.

When, on 2 May, Coote was killed, Grenville assumed command of the garrison at Trim. He displayed his presence of mind when, critically short of match, he made more out of bed cords, and beat off a determined Irish assault on the town. Basking in this success, Grenville persuaded the king's Lieutenant, the Earl of Ormonde, to appoint him Governor of Trim, pointing out with typical self-confidence: 'I hope that none will be placed over me, since I was the principal man in both the gaining and defending of this town'. If he was given £10,000, Sir Richard promised to make Trim 'a terror to the rebels in all the surrounding area'[18]

Much was made of Grenville's alleged savagery in his Irish war. A principal accuser was Clarendon, who wrote that Sir Richard was:

> much esteemed by him [the earl of Leicester] and the more by the Parliament, for the signal acts of cruelty he did every day commit upon the Irish; which were of so many kinds, upon both sexes, young and old, hanging old men who were bedrid, because they would not discover where their money was that he believed they had, and old women, some of quality, after he had plundered them and found less than he expected, that can hardly be believed, though notoriously known to be true.[19]

Some support for Clarendon's claims may be found in a letter by another veteran of Ireland, Dan O'Neill, written after Grenville had joined the Royalists in the West of England, who remarked: 'Sir Richard Grenville is left to block up Plymouth. He is not so bloody as he was in Ireland, but nothing lessened in the rest of his qualities.'[20]

Yet this must be looked at in context of the nature of the conflict. The Irish rebels had been accused in English propaganda of widespread killings and atrocities against the English settlers. Many of these horror stories were groundless, but they served, along with the long-standing fear in England of Catholicism, to create an atmosphere in which the English forces in Ireland sought to exact a bloody vengeance on the Irish population. In Dublin, the Lords of the Council told Ormonde to 'burn, spoil, waste, consume, destroy and demolish all the places, towns, and houses where the said rebels are and to kill, and destroy all the men there inhabiting able to bear arms.'[21] It became routine practice for English and Scots soldiers on punitive expeditions to kill all Irish, regardless of age and sex, who in any way incurred their suspicion or displeasure.[22]

In this respect Grenville seems to have differed little from many other commanders. After examining the evidence against him, Grenville's most recent biographer concludes that, while it is probable that Grenville was guilty of similar atrocities to those of many of his fellow officers, there is no hard evidence to prove that he was any worse.[23]

Trim lay on the River Boyne, about 29 miles north-west of Dublin. Grenville was reinforced by about 900 foot under a somewhat disgruntled Colonel Richard Gibson, who had expected the command at Trim for himself, an important addition, for Trim's medieval defences were in some disrepair.

Concerned by the vulnerability of his garrison, Grenville acted vigorously, but not unduly ruthlessly in the context of the Irish war, to deal with any threat of treachery. One woman and her maid were hanged, and other citizens were expelled and their houses burned. Over the next few months Grenville was in continuous action. After storming one rebel garrison, Sir Richard hanged most of the captured defenders, reporting with satisfaction to Ormonde: 'No rebels have or shall have with me any quarter.'[24]

Foreshadowing his later practices in England, Grenville operated what he called 'Trim Law'. This involved treating the people in the immediate vicinity of the garrison reasonably well in order to keep their support and obtain information from them regarding rebel movements. Not only did Grenville have a measure of success in this, but he also seems to have been popular among his men.

Like all English commanders in Ireland, Grenville was hindered by lack of money and supplies, and by the continuous attrition of combat, sickness and desertion, as a result of which the strength of the Trim garrison steadily dwindled. Despite his difficulties, Grenville worked energetically to strengthen his defences and to keep his men supplied. Sir Richard's men were the subject of a number of complaints from civilians regarding looting. Significantly in the light of later events, one of the main culprits was named as Lieutenant Thomas Roscarrock, a cousin of Grenville.

Meanwhile Grenville's reputation as a military commander continued to grow. In February 1643, at Rathconnell, commanding a force of 2,000 men, and making well-coordinated use of musketeers and cavalry, he won a significant success over a rebel force of twice his numbers. Among Grenville's prizes were 11 enemy colours and the head of one of the rebel commanders, a deserter from the English forces, which Sir Richard proudly despatched to Ormonde in Dublin. On 18 March Grenville acted as second in command of the English cavalry under Lord Lisle at the battle of Ross, where Grenville's rallying of some disordered English horse helped secure the victory.

For King or Parliament?

In August 1643 Grenville returned to England. A number of English officers serving in Ireland had returned since the start of the Civil War and offered their services to the opposing sides. Mostly, though by no means invariably, their sympathies lay with the king. Grenville's motives were more complex. In part he seems to have been disillusioned by the conduct of the war in Ireland, the 'Cessation' or truce made by Ormonde on the king's instructions with the Irish rebels, and by lack of further prospects for his own advancement.

Significant in Grenville's timing may have been his brother Bevil's death at Lansdown on 4 July. Although Sir Bevil's heir was his eldest son, John, the latter was still a teenager, and Sir Richard may have sensed a long-term opportunity to fill a vacuum in the Cornish Royalist leadership.

For the moment, however, Grenville's proclaimed sympathies were with Parliament. Late in August, Sir Richard, with his old commander, Lord Lisle, landed at Parliamentarian-held Liverpool. Grenville was suspected of planning to defect to the Royalists at Chester, and with Lord Lisle and his brother, Captain Sidney, was despatched under escort to London.

Lisle claimed that he had had to dissuade Grenville from giving his guards the slip and heading for the Royalist capital of Oxford, but Richard for the moment decided to pledge allegiance to Parliament. Not unconnected with his decision was Parliament's promise to settle all the arrears in pay of officers from Ireland who joined them. On reaching London, Grenville made a pledge of loyalty. Just how firm this was is unclear; according to one version, Grenville stipulated that he would 'never serve against the King, but would against the Queen in defence of the Protestant religion, and would never serve against the Parliament'[25] It seems unlikely such a lukewarm pledge would have been acceptable, and he was publicly thanked by the House of Commons for his services in Ireland, and, in December, ' a man of approved fidelity to Parliament and a gallant soldier',[26] was appointed Lieutenant-General of Horse to Sir William Waller, and commissioned to raise a regiment of horse in Kent, Surrey and Sussex.

Grenville became a close confidante of Waller, who had served with him in the Palatinate, and, as member of his Council of War, had full access to plans for the coming campaign. According to Clarendon, he received from Parliament ' a great sum of money for the making of his equipage in which he always affected more than ordinary lustre.'[27] However, Grenville found difficulty in raising his regiment of horse, and, according to his own account, was disillusioned with some of the more radical aspects of the Parliamentarian programme. He still retained Waller's confidence, however, and early in March was given the task of supporting Lord Paulet, brother of the Marquis of Winchester, in a plot to betray the key Royalist garrison of Basing House to the Parliamentarians.

On 2 March Grenville left London in style, with servants, a coach and six, a wagon loaded with possessions and £600 intended for the fitting out of his regiment. But on meeting his troops at Bagshot, Grenville declared his hatred of the rebels and their wickedness in fighting against their anointed monarch, announcing his intention of joining the king. The majority of his own troop agreed to serve with him, and Grenville rode into Oxford to a warm welcome, particularly as his information foiled the plan to betray Basing.

On 8 March Grenville wrote to the Speaker of the House of Commons, justifying his decision to defect to the Royalists. He claimed that on leaving Ireland he had intended to take no part in the war: 'I contented myself to think I had served both without dislike of either, and that therefore I might [attend] my own particular, and if before I, in any way, engaged myself (if I should do so in the future) do it upon knowledge, not report.' Grenville wrote that he became increasingly disillusioned with the Parliamentarian cause after arriving at London, and, after Parliament had failed to keep its promise regarding the payment of his arrears: 'therefore I withdrew myself to my becoming and lawful duty to his Majesty at whose feet I have now laid myself from whence no fortune, terror or cruelty shall make me swerve. This Sir, in satisfaction to you and the world I rest, as I expect you should term me, your malignant servant, Richard Grenville'.[28]

Just how much truth there was in Grenville's words is debatable. For some weeks rumours had been circulating that he planned to defect, while Clarendon felt that he had all along intended to join the king, once he had received the money owed to him by Parliament. Grenville's own sympathies, so far as he allowed them to govern his actions, seem to have been strongly Royalist in the traditionalist way typical of the majority of the Cornish gentry.

His letter enraged the Parliamentarians. Grenville was the subject of a torrent of abuse in the London news sheets, 'Skellum' (scoundrel) and 'Red Fox' being among the many epithets applied to him. As a symbol of its detestation of Grenville, Parliament had two gibbets erected, carrying signs announcing that both were reserved for the hated 'Skellum' when he fell into their hands!

For the Royalists Grenville's action was a highly welcome propaganda coup. One of their newspapers gloated triumphantly: 'O credulous Parliament, if Sir Grenville was indeed a Red Fox, what were the sagacious ones who hearkened to him?'[29]

Command in the west

There seems to have been uncertainty on how best to employ Sir Richard. Grenville was anxious to return to the West Country, where he felt his greatest influence lay. The Royalist high command hoped that Grenville's presence might revitalize Cornish support for the war effort and he was sent to the West to raise troops.

Typically, Grenville's first action on arrival was to revenge himself on the retainers of his former wife. Mary's presence in London was held to prove her Parliamentarian sympathies, and her lands in Devon and Cornwall were confiscated and placed in Grenville's hands. Late in March Prince Maurice gave Grenville a warrant authorizing him to arrest Mary's steward, George Cuttford, for sending to London money which he had received from the estates.

Cuttford would remain a prisoner until the following November, and was perhaps fortunate to escape with his life, for Grenville also arrested an attorney who had acted for Mary and the Earl of Suffolk, and hanged him as a spy. Clarendon related that when taxed with this, Sir Richard replied impenitently that :

> Yes, he had hanged him, for he was a traitor and against the King, and that he had taken a brother of his, whom he might have hanged too, but he had suffered him to be exchanged he knew the country talked that he hanged him for revenge, because he had solicited a cause against him; but that was not the cause, though having played the knave with him; he added, smiling, he was well content to find a just cause to punish him.[30]

Grenville, like other officers who had served in Ireland, had brought its ruthless methods back with him to England. Clarendon reported one incident shortly after Grenville's arrival in the West, when, returning from dining with Colonel John Digby, commanding the Royalist forces besieging Plymouth, Grenville and his escort captured five Parliamentarian soldiers from the Plymouth garrison who had been foraging. Grenville forced one of them to hang the rest.[31]

When Digby was wounded on 15 March Grenville took over operations against Plymouth. The port had been in Parliamentarian hands since the beginning of the war, and a Royalist blockade had made little impression. It remained to be seen if Grenville would fare any better.

A complete blockade was impossible because of the width of Plymouth Sound, defended by the fortified St Nicholas Island, and the overwhelming superiority of the Parliamentarian Navy which kept open the garrison's communications by sea. The town was situated in a naturally strong defensive location on a peninsula between the Rivers Tamar and Plym, and was further protected by a series of creeks. These natural defences covering three sides of Plymouth helped shorten the line which the defenders needed to hold, and enabled them to concentrate their efforts on the northern side of the town, where a number of ridges overlooked Plymouth. Here the garrison constructed a series of forts or 'mounts', connected by breastworks, their keystone being the Maudlyn Fort in the centre of the line on North Hill.

The Royalists had long been anxious to reduce Plymouth, both because of the threat it presented and also because the Cornish troops were reluctant to march further eastwards so long as it remained in enemy hands. Immediately after assuming command Grenville on 18 March summoned Plymouth to surrender, appealing to its citizens not to fight on for a 'hopeless cause.This my affection urgeth me to impart unto you out of the great desire I have rather to regain my old friends by love than by force to subject them to ruin.' The summons was rejected, with a contemptuous reference to a report that, prior to his defection, the Parliamentarians had considered making Grenville Governor of Plymouth: 'we accounting ourselves safer to have you an enemy abroad than a pretended friend at home.'[32]

Grenville established his headquarters at his wife's house at Fitzford, 15 miles to the north of Plymouth, with outposts at Mount Stamford and Mount Batten, overlooking Plymouth Sound, from whence batteries could fire at Parliamentarian ships entering the port. The Royalist blockade was maintained for the next few months, with little serious action. Grenville made no attempt to carry Plymouth by assault, probably because he lacked sufficient troops. The garrison reportedly totalled about 3,000 foot and 500 horse; Grenville probably had fewer men. A Parliamentarian writer scoffed: 'We are informed that the said renegade, Grenville, builds very much at Fitzford (I hope castles in the air or houses without foundation) and boasts that he little doubts of having Plymouth, but the garrison and Plymouth will not believe him'.[33]

Grenville had some success in keeping Plymouth sealed off on its landward approaches, but his artillery could do no more than harass resupply from the sea. In any case, events in the wider theatre of the war now intervened.

The decision on 6 June by the Earl of Essex to advance into the West compelled Prince Maurice to raise his siege of Lyme and fall back on Exeter. Grenville made energetic attempts to raise more troops to meet this new threat, and was eventually able to persuade about 1,500 Cornish recruits to cross the Tamar and join Maurice at Okehampton. The Parliamentarians claimed that Grenville was ruthless in his recruiting methods: 'The country groans under extreme misery under the barbarous tyranny of Grenville'[34]

On 18 July Essex decided to push on to relieve Plymouth. Grenville was in no condition to meet the threat without assistance.

Five days later, Essex's arrival at Tavistock forced Grenville to abandon the blockade of Plymouth and pull back to Horsebridge in an attempt to hold the crossings of the River Tamar into Cornwall. He left a garrison of 150 men to hold Fitzford, which on 23 July was stormed by the Parliamentarians, who hanged a number of alleged 'Irish' prisoners.

Essex now made his fateful decision to invade Cornwall, and after a 'hot dispute' brushed aside Grenville's attempt to hold the Tamar crossing at Horsebridge. The Cornish were showing little of their spirit of the earlier days of the war. Many of Grenville's troops disbanded and went home, and on 28 July, as Essex approached Bodmin, Grenville abandoned the town, along with forty barrels of powder, and pulled back to Truro.

He was incapable of mounting serious opposition to Essex, and a Parliamentarian newspaper proclaimed 'It cannot be possible that Grenville can ever rally his men again to any purpose but is fled either to Pendennis Castle or the Mount.'[35] Another writer, relishing the discomfiture of 'Skellum', described him 'fleeing like a guilty Cain from every shadow, frightened by his fancies and tormented by a prickling galled conscience for symptoms of misery; a hell within and a halter at Westminster that makes the man as a March hunted hare.'[36]

The Royalist Sir Edward Walker claimed that 'Sir Richard Grenville, like a man of honour and courage, kept a good body together and retreated in good order to Truro, endeavouring actively to raise a force to resist Essex's further advance.'[37] But Grenville seems to have exaggerated his success. He reached Truro with about 1,000 men. Pulling back further west to Penrhyn, he issued warrants calling out the militia to resist the invasion, and made energetic efforts to obtain mounts for his small force of cavalry. Among the horses summarily requisitioned were six belonging to the Earl of Bath, who later protested to the king, receiving in return, not the horses, but a placatory letter from Lord Digby, advising him not 'to take too much to heart the roughness of a soldier.'[38]

Grenville met with limited success until 3 August when he received a letter from King Charles announcing that he and his forces had crossed into Cornwall in pursuit of Essex. This rallied the Cornish, 'and put new life into them.'[39]

Grenville was ordered to advance eastwards to Tregony in order to hinder the foraging of Essex's army, which was now around Lostwithiel and Fowey. Bringing with him only 600 horse and 1,800 foot, not the 8,000 men he claimed to have raised,[40] Grenville occupied Bodmin on 10 August, and next day linked up with the main Royalist forces. That night he was instructed to occupy Lanhydrock House and secure Respryn Bridge over the River Fowey, which he did against light opposition.

Grenville's men took an active role in the remainder of the Lostwithiel campaign. On 21 August, during the battle of Beacon Hill, they secured the ruins of Restormel Castle, meeting with only slight resistance, and were again in action at Castle Dor on 31 August, in the final engagements which led to the surrender of Essex's infantry. However on 2 September, Grenville's action in pausing to secure the town of Saltash was held to have played a part in allowing the Parliamentarian horse under Sir William Balfour time to escape.

King Charles, however, was satisfied enough with Grenville's conduct to grant him more of what he seems to have craved most – land. He was now given possession of estates around Buckland Abbey and Werrington in Devon which had been held by the Parliamentarian Sir Francis Drake.

KEY ACTION: THE SIEGE OF PLYMOUTH, 1644–45

King Charles summoned the garrison of Plymouth to surrender, but when rebuffed decided he could spare neither time nor casualties in assaulting the town. Once again Grenville was left to conduct the siege. He now faced a more formidable task than in the spring. Plymouth's garrison had been reinforced, and its new Governor, Lord Robartes, was 'one who must be overcome before he could believe he could be so.'[41] With an initial force of only 3–800 foot,[42] Grenville had no prospect of taking Plymouth by assault. He established his headquarters at his new acquisition of Buckland Abbey, and reoccupied his former outposts at Plympton and Saltash, while setting out to recruit more troops from war-weary Devon and Cornwall.

Grenville had considerable success, though employing means which caused considerable resentment among other Royalist commanders. According to Clarendon, when the King's forces had marched away eastwards, Grenville had encouraged Prince Maurice's Cornish troops ' to stay for some time in Cornwall, and then to repair to him: as many of them did, for his forces suddenly increased;

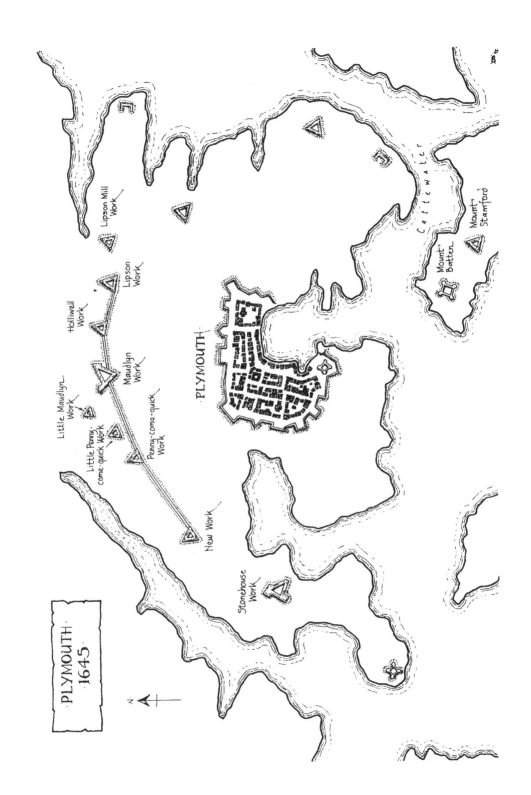

PLYMOUTH · 1645

N

PLYMOUTH

Lipson Mill Work

Lipson Work

Holliwell Work

Little Maudlyn Work

Maudlyn Work

Little Penny-come-quick Work

Penny-come-quick Work

New Work

Stonehouse Work

Mount Batten

Mount Stamford

C a t t e w a t e r

and the truth is, few of the Cornish marched outward.'[43] By the autumn some Parliamentarian writers were claiming that Grenville was operating to his own agenda. Probably, however, he was motivated by a desire to build up a respectably-sized force, if need be at the expense of other Royalist commanders.

Grenville, far from the always uncertain authority of the Royalist high command, also adopted methods reminiscent of the 'Trim Law' he had practised in Ireland. Throughout the autumn he concentrated on developing good relations with the ordinary Cornish people. Grenville was a notably better disciplinarian than many other contemporary commanders, and he made strenuous efforts to ensure that the only looting carried out was authorized by him. He also endeavoured to see that his men were regularly paid and well fed, and, although they possibly never received uniforms, the men of what became known as Grenville's 'New Cornish Tertia' were better cared for than almost any of their contemporaries apart perhaps from Parliament's New Model Army. Mark Stoyle writes that of all the Royalist commanders in the later stages of the war 'it was Grenville who came closest to building an effective, well-balanced and potentially sustainable infantry force'.[44]

The core of Grenville's New Tertia were about 2,000 deserters from Maurice's forces, who formed the basis of four new infantry regiments recruited during the autumn. To these were added various units based on the Cornish Trained Bands, and other volunteer formations, so that by early 1645 Grenville's forces around Plymouth reached a maximum strength of about 5,000 foot and 1,000 horse.

For most of the autumn, however, Grenville's forces remained too weak to mount any direct attack. In mid-September Sir Richard attempted to gain Plymouth by means of treachery. Joseph Grenville, a 16-year-old kinsman, possibly an illegitimate son of Sir Richard, entered the town, posing as a deserter. He then offered £3,000 to a Parliamentarian officer, Colonel Searle, if he would betray Plymouth's outworks to the Royalists. However Searle informed the Governor, and Joseph Grenville was arrested and executed, despite Sir Richard, with unwonted generosity, offering any ransom or exchange demanded for his life.[45]

Perhaps this personal loss, if such it was, darkened Grenville's mood further. He soon found opportunity to exact a characteristically bloody revenge. On 4 October a force of 700 troops from Plymouth seized Saltash in a surprise attack by boat. This was a serious blow for Grenville, threatening his links with Cornwall, and the Royalist commander had to retake the town. His first assault, on 5 October, was repulsed. Next day the Royalists managed to establish a foothold in the lower town, but were thrown back by fire from a ship in the river and by the fierce resistance of the Parliamentarians holding the upper town, who, when ammunition ran short, hurled rocks at their attackers.

On the night of 8 October Grenville launched a third assault. He claimed later that he had made three calls on the defenders to surrender, but all had been rejected, so that he 'resolved to storm them, having 500 stout Cornish foot'. At about 1am the Royalists attacked Saltash on two sides, and in two hours of fierce fighting drove the Parliamentarians down the steep main street to the banks of the Tamar, where some managed to escape by boat. The Royalists claimed to have killed about 4–500 of the enemy and to have taken 300 prisoners.[46]

If the Parliamentarians had rejected a summons to surrender, they had by the laws of war forfeited their right to mercy, and Grenville was not in any case minded to grant clemency. He declared that 'after he hath given God thanks for his victory, he intends to hang 300 of the prisoners'.[47] King Charles apparently wrote to Grenville urging him to spare them, but was too late, for a Cornish Royalist who may have been present reported that Grenville 'hanged many in cold blood'[48] It was one of the major Royalist atrocities of the war, and did much to confirm Grenville's bloody reputation. Significantly, it came at a time when similar actions by Royalist troops elsewhere, which had increased after the arrival of forces from Ireland, had largely ceased, largely because of condemnation by King Charles. It was an illustration of how Grenville was operating effectively outside royal control.

His harshness was also making itself felt in other ways. Apparently on his own initiative, Grenville had given himself the title of 'the King's General in the West', and, appointed High Sheriff of Devon, was making vigorous efforts to raise financial contributions to support his growing army. Although Sir Richard rigorously suppressed unauthorized plundering by his troops, Clarendon felt that he was:

> in truth the greatest plunderer of the war, for whenever any person had disobeyed any of his commandments, or whenever anyone failed to appear at the posse (which he summoned very frequently after he became sheriff of Devon) he presently sent a party of horse to apprehend their persons and to drive their grounds. If the persons were taken, they were very well content to remit their stock to redeem their persons. For the better disposing of them thereafter he would hang a constable or some other poor fellow [as a result] he had a greater stock of cattle of all sorts upon his grounds than any person in the West of England.[49]

Many of Grenville's victims were imprisoned in the remote Norman stronghold of Lydford Castle, where their treatment, amounting in some cases to death by starvation, became a dark West Country legend. A Tavistock poet, William Brown, wrote after visiting a prisoner there in 1644:

> I oft have heard of Lydford law;
> How in the morn they hang and draw,
> And sit in judgement after;
> At first I wondered at it much,
> But since I find the matter such
> As it deserves no laughter[50]

The accusations are given support by the register of burials for Lydford parish. During this time the number of burials recorded trebled.[51]

Grenville might have set himself up as one of the most powerful and terrifying of the king's regional warlords, but he was still no closer to making good his boast of capturing Plymouth. Early in 1645 he felt strong enough to mount his most serious effort. Grenville launched a major assault on Plymouth's outworks on the night of 10 January.

The main blows were directed at the key fort of Maudlyn, and its western neighbour Little Penny-come-quick. Colonel John Birch's Regiment of Foot was responsible for the defence of Maudlyn when, at about 2am, Royalist guns opened fire. Then the Royalists moved forward, with the New Cornish Tertia, in three bodies, leading the advance, supported by two more divisions of foot, each 1,500 strong. Birch and most of his regiment were in reserve, but the colonel immediately set off for Maudlyn with eight companies 'in as good order as that black and dark night would permit.' He found that the attackers had already been repulsed, according to one Parliamentarian account no less than thirty attackers having been killed by one discharge of case shot fired by the captain of the fort.

Birch noticed however that the guns of Little Penny-come-quick Fort had fallen silent, and suspecting the worst, led his reserves in that direction. When the Parliamentarians had come within pike-length, those within the fort called 'Stand, who are you for?' 'For the Parliament!' Birch replied, and the Royalists, who had indeed taken the fort, opened fire. Telling his troops that it was 'safer to go on than retreat', Birch stormed the ramparts, and retook the fort, killing or capturing twenty Royalists, among them a Colonel Arundell, whose sword Birch kept for himself.[52]

Elsewhere Grenville's assault petered out, and its failure became the subject of heated recrimination in the Royalist camp. On 17 January, in his own terse account, Grenville wrote: 'I have lately in the night attempted to force Plymouth works and took one of them nigh the Maudlyn work, and had my seconds performed their parts Plymouth in all probability had now certainly been ours'.[53]

The Parliamentarians claimed that matters came to a head at a Council of War held in Plympton. Grenville reportedly ordered Colonel Phillip Champernown, commanding Prince Maurice's Regiment of Foot, to renew the assault. On the latter's refusal, the dispute escalated into an exchange of pistol shots, in which Grenville 'fired his own pistol upon the Colonel and slew him dead upon the place, which the Colonel's brother seeing, fired off his pistol upon Grenville and missed him, whereat Grenville drew his sword and ran him through'.[54] While it seems a pity to spoil a good story, it has to be said that the reports of Phillip Champernown's death were exaggerated. He lived until 1684.[55]

Further smaller attacks by Grenville during the course of February achieved no better success, and it was obvious that the defences of Plymouth were too strong for the forces available.

For King, Cornwall or Grenville?

At the end of February Grenville received orders from Prince Rupert to assist Goring in the siege of Taunton. Grenville did not obey until later in March, and then only on receiving a direct command from the king. He would claim that he had been transferred as a result of the jealousy of Sir John Berkeley, Governor of Exeter, and, despite ample evidence to the contrary, that Plymouth had been so reduced 'by a strict blockeering that the enemy horses were almost starved and lost and their foot grown almost to desperation, in such sort that if the said army had been suffered to remain but two months longer before that town, very probably Plymouth had been thereby reduced to obedience.'[56]

Grenville left 400 horse and 1,200 foot to maintain a blockade of Plymouth, and took the rest, including the New Cornish Tertia, eastwards. By now the 15-year-old Charles, Prince of Wales, was nominally in command of Royalist forces in the West, assisted by the Council of the West formed from a number of the King's senior advisers. But this body found it impossible to resolve the differences among what was rapidly becoming a devil's brew of rival Royalist commanders, with unclear and often overlapping authority.

Sir Richard joined in the disputes with alacrity. He refused to serve under Goring's command in opposing the incursion into the West of Waller and Cromwell, telling the Council that 'his men would not stir a foot, and he had promised the Commissioners of Devon and Cornwall, that he would not advance beyond Taunton until Taunton were reduced, but that he made no question, if he were not disturbed, to make a good account of that place.'[57] Like many of Grenville's claims, this was partly true. The Cornish troops were notoriously unwilling to serve far from home, particularly in the later stages of the war. It is unclear if Grenville could in fact have prevailed upon them to do so, had he been so inclined.

There seemed no prospect of Goring and Grenville cooperating, though they had little opportunity, for shortly after arriving Grenville was seriously wounded by a shot in the thigh while supervising an attack on a Parliamentarian outpost at Wellington House. His recovery in doubt, Grenville was taken in a litter to Exeter, but not before, Clarendon alleged, he had instructed his officers not to cooperate with Sir John Berkeley, who had taken over command. From Exeter, fighting off the effects of his wound with customary fierce determination, Grenville wrote disingenuously on 23 April to the King's Secretary of State, Lord Digby:

> I only desire my recovery and life that I may employ it in his Majesty's service. I heartily wish all other men's intentions were as clearly without their own private ends.[58]

The Council of the West examined the grievances of Grenville and Berkeley, only to discover that their commissions and areas of command were virtually identical, 'so that each might reasonably think he had power over the other.' They offered Grenville command of the proposed new army of the Western Association, obviously believing that, despite his faults, Sir Richard was the most capable soldier available, and that only he could stem the tide of desertion among the Cornish and Devon troops before Taunton. They were also influenced, albeit with growing misgivings, by Grenville's obvious popularity with the ordinary people of Devon and Cornwall, which even the Parliamentarians grudgingly admitted to:

Grenville, that unjust Skellum, hath by the serpentine policy overawed these parts, he hath gained the country's love by hanging men for plundering; for it is verified that he pays every soldier his pay every Saturday night, and each foot soldier duly receives three shillings six pence, but he hangs every constable that brings not in the unreasonable assessment. He hath hanged 100 constables and like the fox he preyed furthest from home, for he allows his horse to fetch in what they can get, so it be but five miles from his quarters.[59]

A Western Association army under Grenville might have proved a formidable force, but in May Grenville's appointment was revoked by the king in favour of George Goring. Grenville was to serve as his Major General of Foot, a demotion and loss of independence which there was never any chance of Sir Richard accepting. It was mid-June before Grenville was fit enough to return to the field, and he was ordered by the Council of the West to blockade Parliamentarian-held Lyme.

Grenville had no intention of obeying. He refused the commission of Major General, and retired to Ottery St Mary in Devon, despatching a defiant letter to the Prince's Council:

I find myself now ordered to a by-corner, in the condition of an unworthy person in respect of my present charge having neither men fit for service, and very hardly finding means to give these substance through the poverty of the country occasioned by the newly raised forces that were only the devourers of their friends.[60]

Grenville was called to account before Prince Charles, and: 'Sullenly extolled his services and enlarged his sufferings', but was sharply rebuked.[61]

But because of his popularity with the Cornish forces, Grenville remained indispensable. He was sent back to Cornwall to round up the men who had deserted from the forces before Taunton, and given command of the Cornish Trained Bands. Although Grenville had considerable success in collecting deserters, he claimed that the majority were only willing to fight for the Prince within Cornwall itself, and from now on his attitude began to take on overtones of what has been suggested to be a form of Cornish nationalism.[62] Grenville's actions over the next few months are open to several interpretations. Was he attempting to place himself at the head of a distinctly Cornish movement, trying to preserve his own independent Western command, or acting in what he saw as the best interests of a dying Royalist cause?

By the autumn of 1645 it was clear that the remnants of the Cornish forces east of the Tamar were only willing to serve under Grenville. The Prince of Wales had to cooperate with Grenville in fostering a Cornish sense of national identity in order to encourage them to continue the fight. During October and November Grenville remained at Okehampton with the New Cornish Tertia and some of the Trained Band, about 2,500 men in all. At this time he presented the Prince's Council with what Clarendon described as a 'strange design' to dig a

40-mile long trench from Barnstaple south to the Channel coast, behind which he would defend Cornwall and part of Devon. Grenville himself explained the scheme more plausibly as a proposal to establish a 25-mile-long chain of strong points at Ashburton, Okehampton and Chimleigh, linked by a line of communications, and designed to block the advance eastwards of Fairfax and the New Model Army.

It was too late for such a plan to be feasible, and the Prince's Council, already suspicious of Grenville's intentions, were even more alarmed by the proposals which he put forward for reaching a truce with Parliament:

> our late losses have brought us nigh despair, and we truly say His Majesty hath no obedience left but poor little Cornwall, and that in a sad condition by the miserable accidents of war under which it hath long groaned. The country is impoverished by the obstruction of all trade, and in my opinion it is not to be hoped that Cornwall, with our ruined county of Devon, can long subsist and maintain the vast number of men that are requisite to oppose the enemy's army in case they advance upon us. Sir, what we wish is not in our power to act. It rests that we hold on the occasion that offers the fairest face. And who knows but some overture well managed by God's blessing in a short time produce a longed-for peace to this languishing kingdom.[63]

Grenville went on to urge seeking a truce by which Cornwall became neutralized and virtually autonomous under the Prince of Wales. There was, of course, not the slightest possibility of Parliament agreeing to this, and the main interest in the scheme lies in guessing what Grenville's motives were. It certainly demonstrated a lack of political awareness; what is less apparent is whether it represented latent Cornish nationalism, which Grenville hoped to place himself at the head of, or, perhaps more likely, a bid by Grenville to set himself up as regional warlord with the prince under his effective control. It clearly stood no chance of acceptance by the leadership of either side.

Sir Richard had now isolated himself from the prince and his Council. Indeed, with his encouragement, Cornish troops were now attempting to prevent other Royalist forces from entering the county. When, in January 1646, Hopton was appointed as commander of the remnants of the Royalist forces in the West, Grenville refused to serve under him. On 19 January he was stripped of all his commands, and two days later imprisoned on St Michael's Mount.

Grenville's removal and arrest caused a wave of unrest among the Cornish troops, though in another example of his ambiguous nature, Grenville rejected an offer by Colonel Edward Roscarrock of the New Cornish Tertia to raise his troops in his support, and ordered him to obey the Prince of Wales. It made little difference; without Grenville the heart had gone out of Cornish resistance. A Parliamentarian newspaper reported how, after Hopton's defeat at Torrington on 15 February: 'These foot which Sir Richard Grenville hath got together do refuse to obey either the Lord Hopton or any other save Sir Richard himself'.[64]

If he had fallen into Parliamentarian hands, Grenville's life would almost certainly have been forfeit, and, in March, as the Royalist army in the West surrendered, he was allowed, still protesting his innocence, to depart for the Continent.

Aftermath

Grenville's remaining years were ones of bitterness and frustration. He remained for some time on the fringes of Royalist conspiracy. In 1650 Charles II agreed to Grenville being appointed as Lieutenant General under the Marquis of Hertford in a proposed Western Rising. This never took place, and Grenville's appointment was quashed by the intervention of Edward Hyde (Clarendon). Soon afterwards Grenville was making a comfortable living operating a fleet of privateers out of St Malo, but he became increasingly obsessed by a bitter feud with Hyde, who continued to veto his involvement in Royalist plans.

An embittered Grenville, commenting that 'So fat a Hyde ought to be well-tanned', unsuccessfully accused Hyde of treachery, and as a result for most of the remainder of his life was barred from the Royalist court in exile. On 21 October 1659, impoverished, and possibly slightly mentally unbalanced, Grenville died in Bruges. His grave, its site since lost, was said to have born the inscription of 'The King's General in the West'.

Sir Richard Grenville was indisputably a courageous, competent professional soldier. Though he was ruthless, demanding, and highly vindictive towards any who crossed him, Grenville was also an inspirational leader who won the devotion of his troops and yet remained a highly effective disciplinarian. Although he never commanded an army in a major engagement, Sir Richard's performance at the siege of Plymouth suggested both determination and ability.

But Grenville's undoubtedly remarkable qualities were largely negated by his defects of character. Probably too unreliable ever to make a good commander-in-chief, he was equally unsuitable in a subordinate role, thanks to his inability to place a common cause above his own frequently narrow and selfish interests. Of all King Charles' generals, Grenville's story was perhaps the greatest example of wasted talents.

Chapter Ten
William Cavendish, First Marquis of Newcastle

William Cavendish, successively Earl, Marquis and Duke of Newcastle, and Captain-General of the King's northern forces in 1642–44, has been almost universally condemned by his contemporaries and later historians. He is generally viewed as a pleasure-loving, ineffectual and self-obsessed dilettante, who, in a fit of pique, lost both his army and the north at the Battle of Marston Moor.

In portraits of Newcastle, we see a man of obvious refinement and impeccable taste in dress, with pleasant, but somewhat distant, features. A thinker, perhaps, rather than man of action. But there was more to William Cavendish.

Best-known of contemporary assessments, perhaps, is that of the Royalist courtier Sir Philip Warwick, who knew Newcastle, and, while conceding that he was 'a gentleman of grandeur, generosity, loyalty and forward courage, added that: 'His edge had too much of the razor in it, for he had a tincture of a romantic spirit, and had the misfortune to have somewhat of the poet in him.'[1] Clarendon was more dismissive:

> He liked the pomp and absolute authority of a general well, and preserved the dignity of it to the full; and for the discharge of the outward state and circumstances of it, in acts of courtesy, affability, bounty, and generosity, he abounded; which in the infancy of a war became him, and made him for some time very acceptable to men of all conditions. But the substantial part, and fatigue, of a general, he did not in any way understand, (being utterly unacquainted with war) nor could submit to, but referred all matter of that nature to his lieutenant-general, King.[Though brave and inspiring in battle] such articles of action were no sooner over, than he retired to his delightful company, muses or his softer pleasures, . . . that he would not be interrupted upon what occasions soever, insomuch as he sometimes denied admission, even to General King himself, for two days together, from whence many inconveniences fell out. . . [2]

To Prince Rupert and the matter-of-fact soldiery of his immediate circle, Newcastle's cultural interests, his courtliness and flowery prose, were objects of derision. It was from the prince's supporters that the jibe originated that Newcastle 'rose at eleven, combed his hair until noon, and so the work was done.' This rather ludicrous image seemed confirmed when after the Restoration, his eccentric, bluestocking second wife, Margaret 'Mad Meg' Cavendish, published a laudatory and highly uncritical biography of her husband,[3] which Samuel Pepys felt 'showed him but an ass to suffer her to write it'.[4]

Modern historians largely concur with Newcastle's contemporaries. Peter Young and Alfred Burne felt that 'in general his operations were too methodical, and he seems to have been somewhat lacking in that element of robustness which Lord Wavell has declared is so essential a quality in a general.'[5] Austin Woolrych saw Newcastle as 'the sort of *grand seigneur* to whom the professional parts of soldiering . . . were rather below a nobleman's dignity.'[6] Some writers have been slightly more charitable: Patrick Morrah felt that Newcastle was 'a grandee with many admirable qualities but little military experience'[7], others such as Stuart Reid and the leading authority on the Northern Royalist armies, Peter Newman, have credited Newcastle with rather more toughness and ability.[8]

Early life

William Cavendish was born into one of the great noble families of England, though as a member of a cadet branch, William inherited little of their wealth. His great estates which extended across wide areas of the North Midlands and north-east England came from his wife, his mother and his grandmother. He was created a viscount – in return for £4,000 – by James I, and by Charles I Earl of Newcastle. By then Cavendish had come to exemplify the complete 'Renaissance man.' Handsome, impeccably dressed and mannered, he was a lover of the arts, a poet and prolific (if mediocre) playwright, a skilled dancer, and friend and patron of philosophers and thinkers such as Thomas Hobbes. At the same time, Newcastle had a reputation as a swordsman, and a master of horsemanship. His love of the fine arts and architecture were reflected in building work at his residences such as Welbeck House and Bolsover Castle in Derbyshire, where he lavishly entertained Charles I in the halcyon days of the 1630s.

Newcastle was a traditionalist, and strong supporter of the ideals of monarchy. Clarendon wrote of him that:

> He loved monarchy, as it was the foundation and support of his own great-
> ness; and the Church, as it was well constituted for the splendour and
> security of the Crown; and religion, as it cherished and maintained that
> order and obedience that was necessary to both; without any other passion
> for the particular opinions which were grown up in it and distinguished it
> into parties, than as he detested whatsoever was like to disturb the public
> peace.[9]

For all his wealth, accomplishments and evident loyalty to the Crown, Newcastle, for reasons which remain obscure, was not part of the king's inner circle. In 1638, after a good deal of lobbying, Newcastle was made Governor to eight-year-old Charles Prince of Wales, a post which seems to have given a good deal of satisfaction to both those principally involved. Charles relished his governor's accomplishments, and his lenient approach, concentrating on subjects such as riding and fencing which the prince most enjoyed, pointing out in justification that 'I would not have you too studious . . . the greatest clerks are not the wisest men.'

But the balmy days of the king's 'Personal Rule' came to an end with the disputes with Scotland, and Newcastle found himself involved in military affairs. He was one of the first to offer his services to the king, and in 1639 raised a troop of horse, consisting of 120 of his dependents, relatives and tenants, known as the Prince's Troop. But Newcastle was quick to demonstrate that touchiness and sensitivity to slights, real or imagined, which was to plague his military career. Feeling that he, and the Prince's Troop, should be answerable only to the king, Newcastle challenged the Earl of Holland, General of Horse, to a duel!

In May 1641 Newcastle was forced to resign as Governor to the Prince of Wales because of his apparent involvement in the 'Army Plot' by a number of ultra-Royalist officers to use the army raised against the Scots to suppress the English Parliament.

General in the north

The outbreak of Civil War brought Newcastle to the forefront of events. As the leading magnate in the north of England, Newcastle, whatever the king's personal feelings about him, was indispensable to the Royalist war effort. Predominantly, though far from entirely, Royalist in sentiment, the north of England, with its great resources in material and manpower, was vital for the King's cause. Its ports provided landing points for the men and munitions which Queen Henrietta Maria was endeavouring to obtain on the Continent. On 29 June the 50-year-old Earl of Newcastle was commissioned as Governor of Newcastle-upon-Tyne and General of Northumberland, Durham, Cumberland and Westmoreland. His task was to secure Royalist control of this area, and in particular, to secure its ports for the landing of the queen and her supplies. There was at this stage no intention of using Newcastle's forces any further south.

Newcastle carried out his initial task with commendable efficiency. Though some areas, such as Durham, and the town of Newcastle, were at first apathetic or potentially hostile, the earl was able to re-raise his old troop of horse, together with a regiment of foot, later to win fame as the 'Whitecoats', from among his own neighbours and tenants in the north-east. The town of Newcastle was summarily brought into line by exercising the Whitecoats in its streets, and a pro-Royalist Mayor was appointed by Newcastle. When the Durham Trained Bands proved reluctant to serve, they were overawed by a visit from Newcastle and his troops from Northumberland.

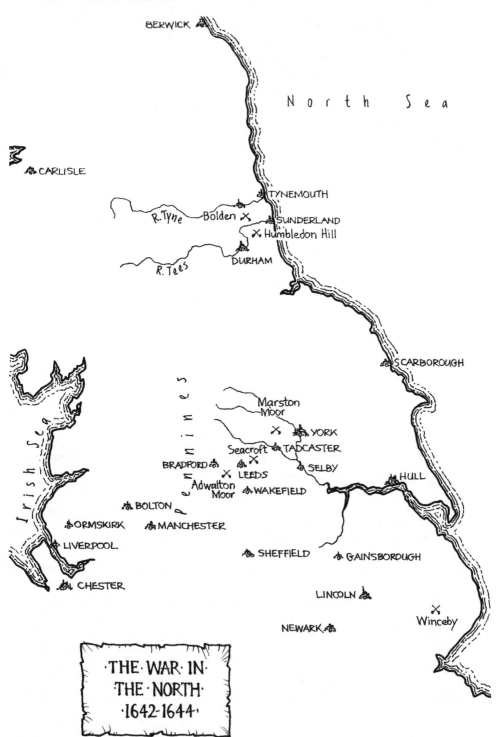

BERWICK

North Sea

CARLISLE

TYNEMOUTH

R. Tyne   Bolden   SUNDERLAND
                     Humbledon Hill

R. Tees   DURHAM

SCARBOROUGH

Marston Moor

YORK
Seacroft   TADCASTER
BRADFORD   SELBY
            LEEDS
Adwalton   WAKEFIELD
Moor

Irish Sea

BOLTON

ORMSKIRK   MANCHESTER

LIVERPOOL

SHEFFIELD   GAINSBOROUGH

CHESTER

LINCOLN

NEWARK   Winceby

Pennines

HULL

·THE·WAR·IN·
THE·NORTH·
·1642-1644·

An initial lack of arms was eased by the arrival of a cargo of weapons from Denmark, although for some time Newcastle had difficulty in arming all of his recruits. In her 'Life' of Newcastle, the Duchess gives inflated figures of the number of troops her husband was able to raise in the autumn of 1642; the true total was probably about 3,000 foot and 2,000 horse and dragoons, some of whom would be required for garrison duty.[10]

Following instructions from the king that 'I do not only permit, but command you to make use of all of my loving subjects' service, without examining their consciences (more than their loyalty to me) as you shall find most to conduce to the upholding of my just legal power.'[11], Newcastle began recruiting among the large Catholic population of the north-east, justifying his actions in a published 'Declaration' by the rather dubious claim that Parliament had recruited foreign Catholic mercenaries first.[12] One result was that Newcastle's army, inaccurately, for the majority of its men were Protestant, became known to Parliamentarian propagandists as the 'Popish Army'.

In late July 1642 the king greatly enlarged Newcastle's powers, making him General of all Royalist forces raised now or in the future north of the Trent, together with the counties of Lincolnshire, Nottinghamshire, Derbyshire, Lancashire, Cheshire, Leicestershire and Rutland. Eventually the counties of the Parliamentarian Eastern Association would also be added. Newcastle was granted more autonomous powers than any other of the king's generals.

The powers granted to Newcastle were a recognition by the king that it was impossible for he himself adequately to direct the war effort in so remote an area. Newcastle's area of command was actually too extensive for him to control effectively either. Theoretically subordinate commanders, such as Henry Hastings in the Midlands and the Earl of Derby in Lancashire, would in practice largely go their own way.

By the late summer of 1642, having accomplished his original mission, Newcastle found himself faced with a new problem. The Yorkshire Royalists were commanded by the Earl of Cumberland, and not directly under Newcastle's control. However, Cumberland was rapidly losing ground to Parliamentarian forces under Lord Fairfax and his son, Sir Thomas, based in the woollen towns of the West Riding, and appealed to Newcastle for assistance. The earl was unenthusiastic about this additional responsibility.

He demanded the assurance of the Yorkshire County Commissioners that his troops would receive regular payment and supplies, and also pointed out:

> That since this army was levied a purpose to guard her Majesty's person, that it shall not be held a breach of any engagement betwixt us if I retire with such numbers as I shall think fit for that service.[13]

When the Yorkshire authorities proved evasive in some of their assurances, Newcastle replied firmly in a way which demonstrated a keen awareness of some of the realities of soldiering:

> I am very sorry you pleased to leave out the article for the officers' pay or

coldly referred it to your committee, being the principal thing in all the articles, for you know the soldier is encouraged with nothing but money, or hopes of it, and truly last night, when I was going to bed, there came colonels and lieutenant-colonels, and said they heard you had left it out, and for their parts that they must think that if you were so cautious not to grant it in paper before we came in, they doubted very much of it in money when they were there, and that the workman was worthy of his hire, and suchlike discontented words; So the truth is, rather than not come cheerfully to serve you, I shall not come at all, for I see beforehand I shall either disband with a mutiny, or fall of plundering without distinction, either of which would be destructive to me.[14]

Newcastle knew that he had no option but to go to Yorkshire. If York, England's second city, fell into enemy hands, not only would his links with the south be rendered yet more tenuous, but he would also be exposed to attack by the Yorkshire Parliamentarians.

The War in Yorkshire, 1642–43

Newcastle's troops dispersed a small Parliamentarian force which attempted to block their passage at Piercebridge, and reached York on 30 November. Newcastle now moved against the Fairfaxes, who were pulling back towards their West Riding heartland. The Royalists had the better of a rather untidy rearguard action on 1 December at Tadcaster, but the chance of a decisive victory was lost as a result of the failure of Newcastle's Lieutenant General of Horse, the Earl of Newport, to act promptly.

The king wrote optimistically to Newcastle in December that 'the business of Yorkshire I account almost done', while Lord Fairfax admitted him to be 'absolute master of the field.' But Newcastle proved unable to carry the campaign through to a decisive conclusion. This partly resulted from the onset of winter, but the earl also faced other problems. Following his arrival in Yorkshire he had begun to expand his army, but had continuing difficulties arming his recruits. In February 1643 orders were given for all 'private arms' in Yorkshire to be brought to a central magazine at York, and the county Trained Bandsmen were to serve either in person or to provide a substitute.

To his credit, Newcastle was also aware that, faced now by a prolonged campaign, he and most of his officers lacked the necessary military experience to conduct it. As a result, he appointed to senior positions a number of professional soldiers brought over from Europe. Most controversial was a Scotsman, James King, whom Newcastle appointed as his Lieutenant General, effectively his chief of staff. As with the similar appointment of Patrick Ruthven as Lord General to King Charles in the Oxford Army, it is sometimes difficult to discern the actual share of responsibility for military decisions between Newcastle and King, but in general it seems that Newcastle deferred to his professional adviser.

Opinions of King were generally unenthusiastic. Clarendon spoke of his 'extraordinary success' in the service of Gustavus Adolphus of Sweden, but another Scots professional, James Turner, said that King was 'a person of great honour, but what he had saved of it in Germany, where he made a great ship-wreck of most of it, he lost in England.'[15] Hitherto King had been best known for his equivocal role at the battle of Lemgo in 1638, as a result of which, some claimed, Prince Rupert had been captured by the Imperialists. Overall, the evidence points to King being a competent, if somewhat cautious and un-imaginative, soldier.

Also arriving at the same time was the erratically brilliant George Goring, appointed by Newcastle as his General of Horse. Major General of Foot was another career soldier, Sir Francis Mackworth. General of the Ordnance was William Davenant, the playwright who had been a pre-war friend of Newcastle. However, criticism of his choice should be balanced against the fact that Davenant had occupied a similar position in the English forces during the Scots Wars.

With his team in place, Newcastle was able to consider his next move. Minor operations against the West Riding during the winter had met with little success, and had depleted Newcastle's limited supplies of ammunition, while he also had to man a number of garrisons, including Pontefract Castle and Newark.

Newcastle was distracted by his primary mission of protecting Queen Henrietta Maria and her great munitions convoy, which was brought safely into York late in February. Although most of the munitions were destined for the Oxford Army, some, including the pair of Dutch demi-cannon known as 'Gog' and Magog' or the 'Queen's Pocket Pistols', were made available to Newcastle's forces.

By March the 'Popish Army' was able to begin active operations, highlighted on the 30th of that month by Goring's victory over Sir Thomas Fairfax at Seacroft Moor. Newcastle remained however, at least in his own eyes, effectively hobbled by his responsibilities towards the queen, and General King was not one to urge him to take risks. In April the Northern Army had to detach 1,500 'commanded' foot from various regiments to escort the first consignment of munitions to Oxford. At about the same time, in a demonstration of his chivalrous, if some-what unworldly, approach to warfare, Newcastle sent Lord Fairfax an optimistic challenge to give battle 'after the examples of our heroic ancestors, who used not to spend their time in scratching one another out of holes, but in pitched fields determined their doubts.' Fairfax, to whom the adjective 'heroic' was never applied, declined 'to follow the rules of Amadeus de Gaule, or the Knight of the Sun, which the language of the declaration seems to effect in offering pitched battles.'[16]

In May Newcastle at last took the field, sending his energetic Lieutenant-General of Horse, and relative, Charles Cavendish, to strike into Lincolnshire, while Newcastle himself advanced into South Yorkshire. Sheffield, with its iron-works, which would be a useful addition to Newcastle's munitions manufacturing capacity, and Rotherham were taken, but this success was counterbalanced on 21 May when Sir Thomas Fairfax stormed Wakefield, capturing George Goring and 1,500 prisoners, described by the Duchess of Newcastle as 'a very great loss and hindrance to my Lord's designs, it being the moiety of his army, and most of his ammunition.'[17]

The loss of men was not as serious as the duchess alleged, for most of them were quickly exchanged. The departure for Oxford of the queen and the rest of her convoy, while depriving Newcastle of more troops required to escort her, freed him for other enterprises. It was apparently briefly debated whether the Earl and his entire army should accompany her, until it was pointed out that their departure would leave the entire north of England open to Lord Fairfax.[18]

On 22 June Newcastle took the field with an army of approximately 3,000 foot and 4,000 horse, and advanced into the West Riding. His first target was the Parliamentarian outpost of Howley Hall. After its Governor, Sir John Saville, refused to surrender, the garrison was stormed. Contrary to Newcastle's orders Saville was spared on capture. In an incident illustrating Newcastle's rather confused approach to war, the officer who had granted Saville mercy was reprimanded:

> and though he resolved to kill him, yet my Lord would not suffer him to do it, saying, it was inhuman to kill any man in cold blood. Hereupon the governor kissed the key of the house door and presented it to my Lord: to which my Lord returned this answer: 'I need it not', said he, 'for I brought a key along with me which yet I was unwilling to use, until you forced me to it.[19]

The Royalists advanced towards Bradford, and on 30 June on Adwalton Moor, to the east of the town, encountered the Fairfaxes. The armies may have been roughly equal in numbers, but many of the Parliamentarians were poorly armed, untrained countrymen. The Fairfaxes had hoped to surprise the Royalists in their quarters, but Newcastle, although unaware of his opponents' intentions, was already on the march.

The Parliamentarians took up position on the eastern edge of the Moor, where they hoped the enclosed terrain would negate the Royalist advantage in horse, and enable them to make maximum use of their own superiority in musketeers. Newcastle deployed his own musketeers on the eastern fringes of the Moor and his horse and pikes to their rear.

Several attacks by the Royalist horse were thrown back. Newcastle's musketeers also had the worst of their exchange with their opponents, and the Parliamentarian advance threatened to overrun the Royalist gun line. Most accounts pay tribute to Newcastle's courage in battle, and he seems to have taken a personal part in rallying his men. However the decisive role was played by one of his commanders, possibly leading the pikes of Newcastle's own Regiment of Foot, as Sir Thomas Fairfax describes:

> while they [the Royalists] were in this wavering condition, one Colonel Skirton [Postumous Kirton] a wild and desperate man, desired his General to let him charge once more with a stand of pikes, with which he broke in

upon our men, and they not relieved by our Reserves, commanded by some ill-affected officers, . . . our men lost ground, which the enemy seeing, pursued their advantage by bringing on fresh troops. Ours herewith discouraged, began to flee, and so were soon routed.[20]

Adwalton Moor saw the eclipse for the moment of the Parliamentarian army in the north, with over 2,000 casualties. Bradford and Leeds fell to the Royalists, and the Fairfaxes fled to Hull. The courtly Newcastle was in his element when Sir Thomas's wife was captured. The earl sent her on her way to Hull in his own coach and six.

Failure at Hull

Newcastle seemed to have triumphantly achieved his main tasks. But the victory at Adwalton Moor brought with it ultimately insuperable problems. Fears of the 'Popish Army' driving south into the Eastern Association were a major factor in Parliament allying with the Scots, which presented Newcastle with the threat of a 'second front' in the north.

So far, Newcastle and King had discharged their military responsibilities, if not with particular boldness and élan, at least competently. Newcastle used the wide powers granted to him with discretion. He only, for example conferred twelve knighthoods, usually for gallantry in the field, during the entire period of his command. It was claimed that he granted too many commissions to raise regiments, with the result that his army contained a large number of weak, over-officered units, which were expensive to maintain. The duchess claimed that colonelcies were only granted to those with sufficient means to maintain the units raised, although this proved no easier for many of Newcastle's officers than it did in other Civil War armies. He had also by now, thanks to continued imports from the Continent and a limited local manufacturing capability, succeeded in at least adequately arming and equipping his troops.

After Adwalton Moor the Northern Royalists faced no effective resistance east of the Pennines other than Hull. A common criticism of Newcastle is that he should have followed up his success by a thrust into Parliament's Eastern Association. He displayed no apparent haste in his next moves. His advance into Lincolnshire was as much a reaction to the defeat and death of Charles Cavendish at Gainsborough (28 July) as part of a long-term strategy, although it did result in the capture of Lincoln.

Newcastle informed the king that he could not advance any further south because of the unwillingness of the Yorkshire Royalists to permit their forces (which made up about half of Newcastle's army) to take part so long as Hull remained unreduced. Newcastle never had unconditional control of the Yorkshire troops and he was probably encouraged in this cautious approach by General King, (soon to be made Lord Eythin). It is also unclear whether King Charles ever sent Newcastle any firm orders to march south; if he had done so, it is difficult to believe that the earl would have ignored them. The nearest hint we have comes in a letter written sometime that summer from the queen to Newcastle:

> He [the king] had written me to send you word to go into Suffolk, Norfolk or Huntingdonshire. I answered him that you were a better judge than he of that, and that I should not do it. The truth is that they envy your army.[21]

The real significance of this letter, so far as Newcastle was concerned, lay in the final sentence. He had always, even before the war, been on the fringes of the Court, and he remained suspicious of many of its intimates. He seems, probably because he had heard some of the jibes directed at him, to have been particularly resentful of the circle around Prince Rupert. Sir Philip Warwick may, up to a point, have been correct when he suggested that :

> There was nothing he [Newcastle] apprehended more than to be joined to the king's army, and to serve under Prince Rupert; for he designed himself to be the man who should turn the scale, and to be a distinct, self-subsisting army, wherever he was.[22]

In reality, there was no way in which Newcastle could have gone further south with Hull unreduced to his rear, and at the end of August the Northern Army settled down to besiege it. But, as Newcastle probably realized from the start, so long as the port's strong fortifications remained unbreached, and it could be supplied from the sea, there was no chance of success. The defenders were never seriously threatened, and Royalist prospects were reduced still further when heavy rain flooded their siegeworks, leading to a rare example of Newcastle's wit, when he commented wryly: 'You hear us called the 'Popish Army', but you see we trust not in our good works.'[23]

It may have been an attempt to put a brave face on failure. On 11 October Newcastle's hopes suffered a double blow with a major Royalist defeat in Lincolnshire at Winceby and a successful large-scale sortie by the Hull garrison. Over the next few days the Royalists retreated over the Humber.

The failure at Hull undoubtedly cost Newcastle men and munitions he could ill afford to lose, but it is hard to see, with the imminent threat of Scottish invasion, that he could have mounted a sustained campaign in the Eastern Association. As Stuart Reid points out: 'Clearing the Eastern Association would have cost at least one campaigning season, and it is unlikely that Newcastle could have been established in Essex before late 1644 or 1645. And the Scots invasion was only months away.'[24]

The Scots invasion

With the Scots mustering an army to invade north-east England, Newcastle now faced a war on multiple fronts. Throughout the autumn he was aware of the threat, but lacked adequate resources to meet it. On 19 January 1644 the expected invasion, by a Scottish army about 20,000 strong, began. Newcastle had only been able to spare a handful of troops under Sir Thomas Glemham to guard his northern frontier, and they, attempting to carry out a 'scorched earth' strategy, fell back on Newcastle-upon-Tyne.

It was essential to save the port, and Newcastle, raised to the rank of marquis by the king in the previous October, hurried north from York with all the troops he could spare. To hold Yorkshire against the increasing threat from Parliamentarian forces to the south and east, he left John Lord Belasyse with the bulk of his Yorkshire troops, 1,000 horse and 5,000 foot. This, like the force which Newcastle took north, was woefully inadequate for the task facing it.

After a forced march through bitter wintry conditions, which should have silenced any doubts regarding his personal stamina, the marquis reached Newcastle a few hours ahead of the Scots, in time to beat off an attack on its outworks. But, as he warned Prince Rupert five days later:

> I know they tell you, sir, that I have great force; truly, I cannot march five thousand foot, and the horse not well-armed. The Scots advanced as far as Morpeth, and they are fourteen thousand as the report goes. Since I must have no help, I must do the best I can with these . . . [25]

Hoping for reinforcement by Byron's troops from Ireland, Newcastle's strategy in the meantime was to attempt to hold the line of the Tyne, and wear down the largely inexperienced Scots army with raids by his superior cavalry. On 19 February his horse under Sir Marmaduke Langdale engaged the Scots in a close-fought engagement at Corbridge. Sir James Turner, who was with the Scots army, felt that a strong follow-through might have caused the invaders to retreat back across the border, and blamed the failure upon Lord Eythin (James King). Bearing in mind Eythin's known caution, this is possible, but the Duchess of Newcastle indirectly went further, alleging that:

> there was so much treachery, juggling, and falsehood in my Lord's own army, that it was impossible for him to be successful in his designs and undertakings.[26]

This presumably was aimed principally at Eythin, and written when Newcastle had fixed upon the Scotsman as the principal scapegoat for his failure. But Eythin had never shown any sympathy for the Covenanters, staying loyal to the king during the Scots Wars. He was probably not particularly bothered about fighting against his own countrymen. He was, however, notoriously cautious and it would have been true to his known character if he dissuaded Newcastle from an overly aggressive strategy in the north-east.

On 28 February, having shifted upstream, the Scots army, commanded by the vastly experienced old soldier, Alexander Leslie, Earl of Leven, crossed the Tyne at four points which Newcastle's forces had been too few to guard. The Scots reached Sunderland on 4 March. Here they could be supplied by sea. Newcastle had warned the king on 16 February of what he saw as a rapidly deteriorating situation:

> If your Majesty beat the Scots, your game is absolutely won . . . [but, he warned of] a great army at Newark behind us, and a great Scotch army before us, and Sir Thomas Fairfax very strong for the West Riding of Yorkshire, and his father master of the East Riding, so we are beset, not able to encounter the Scots, and shall not be able make our retreat for the army behind us . . . [27]

Although reinforced by some newly raised Durham levies, and eventually by a brigade of horse from the Midlands under Sir Charles Lucas, Newcastle had not felt strong enough to interfere with Leven's march to Sunderland. However, he was aware that time was short; at any moment Belasyse's small force in Yorkshire, which had not been reinforced despite the promises of the Yorkshire Commissioners, might be overwhelmed. So, amidst blizzards, on 7/8 March, at Penshaw Hill, Newcastle attempted to draw Leven into the decisive action the Royalists so urgently needed. There were two frustrating days of skirmishing which never quite escalated into major fighting, as Leven declined to be lured out of his strong defensive positions. By the evening of 8 March it was obvious to Newcastle that he had failed: 'By this time, the enemy caused us to withdraw to the higher ground, where being saluted with cold blasts and snow, our horses' sufferance with hunger, that we seemed so far to become friends as in providing against these common enemies.'[28]

Next morning Newcastle withdrew to Durham. He had not brought on the decisive action which was urgently needed. As the Earl of Leven was evidently aware, he needed only to keep the Scots army intact until help arrived from the Parliamentarian forces to the south, while Newcastle had to beat him before disaster struck Belasyse in Yorkshire. Probably stung by a smug assurance from King Charles that 'I profess the Scots rebels to be in much worse case than your army'[29], Newcastle in desperation pleaded for assistance from Prince Rupert:

> the Scots are as big again in foot as I am, and their horse, I doubt not, much better than ours are, so that if your Highness do not please to come hither, and that very soon too, the great game of your uncle's will be endangered if not lost.[30]

On 13 March Newcastle was approached by the Marquis of Montrose, newly established in favour as King Charles's Scottish champion, with a request for supplies. Montrose was told:

> For arms and ammunition he had not to the two parts of his own, but had been so long expecting them beyond sea, as he was now out of hopes.[31]

Nevertheless, on Sunday 23 March, Newcastle made another attempt to bring Leven to battle. Moving along the north bank of the River Wear, the Royalists, according to the Scots, hoped to catch their opponents unawares engaged in Sabbath devotions in their quarters. However, the Scots were on the alert, and took up position on the hill known as Whitburn Lizard, with Newcastle deployed three miles to the south-east on Bolden Hill. Between the opposing armies lay an area of flat enclosed ground, containing three villages. Both sides advanced their musketeers and a hot exchange of fire continued until after midnight, and, according to Newcastle: 'Many Officers who have been old Soldiers, did affirm that they had never seen so long and hot service in the night time.' Next morning, after both sides had suffered several hundred casualties, Newcastle decided the Scots position was too strong to assault, and pulled back again into Durham.

So far, Newcastle had avoided defeat, although it could be argued that the destruction of the Northern Royalist army was at this stage a secondary consideration for Leven. It is debatable whether Newcastle, certainly in horse, was by any means as out-matched as he apparently believed. His operations had been marked by a lack of enterprise and imagination which bear the hallmarks of Lord Eythin as much as Newcastle himself.

Utterly frustrated, and with apparently little hope of success, Newcastle and his Lieutenant General appear to have offered their resignations. They were dissuaded in a letter from the king which by implication seemed to confirm many of Newcastle's darkest suspicions:

> The truth is, if either you or My Lord Eythin leave my service, I am sure all the North is lost. The Scots are not the only, or (it may be said) the least enemies you contend with at this time. All courage is not in fighting, constancy to a good cause being the chief, and the despising of slanderous tongues and pens being not the least ingredient.[32]

But on 12 April came the news which Newcastle had been dreading. Lord Belasyse and his little force had been overwhelmed at Selby, and York itself was in peril.

Newcastle had been intending to make a further stand against Leven on the line of the Tees, but it was essential to save the northern capital. Harried by the Scottish horse, he made a desperate forced march south. During it most of his raw infantry levies from Durham were lost, but on 19 April Newcastle, with about 3,000 horse and 4,000 foot, reached York narrowly ahead of his pursuers and the Fairfaxes, coming up from the south. On the previous day Newcastle had warned the king:

> the Scots and Fairfax having joined near Wetherby, are now too strong for us in matters of the field . . . they have already put themselves in such a posture as will soon ruin us, being at York, unless there is some speedy course taken to give us relief, and that with a considerable force, for their army is very strong . . . We shall be distressed here very shortly.[33]

Newcastle sent the bulk of his horse out of York, with orders to join any relief force, and, with his foot, prepared to hold out until assistance arrived. By 23 April York was under partial blockade, but it was not until the arrival of Parliament's Army of the Eastern Association on 3 June that a full siege began. Newcastle's aim now was to spin out time until Prince Rupert, now embarked upon his campaign in Lancashire, came to his assistance. With this object, and also perhaps to spur the prince into action, Newcastle spent several days in desultory negotiations with the besiegers, which continued until 15 June.

These were followed next day by a serious attempt to storm York's defences, in repulsing which Newcastle's own Whitecoats, led by the marquis himself, played a leading role. After that there was little action until the morning of 1 July, when the Royalist sentries on the walls of York looked out to find the besiegers' camps empty. Though they did not yet know it, York had been relieved.

Key Action: Marston Moor, 2 July 1644

Definite news of Rupert's approach arrived at about noon, and Newcastle greeted the prince with a letter which displayed all his elaborate, courtly, and to a soldier, thoroughly exasperating, characteristics:

> You are welcome so many several ways, as it is beyond my Arithmetic to number, but this I know you are the redeemer of the North and the saviour of the Crown. Your name, sir, hath terrified the great Generals and they fly before it. It seems their design is not to meet your Highness for I believe they have got a river between you and them but they are so newly gone as there is no certainty at all of them or their intentions, neither can I resolve any things since I am made of nothing but obedience and thankfulness to your Highness's commands.[34]

A probably irritated Rupert may have made the mistake of taking Newcastle's assurances of obedience literally, and this helped confuse further an already uncertain command situation. Rupert clearly felt that he had seniority to Newcastle, although this was by no means obvious, and should have been clarified earlier by the king. Rupert appears to have made no attempt that night to meet with Newcastle, but instead sent Lord George Goring, now once more in command of the Northern cavalry, into York with curt orders for the Marquis and the Northern foot to join him on Marston Moor by 4am next morning.

Newcastle was undoubtedly offended by this brusque treatment, and his discontent was fanned by some of those about him. But his concerns extended beyond his personal feelings. Both Newcastle and Eythin were opposed to Rupert's desire to bring the Allies to immediate battle. Newcastle claimed that the Allied commanders were at loggerheads, and their armies about to go their separate ways. He also said that he was expecting 3,000 reinforcements from the north over the next few days.

Neither claim was entirely accurate. The Allied commanders had pulled back from the Siege of York with the intention of taking up position in the area of Marston Moor, about six miles west of York, to block Rupert's relief march. They had, however, been frustrated, and early on 2 July, covered by a screen of cavalry, began withdrawing towards Wetherby. This was not, however, seen as the beginning of a general dispersal, but more as a tactical withdrawal until they were joined by expected reinforcements from the Midlands.

When the Royalist troops from the north under Clavering eventually joined Rupert on 3 July, they numbered only half the total claimed by Newcastle, not enough to have had any decisive effect.

Newcastle and Eythin's real motives lay deeper. During the first half of 1644 the northern Royalist Army had suffered horrendous losses. The few thousand foot in York, together with the Northern horse under Goring, effectively represented the last of Newcastle's army. If they were lost, it would be the end, not only of Newcastle's command, but of Royalist hopes in the north. It was an outcome Newcastle was desperate to avoid.

Nevertheless, he seems to have begun an attempt to obey Rupert's orders, though he pointed out, rather unconvincingly, that it would take some time to unblock one of the city gates, barricaded during the siege, and, more significantly, that a large number of his foot had absented themselves to loot the abandoned enemy camp, and were still either there or spending the proceeds of their booty in the alehouses of York.

At this stage Lord Eythin apparently took a hand. A Royalist eyewitness claimed that at 2am the bulk of the Northern foot had been drawn up ready to march 'when there came an order from General King that they should not march till they had their pay, whereupon they all quit their colours and dispersed.'[35] King later denied that he had sent such a message, but it seems highly likely, that, with or without Newcastle's knowledge, he was endeavouring to delay the commitment of the Northern foot for as long as possible.

On the morning of 2 July, Rupert reached Marston Moor by 9am. On the ridge to the south of the Moor the screen of enemy cavalry remained, and they sent urgently for the rest of the Allied forces to return. Throughout the morning the prince deployed his troops as they came up, fretting at the non-arrival of Newcastle and his foot, and sending repeated messages to hasten them. Rupert had hoped to attack the Allies while they were still deployed in line of march, but, as more of them returned to the ridge in front of him, his opportunity was fast disappearing: 'He would have attacked the Enemy himself in their Retreat [but] if the Prince had fallen upon the Rear, and miscarried, it would have been objected that he should have stayed for Newcastle'.[36]

The marquis seems to have left York at about 9am, surprisingly for such a fine horseman, and reinforcing doubts as to his degree of commitment, travelling in his coach. It may have been about noon when he met up with Rupert on the western edge of Marston Moor. The encounter was understandably tense. 'My Lord', commented Rupert, 'I wish you had come sooner with all your forces, but I hope we shall yet have a glorious day.'[37] But there was still no sign of the Northern foot, and Newcastle explained that because of their plundering, 'it was impossible to have got them together at the time prefixed, but that he had left General King about the work, who would bring them up with all the expedition that might be.'[38] Rupert, still set on battle, 'would with his own foot, have been falling on the enemy, but that the Marquis dissuaded him, telling him that he had 4,000 as good foot as were in the World.'[39] The views of Newcastle and Rupert were sharply at odds. Newcastle outlined his belief that the Allies were about to split up, and the reinforcements which he expected, but Rupert, using as his justification the letter he had received from the king,[40] replied that he had:

> A positive and absolute command to fight the enemy, which in obedience, and according to his duty he was bound to perform. Whereupon my Lord replied; 'That he was ready and willing, for his part, to obey his Highness in all things, no otherwise than if his Majesty was in person there himself, . . . for he had no other ambition but to live and die a loyal subject to his Majesty.'[41]

None of this amounted to much without the Northern foot, and it may have been as late as 4pm that the first of them, fewer in numbers than Newcastle had claimed, and 'all drunk', began to straggle onto the field with Eythin at their head. Another acrimonious encounter ensued:

> The Prince demanded of King how he liked the marshalling of his army, who replied that he did not approve of it being drawn too near the enemy, and in a place of disadvantage, then said the Prince, 'They may be drawn to a further distance.' 'No Sir,' said King, 'It is too late.' It is so, King dissuaded the Prince from fighting, saying 'Sir, your forwardness cost us the day in Germany, where yourself was taken prisoner.'[42]

Rupert and Eythin seem to have been circling each other like two bristling dogs, and the duchess, who probably gained her information from Newcastle, adds further details:

> When Major-General King came up Prince Rupert showed the Marquis and the Earl a paper, which he said was the draught of the battle as he meant to fight it, and asked them what they thought of it, King answered: 'By God, sir it is very fine in the paper, but there is no such thing in the field.' The Prince replied 'Not so' etc.[43]

Both Newcastle and Eythin claimed that it was too late in the day to initiate a battle, and Rupert, seeing that his opportunity of catching the enemy off-balance had now gone, reluctantly agreed. 'The Marquis asked the Prince what he would do? His Highness answered 'we will charge them tomorrow morning. My Lord asked him, whether he was sure the enemy would not fall on them sooner; he answered 'No!'[44]

Some of this seems suspiciously like hindsight, but it was illustrative of the low ebb in relations between the Prince and Newcastle that, as their men stood down, they chose to eat separately, Newcastle retiring to his coach to enjoy a pipe of tobacco.

He had scarcely settled down when, at about 7pm, a burst of cannon fire announced a general attack by the Allies. Neither Rupert nor Newcastle got to grips with the ensuing battle. Newcastle displayed his customary bravery. Hoping to join his own regiment of foot, he placed himself at the head of his small Lifeguard of Horse, and:

> Passing through two bodies of foot, engaged with each other not at forty yards distance, received not the least hurt, though they fired quick upon each other; but marched towards a Scots regiment of foot, which they charged and routed; in which encounter my Lord himself killed three with his page's half-leaden sword, for he had no other left him . . . At last, after they had passed through this regiment of foot, a pikeman made a stand to the whole troop; and though my Lord charged him twice or thrice, yet he could not enter him; but the troop despatched him soon.[45]

By now the battle was lost, and as night fell, Newcastle withdrew to York. Early the following morning, the defeated Royalist commanders had a final bleak encounter. It seems that the marquis had initially considered going to the north-east of England in an attempt to rally his forces, but was dissuaded by Eythin. By the time that he met Rupert, Newcastle's mind was made up:

> says the Prince: 'I will rally my men.' Says General King; 'Know you what Lord Newcastle will do?' Says Lord Newcastle: 'I will go into Holland (looking upon all as lost)'.[46]

Rupert attempted to dissuade him and 'would have him endeavour to recruit his forces. No (says he) I will not endure the laughter of the Court, and King said he would go with him, and so they did . . .'[47]

At Scarborough, Newcastle and Eythin, with many of their associates, embarked for the Continent. Although Rupert, belatedly, sent a message ordering Eythin's arrest on a charge of treason, King Charles does not seem to have attached any particular blame to Newcastle. Clarendon perhaps summed up the general view, when he wrote:

> All that can be said for the Marquis is, that he was so utterly tired with a Condition and Employment so contrary to his Humour, Nature, and Education, that he did not consider the means or the way, that would let him out of it, and free him forever from having more to do with it.[48]

Aftermath

Newcastle spent his years of exile in relative poverty, using his considerable charm to appease his creditors. He also found time to marry his second wife, the talented and eccentric Margaret Lucas, over thirty years his junior, and to set up a flourishing riding school in Antwerp. The marquis also resumed his literary interests, writing a book on horsemanship, a couple of plays, and a book of advice on kingship for Charles II, in which he recommended that books of a controversial nature, including the Bible, should be available only in Latin, to avoid causing unrest among the common people!

At the Restoration, Newcastle returned to England, temporarily leaving Margaret in Holland as security for his debts. Though granted a dukedom in 1662, Newcastle received no other recompense for his sacrifices in the Royalist cause, and spent little time at Court, retiring with his wife to his estates, where both spent their remaining years in increasing eccentricity, producing a steady stream of literary offerings of a wide variety.

Newcastle's generalship, although judged over-harshly by some of his contemporaries, was, on the whole, unremarkable. Although, to his credit, he recognized his own inexperience, Newcastle lacked the energy and decision to ensure that those whom he employed to do the work did so effectively. As a result Royalist operations in the north were too often over-cautious and methodical, and, as in early 1643, valuable opportunities were lost.

Newcastle was ultimately the victim of his own over-sensitive and touchy nature. His suspicion and intolerance of criticism made him lend too ready an ear to those, like Lord Eythin, who had grudges of their own to settle. As a result, Newcastle and Eythin must bear a major share of the blame for the loss of the battle of Marston Moor, and with it the north of England. More than anyone, they could be said to have lost the war for King Charles in the course of an afternoon.

Chapter Eleven
Henry, Lord Wilmot

Some men, however hard they try, are never taken entirely seriously. One such, who carried the faint aura of a buffoon around him all his life, was Henry, Lord Wilmot. Clarendon, comparing him with George Goring,[1] having given Wilmot lukewarm credit as less fundamentally evil than Goring, summed him up as 'a man of haughty and ambitious nature, of a pleasant wit, and an ill understanding. [He was] proud and ambitious, and incapable of being contented, but with a great power over all of that inclination [hard drinkers] which was a great people.'[2] Largely thanks to Clarendon, he appeared to posterity as an archetypal Cavalier, a lover of mirth and good fellowship, though not very bright, who ultimately ventured too close to the verge of treason, and suffered disgrace as a result.

Wilmot's portraits add to the impression of a lover of good living, with heavy, somewhat indolent, features, a hint of cynical good humour, but little evidence of strenuous intellectual activity. It was said by one modern writer that 'Wilmot was in great place and lived through great events; he fathered a rake, but he was no great person in his own account.'[3] Yet, as Lieutenant General of the Oxford Army horse for much of the war, Wilmot proved to be a capable commander, and on more than one occasion, belied Clarendon's inference of possessing too great a sense of self-preservation.

Early life

Born in 1613, Henry was the third son, and heir, of Charles Wilmot, 1st Viscount Wilmot of Athlone in the Irish peerage, their seat at Addersbury in Wiltshire. Like many young men of his background with limited financial assets, Wilmot took up professional soldiering. In 1635 he was a captain in the Low Countries, and served in 1637 at that great proving ground for English soldiers, the Siege of Breda.

Wilmot was back in England for both of the Scots Wars. During the first, as Commissary General of Horse, he was one of a number of officers involved in disputes amongst themselves. He drew his sword on one of the officers of the

Lord General, the Earl of Arundel, for 'encroaching on his office' and was briefly arrested by none other than George Goring before being freed after an enquiry by the Council of War, which committed Wilmot's opponent instead.

In the Second Scots War, when he was again Commissary General, Wilmot fought at Newburn, the only action of note. With a number of officers he charged the Scottish horse who were crossing the Tweed, and forcing his way into their ranks, 'killed two or three with his own hands after he had received a pistol shot in his face; he charged them alone where his troops was less engaged.'[4] Eventually, unsupported, Wilmot was forced to retire by weight of enemy numbers.

With the end of the war, Wilmot was among the ultra-Royalist officers involved in the 'Army Plot' to employ the troops raised to fight the Scots against the king's opponents in England. Wilmot had recently been returned as MP for Tamworth, but with his role in the intrigue betrayed by George Goring, he was expelled from the House of Commons. He seems to have avoided a worse penalty by providing evidence which assisted the impeachment of the Earl of Strafford.

Cavalry commander

In 1642 Wilmot was one of the first to rally to the king at York. By August he was raising a Regiment of Horse, drawn predominantly from the West Country. With his previous record, Wilmot may have hoped for a senior command, perhaps even that of General of Horse. In the event the post went to the king's nephew, Prince Rupert, whose military experience was no greater than Wilmot's but who had the advantage of royal birth. This rankled increasingly with Wilmot as time went on and he clashed with the abrasive Rupert.

Once again Wilmot was appointed Commissary General of Horse. This post was theoretically third-in-command of the horse, and as no Lieutenant General of Horse had been appointed, Wilmot deputized for Rupert. The contemporary military writer, John Cruso, described the responsibilities of the position:

> The Commissary General commandeth in the absence of the Lieutenant General and therefore must be a man of great experience . . . He must be vigilant, and careful to appease dissensions which grow among the soldiers, as he dealeth most with them. He is to send and distribute the orders, and keep record of the lists of the guards, convoys and other services. He is to go every evening to receive the orders and the word; and having given it to the General and Lieutenant General, he is to give it to the Quarter Master General, that he may distribute it . . . In all actions he is of singular use, entrusted especially with the execution of the orders. In appointing the lodgings; or places in several exploits, he must be free from partiality: and such as at this time have cause of discontent, he must make amends the next, so they may see it was of necessity, not of partiality. His place is of very great use and importance.[5]

Wilmot, in other words, was responsible for much of the day-to-day running of the Royalist horse. It was a post which suited his skills in man-management and his gregariousness, but one in which he had to spend a great deal of time smoothing feathers ruffled by the undiplomatic Rupert.

Wilmot and the troop of horse which he had so far mustered were in action on 23 September at Powick Bridge, where Wilmot apparently received a 'shrewd wound', and was described afterwards by Sir Bevil Grenville as 'my noble friend, the brave Wilmot'.[6] According to his opponents, Wilmot had a summary way of dealing with potentially difficult civilians. During the summer, suspecting some villagers of assisting the Parliamentarians, he threatened to 'string up the men and send the soldiers to their wives and children.'[7]

At Edgehill (23 October) Wilmot led the left wing of the Royalist horse. Outnumbered some three to one, Wilmot's horse faced a more difficult task than Rupert on the right, having 'to charge in worse ground, amongst hedges, and through gaps and ditches, which were lined with musketeers.' However, once the Royalist dragoons had disposed of their Parliamentarian counterparts, Wilmot and his men routed the opposing horse with the same ease as did Rupert's troopers on the opposite wing.

There is no evidence that Wilmot had any more success than Rupert in checking the pursuit, though Sir Charles Lucas of Carnarvon's Regiment did succeed in rallying some of his men and assisting the Royalist foot. Returning belatedly to the field, Wilmot advised against resuming the action, even next day. He told the king's Secretary of State, Lord Falkland: 'My Lord, we have got the day, and let us live to enjoy the fruits thereof.' He has been criticized for what was probably a throwaway remark. The reality was that even next day the Royalist horse were still in considerable confusion. The soldiers had probably not eaten since the battle, while their horses were 'so weak that they would not be able to make a charge.' The officers had 'with much ado prevailed with them to keep the field.' Rather than being the words of an ultra-cautious officer with an eye to his own preservation, Wilmot's comment was probably the realistic assessment of an experienced soldier.[8]

On 3 November Wilmot scored an important independent success, when he captured the town of Marlborough. His summons rejected, he warned the townspeople that if they compelled him 'to enter the town by force, it would not be in his power to keep his soldiers from taking that which they should win with their blood.' And Marlborough was indeed thoroughly pillaged after an action in which Wilmot took 1,000 prisoners and four guns.

The failure of the Edgehill campaign to bring about the anticipated quick end to the war meant that the Royalist army was forced into winter quarters around Oxford. The maintenance and discipline of the cavalry, in the process of rapid expansion, caused considerable problems, and resulted in growing friction between Wilmot and Rupert. On 1 December Wilmot wrote to the prince:

Even now I received a command from your Highness to be tomorrow night at Wantage, where I shall not fail to obey any commands laid upon me, according to my power. But give me leave to tell your Highness, that I think myself very unhappy to be employed in this occasion, being a witness that at other times in the like occasions, troops are sent out without any manner of forecast or design, or care to preserve or quarter them when they are abroad; if I had any place to set up my horses, I should wait on your Highness this night at Oxford. Tomorrow it will be too late, so that I shall obey your Highness in being at Wantage, and there expect instructions how to behave myself, which I shall not fail to see punctually done.[9]

There was a clear difference of opinion between Wilmot and his commander, and possibly only Rupert's frequent absences during the spring and early summer, leaving Wilmot in effective control of the Oxford Army horse during these times, prevented matters coming to a head. In April the rather irregular chain of command was clarified when Wilmot was commissioned as Lieutenant General of Horse and Dragoons.

KEY ACTION: ROUNDWAY DOWN, 13 JULY 1643

Rupert's absence in July, when he was despatched to meet the queen and her vital munitions convoy from the north, provided Wilmot with the opportunity for his greatest exploit. Following their near-defeat at Lansdown, the Western Royalist forces under Hertford, Prince Maurice and Hopton had taken refuge in Devizes, from where, leaving Hopton and the foot under siege by Sir William Waller, Hertford, Maurice and the horse broke out and headed to Oxford to seek assistance. They arrived to find the king and Rupert both absent, and no spare foot available. There was also a shortage of ammunition, particularly as the last convoy sent to the west, escorted by the cavalry brigade of the Earl of Crawford, had been intercepted by the enemy.

Prince Maurice did obtain a pair of 6-pounder brass guns, and on 12 July rendezvoused at Marlborough with the only available reinforcements, the cavalry brigades of Wilmot, Sir John Byron and Crawford. The combined force headed for Devizes.

There seems, at least afterwards, to have been some confusion over who was in command of the expedition. Maurice was Lieutenant General of the Western forces, but he was serving with the expedition purely as a volunteer, accompanied by his Regiment of Horse, though not, apparently, by any other Western cavalry. It seems clear, that, if only by seniority of commission, command lay with Wilmot.

Early on 13 July, as he began a softening-up bombardment of Hopton's defences at Devizes, Waller received word that the Royalists were approaching from the east. Moving up on to Roundway Down, above the town, Waller took up position astride the Marlborough road, with Bagdon (Roundway) Hill to his right and King's Play Hill to the north. According to Clarendon, Wilmot was at a loss to know what to do:

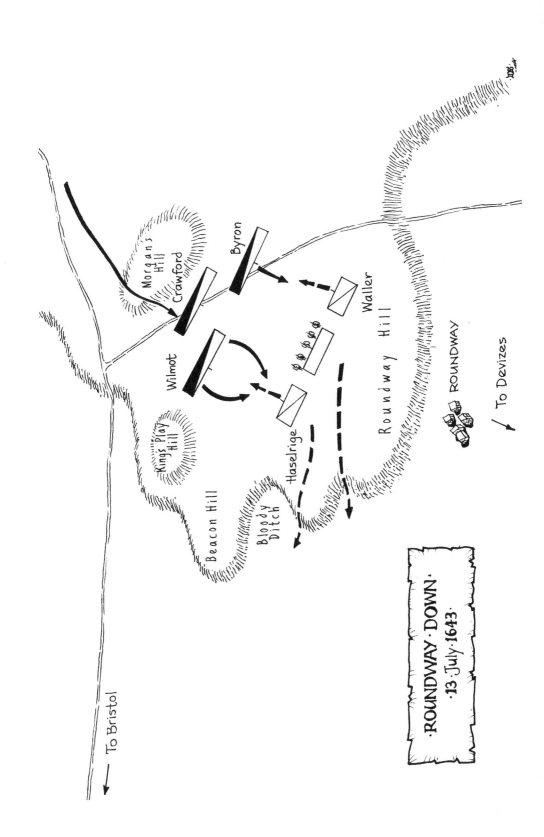

To Bristol

Morgans Hill

Crawford

Byron

Waller

Wilmot

Kings Play Hill

Haselrige

Roundway Hill

ROUNDWAY

To Devizes

Beacon Hill

Bloody Ditch

·ROUNDWAY·DOWN·
·13·July·1643·

finding them in this posture, with horse, foot and cannon much superior to him in number, and hearing nothing of the foot from the town, though he had made all signs to them from another part of the hill, according to what he had appointed them to expect by his messenger, that body of foot being the strength upon which he relied, knew not what to do, but calling his officers together, amongst whom there was the earl of Carnarvon, who was general of horse under the marquis of Hertford in the west, and had been engaged in all the actions with Waller, and so knew his manner of fighting, who came now only as a volunteer in the regiment of Sir John Byron, they all found it necessary to fight, since they could not expect the foot longer than the enemy would give them leave; and observing that Waller had placed all horse in several small bodies at some distance each from other, and all between them were his foot and cannon, Carnarvon said that the regiment of curassiers, which stood nearest to them, were the men upon whom Waller principally depended, and therefore desired Wilmot that their whole body might charge them; and if they could rout them, it was probable it might have a good effect upon their whole army. Which advice being taken, had the effect desired . . . [10]

Clarendon probably intended this as criticism of Wilmot, although in fact it seems to have been an example of a wise commander consulting one of his officers who had considerable experience in action against an opponent with whom Wilmot was unfamiliar.

Waller's army totalled about 2,000 horse, stationed on his flanks, with his five regiments of foot, 1,800 men in all with seven light guns, in the centre. It was at about 2pm that they sighted the Royalists about two miles away, moving down the old Roman Road from Marlborough, and then swinging south on to the 800-foot high Morgan's Hill, where they halted and fired two guns as a signal to Hopton in Devizes of their approach.

A pause of about an hour followed, during which the consultations described by Clarendon between Wilmot and his officers took place. Their decision reached, the Royalists deployed for action. Wilmot had about 1,800 horse, formed up with his own brigade on his right, three ranks deep, and Byron's brigade in the same formation slightly behind and to his left. Crawford's smaller brigade formed the reserve.

At about 3pm, the Royalists began to advance. Fighting commenced with a clash between the opposing 'forlorn hopes', and as the Parliamentarians fell back, Sir Arthur Haselrige and his cuirassiers on Waller's left advanced to support them. His 'lobsters' were formed six deep, and Haselrige possibly hoped to punch his way through Wilmot's opposing lines, but his gunners failed to support him, and Wilmot launched a timely counter-charge. As Captain Richard Atkyns of Prince Maurice's Regiment, who took, part, relates:

All the horse on the left hand of Prince Maurice had none to charge; we charging at the utmost man of their right wing; for though they were above twice our numbers, they being six deep, in close order and we but three deep, and open (by reason of our sudden charge) we were without them at both ends.[11]

Haslerige's outflanked men gave ground, and then rallied, retaking four guns which had briefly been lost, and fighting continued while Byron was in action against the other wing of Waller's horse. As Byron recalled, his men now charged Waller's own brigade:

> Yet they would not quit their ground but stood pushing for it a pretty space, till it pleased God (I think) to put new spirit into our tired horse as well as our own men, so that though it were up the hill, and that a steep one, we overbore them, and with that violence that we forced them to fall foul upon other reserves of horse out of their field, [Haselrige's men] and left their foot naked, and pursued them near three miles over the downs in Bristol way till they came to a precipice, where the fear made them so valiant that they galloped down as if it had been plain ground, and many of them broke their own and their horses' necks. In my return from the chase I took two pieces of their cannon, and divers wagons laden with ammunition, and then rallied together our scattered troops, which were as much broken as the enemy by reason of their hot pursuit . . . [12]

Waller, joining his foot, had meanwhile formed them into 'hedgehogs' which were probably harassed by Crawford's brigade, although no major attack was attempted until Byron and Wilmot returned from the pursuit of the Parliamentarian horse. Initially their attacks made little impression, until the Cornish foot from Devizes at last arrived on the scene. Sighting them, the Parliamentarian foot attempted to march off, but became disordered in the process, and Byron was able to deliver another charge which scattered them. Waller and some mounted officers made their escape, but the Royalists had killed 3–600 of their opponents, and taken some 800 prisoners. Waller's army was broken.

Confusion over the credit for this, the most sweeping Royalist cavalry victory of the war, continued, with Prince Maurice apparently claiming to have been in command, until he discovered that Wilmot, by virtue of the dating of his commission, was senior to him.[13] It is hard not to conclude that the Prince was being somewhat disingenuous; the evidence points to the victory being Wilmot's.

Disputes with Rupert

Roundway Down proved to be the climax of Wilmot's career. Early in August the bulk of the Royalist Oxford Army began the siege of Gloucester. A relief attempt by the principal Parliamentarian army under the Earl of Essex was expected, and Wilmot, who had been left in the vicinity of Oxford with perhaps

2,000 horse, was tasked with harassing his march. On 3 August Wilmot assured Rupert:

> The last night Essex himself lay with his foot at Chilton, and his horse at Wotton; this day, I am informed, his rendezvous is near Bicester. I shall not fail to attend him with as much diligence as I am capable of, and daily to give your Highness an account of his and my motions . . . [14]

Wilmot makes no mention of halting Essex's march, and indeed lacked the strength to do so. He carried out several small-scale attacks on Parliamentarian quarters, but neither he, nor the main force of horse under Prince Rupert, proved able to stop Essex, if such had ever been their intention, and Gloucester was relieved on 5 September.

At the First Battle of Newbury (20 September) Wilmot fought with the main Royalist cavalry in the action on Wash Common, though no record of his actions has survived. On the whole 1643 had been a successful year for Wilmot. In June he had been created First Baron Wilmot of Adderbury, and the king had arranged his marriage to a rich widow. However he became caught up in the recriminations which followed the failure to destroy Essex in the Newbury campaign. Rupert, following his habitual practice of seeking a scapegoat for his own failures, apparently blamed Wilmot for failing to prevent Essex from relieving Gloucester, and the latter responded angrily. Rupert's departure for the north, in February 1644, left Wilmot as Lieutenant General, for the moment in undisputed command of the Oxford Army horse, but ultimately did not improve his mood. Clarendon wrote that Wilmot:

> never considered above one thing at once, but he considered that thing so impatiently that he would not admit of anything else to be worth any consideration. He had from the beginning of the war been very averse to any advice of the Privy Council, and thought that the king's affairs (which depended upon the success of the war) should entirely be governed and conducted by the soldiers and men of war, and that no other councillors should have any credit with his Majesty. While prince Rupert was present, his exceeding great prejudice, or rather personal animosity towards him, made anything that Wilmot said or proposed enough slighted and contradicted: and the King himself upon some former account and observation, was far from any indulgence to his person or esteem of his parts. But now, by the prince's absence, and his being the second man in the army, and the contempt he had of the old general (Forth), who was there the only officer above him, he grew marvellously elated, and and looked upon himself as one whose advice ought to be followed and submitted to in all things. He had by his excessive good fellowship (in every part whereof he excelled, and was grateful to all the company) made himself so popular with all the officers of the army, especially of the horse, that he had in truth a very great interest, which he desired must appear to the King, that he might have the more

interest in him. He was positive in all his activities in council, and bore contradictions very impatiently, and because he was most contradicted by the Secretary and the Master of the Rolls [Digby and Lord Culpeper], who he saw had the greatest influence on the King, he used all the artifices he could to render them unacceptable and suspected to the officers of the army, by telling them what they had said in council, which he thought would render them the more ungrateful; and in the times of jollity, persuaded the old general to believe that they had invaded his prerogative, and meddled more in the business of the war than they ought to do, and thereby made him the less disposed to concur with them in advice, how rational and seasonable soever it was; which put the king to the trouble of converting him.[15]

This unhappy situation worsened during the spring. In April, in an attempt to provide the king with a feasible defensive strategy in the South while he himself countered the Scots in the north, Prince Rupert paid a flying visit to Oxford, and proposed a strategy by which the bulk of the Oxford Army foot should be garrisoned in the ring of fortified towns around Oxford, with the horse employed to strike at the communications of any enemy forces which moved against them. As a plan, Rupert's proposals have sometimes been given more credit than they deserved, for they paid too little account of the numerical weakness of the Oxford Army foot, or that the superiority of the Royalist horse was no longer unquestioned.

Once Rupert had departed, and the Parliamentarian armies of Essex and Waller showed signs of activity, Wilmot and Forth were quick to propose alterations in the king's strategy. On 18 May Reading was evacuated. On the 24th the foot thus released were moved to Abingdon, and the horse to Faringdon, with the intention of using the latter to harass the Parliamentarians, who were now advancing towards Oxford. Clarendon claimed that the results were disappointing, 'all which was imputed to the ill-humour and neglect of Wilmot.'[16]

On 25 May Abingdon was also evacuated. This led to a storm of recrimination, although given the fact that it was currently only held by one 500-strong regiment of foot the town was indefensible. The king, however, wanted to be fully involved in any decisions regarding its fate, and asked Forth to delay any decision until he arrived, but discovered that the evacuation had already been carried out. Though Forth had given the order, the King's Secretary at War, Sir Edward Walker, commented cryptically in his account of events: 'by whose counsel or why he did it is not for me to enquire.' The king, however, had no doubts, adding in an annotation to Walker's manuscript: 'yet I cannot but say that the Lord Wilmot was generally thought to be the chief adviser to quit Abingdon.'[17]

With the Parliamentarians closing in around Oxford, Charles, taking with him Wilmot and the horse, with 2,500 musketeers, evaded the trap by his celebrated forced march across the Cotswolds to Worcester. Wilmot, however, was now regarded by Charles as the chief architect of his misfortunes, and through his enmity towards the king's civilian advisers, had made the fatal mistake of alienating the influential Secretary of State, Lord George Digby.

Tipton Green and Cropredy Bridge

Wilmot, however, added one more military success to his record, and temporarily secured his own position. On reaching Worcester, on 6 June, the king learnt that the important Midlands garrison of Dudley Castle to the north-west was under severe enemy pressure. Its governor, Colonel Thomas Leveson, had taken about 300 horse to reinforce Rupert in his operations in Lancashire, and by 2 June Dudley's weakened garrison was under siege by the Earl of Denbigh with about 750 horse and 1,000 foot.

On 11 June, Charles despatched Wilmot with about 2,500 horse to relieve Dudley. Denbigh learnt of his approach late in the afternoon, as the Royalists crossed Pensnett Chase. The Parliamentarian commander detached a force of horse under Colonel Thomas Mytton to meet Wilmot, who clashed indecisively with him late in the evening. Having taken a few prisoners, Wilmot called a halt for the night.

Denbigh, meanwhile, decided to lift his siege under cover of darkness. However, his siege guns had evidently become bogged down in their emplacements, and at dawn Denbigh's men were still struggling to shift them and pull them to safety along a narrow lane near the Castle. To add to Denbigh's difficulties, the carriage of his largest gun, 'the Stafford Great Piece', broke while within half-musket shot distance of the Castle. Commenting that 'I had rather lose ten lives than one piece of my artillery', Denbigh refused to abandon the gun, but by the time that it was on the move again, Wilmot had arrived.

Denbigh was forced to deploy his forces on Tipton Green, about three-quarters of a mile from Dudley Castle. Reinforced by musketeers from the garrison, Wilmot advanced to the attack, fighting beginning when Royalist musketeers occupied Tipton Green House, which dominated one side of the Green. At the same time, about 300 horse with other musketeers marched down the lane leading from Dudley Castle Hill to engage the Parliamentarians. Wilmot's first charge broke the Parliamentarian forlorn hope, and his second attack routed some Parliamentarian horse moving up in support. However, Denbigh had sufficient reserves to make his own counter-attack, which drove the Royalists back, while some Staffordshire Foot under Colonel Simon Rugeley took Tipton Green House.

A stand-off followed, with neither side anxious to renew the action. Wilmot had achieved his objective of relieving Dudley Castle, and so disengaged. Denbigh withdrew to Walsall, and Wilmot rejoined the king next day, both commanders claiming the victory, Wilmot with marginally more justification.[18]

However, this success did nothing to change the king's view of Wilmot. Charles was still seething over the evacuation of Abingdon, writing to Prince Rupert on 7 June:

> I confess, the best had been to have followed your advice, yet if we had rightly followed our own, we had done well enough; but we too easily quitted Abingdon, and were not so nimble upon their loose quarters as we

might have been, of which errors I must acquit myself and my Lord General.[19]

The inference was obvious, and at about the same time Charles wrote separately to Rupert asking his opinion of the suggestion that Prince Maurice be made General of Horse 'considering how matters stand with Wilmot.'[20] Matters by now stood a good deal worse. Thanks to the decision of Essex and Waller to divide their forces, Waller continuing operations against the king while Essex marched to the relief of Lyme, Charles was able to return to Oxford and re-unite his army. From here he marched to Buckingham, where the Royalists considered their next move. According to Clarendon:

> Wilmot continued still sullen and perverse, and every day grew more insolent, and had contracted such an animosity against Lord Digby and the Master of the Rolls, that he persuaded many officers of the army, especially of the horse, where he was most entirely obeyed, to join in a petition to the King, that those two councillors might be excluded, and be no more present in councils of war, which they promised to do.[21]

This was a major threat to the position of the ambitious Digby, and finally persuaded him to put his considerable influence towards removing Wilmot, but in the interim disputes continued. Some of the king's advisers favoured a thrust into the Eastern Association, but:

> Wilmot, without ever communicating it with the King, positively advised that they might presently march towards London, and, now both their generals and their armies were far from them, make trial what the true affection of the city was: and that, when the army was marched as far as St Albans, the King should send such a gracious message both to Parliament and city as was most like to prevail upon them: and concluded as if he knew that this way of proceeding would be very much approved of by the army. This extravagant notion, with all the circumstances of it, troubled the King very much: yet he thought it not fit absolutely to reject it, lest it might promote that petition which he knew was framing among the officers, but assured them, that such a message should be prepared, and then that he would communicate both that and what concerned his march towards London to the Council at Oxford; that in so weighty an affair he might receive their counsel. To that purpose the lord Digby and the Master of the Rolls were sent to Oxford; who, after two days, returned without any approbation of the march or the message by the lords. But all that intrigue fell of itself, upon the sure intelligence, that Waller had left Worcestershire, and marched out with what speed he could, to find his Majesty.[22]

Whatever merits his proposals may have had, and in reality they were few, Wilmot had now seriously overstepped the mark. Probably only the imminent prospect of battle saved him, and when the Oxford Army clashed with Waller on 28 June at Cropredy Bridge in Oxfordshire, Wilmot behaved himself with his customary bravery, leading a spirited counter-charge which repulsed Waller's attempts to cut off the rear of the extended Royalist column. As on other occasions in his career, Wilmot's tendency to be in the thick of the action resulted in his being wounded – shot in the arm and grazed on either the hand or stomach. He was twice briefly taken prisoner and on the second occasion 'committed to the custody of two Soldiers, who in our disorderly retreat lost him again.'[23]

The Royalist newspaper *Mercurius Aulicus* commented that 'Wilmot's service this day was very eminent.'[24] But more important to the king was that what he saw as the discontented state of his troops following Wilmot's agitation was one of the factors which made him decide against attempting to complete the destruction of Waller's army. As the Royalist army turned to pursue Essex into the West, Lord Wilmot's days were numbered.

Dismissal

The king was now actively planning to replace the elderly and infirm Lord Forth as his Lord General with Prince Rupert. The prince at the same time would resign his post of General of Horse in favour of Lord George Goring. In theory, Wilmot might retain the position of Lieutenant General, but, as Digby, and possibly the king, knew, this was likely to be unacceptable to Wilmot. During the pursuit of Essex into Cornwall Wilmot grew steadily more restive and disputatious. According to Clarendon, the prospect of coming under the command of both Rupert and the almost equally detested Goring would be such a mortification to him as he would never have been able to digest.'[25]

It may have been this prospect which heightened Wilmot's disaffection, and:

> during the whole march he discoursed in all places that the King must send to the Earl of Essex, to invite him to a conjunction with him, that so the Parliament might be obliged to consent to a peace.[26]

Clarendon also claimed that Wilmot had attempted to send Essex a message assuring him 'that the army so much desired peace that it should not be in the power of any persons about the King to hinder it, if his lordship would treat upon any reasonable propositions.'[27] This was close to treason, and was presented 'in full magnitude to the king by the Lord Digby, and his majesty's own aversion kindled any spark into a formal distrust.'[28]

Goring had already been sent for, and once he joined the Royalist army facing Essex at Lostwithiel, the next step was immediate. On the morning of 8 August Wilmot was arrested by the Knight Marshal at the head of his troops:

> in the King's name of high treason, and dismounted him from his horse in the head of all the troops, and putting a guard upon him, he was presently sent prisoner to Exeter.[29]

Charles was concerned about the affects of Wilmot's arrest on the army, particularly the cavalry. The majority of the cavalry field officers signed a petition to the king, 'to request some light from your majesty concerning this business'.[30] The king, unwisely in Clarendon's view, responded with a list of charges laid against Wilmot:

> which though they contained so many indiscretions, vanities and insolences, . . . yet generally they seemed not to make him so very black as he had been represented to be . . .[31]

Wilmot's own response was to deny any intentions of treason:

> The height of my pretended offences (were they confessed by me or proved by them) reacheth no further than words, though of such nature as are as disagreeable to my loyalty and duty, as they were always distant either from my intentions or expressions. . . . the groundwork of their accusations [are] clearly nothing but a too violent expressing mine inclination unto Peace.[32]

It was tacitly agreed that prosecuting Wilmot on such uncertain grounds would merely prolong discontent in the army, and as Wilmot himself was clearly unwilling to serve under Goring, 'his old mortal enemy',[33] a compromise was speedily effected. In November Wilmot was allowed to depart for the Continent, with a letter of recommendation to the queen from King Charles. He was made Gentleman of the Bedchamber to the Prince of Wales, in unspoken recognition of the dubious nature of the charges against him, and perhaps of the problems he could cause had he petitioned the Oxford Parliament for reinstatement.

Aftermath

The after-effects of the affair rumbled on in the Royalist Court in exile for some years, culminating in 1649 in a somewhat farcical duel between Wilmot and Digby, in a confused dispute which began with Wilmot challenging Digby over the accusations of 1644, but actually fought by Digby in defence of Prince Rupert's honour against Wilmot's claim that the Prince had vowed to shoot Digby dead! Digby was wounded, and honour deemed satisfied.

The convivial Wilmot was now a firm favourite of the young Charles II, and accompanied him on the expedition which culminated in the Battle of Worcester on 3 September 1651. Rather surprisingly, Charles selected Wilmot as his companion in his celebrated escape after the battle. Richard Ollard, the historian of Charles's adventures, said of Wilmot's part: 'he was stupid, he was careless, he was forgetful, he was indiscreet.'[34] He would only travel on horseback, accompanied by his manservant, and refused to wear a disguise saying that 'he would look frightfully in it.' However Wilmot was not without his uses. As the fugitives travelled through the West Country, Wilmot's network of former comrades-in-arms, who still retained an obvious affection for their old commander, played an important role in Charles's eventual escape to the Continent.

In 1652 Wilmot was created Earl of Rochester, and made several more clandestine visits to England on the king's business, on one of which he fathered his son, the noted Restoration rake, John, Second Earl of Rochester. Somewhat surprisingly, he managed to escape arrest on all his missions, despite a characteristic indifference to secrecy, and carelessness: 'in making his journeys, . . . he departed very unwillingly from all places where there was good eating and drinking.'[35]

Wilmot would probably have prospered as a boon companion of Charles II after the Restoration, but with typical ill-timing, he died in Ghent, still an exile, in 1658.

Henry Wilmot probably never fully appreciated the reasons for his downfall. He was a competent if uninspired professional soldier, who in battle could be relied upon not to make any major errors. He was apparently a capable and popular commander, well-liked and respected by his men. In the absence of Prince Rupert he would probably have made an adequate General of Horse for the Oxford Army. Wilmot's problem was that his ambition exceeded his intellectual capacities. He was on bad terms with Rupert from the beginning, and his discontent rankled until he ventured too far into the fields of politics and Court intrigue for which he was ill-equipped. Guilty of foolishness rather than treasonable intent, he paid the inevitable price.

Chapter 12
James Graham, Marquis of Montrose

Montrose 'of all the leading Cavaliers came closest to the Renaissance ideal of the Complete Man; the gentleman who is at once a soldier, a scholar and a poet, a gay gallant and a pattern of Christian chivalry.'[1]

This view is typical of the way James Graham, Marquis of Montrose has been portrayed by the majority of those writing about him. To biographers such as John Buchan and C.V.Wedgwood, Montrose was a heroic figure, whose few relatively minor faults were far outweighed by the general nobility of his character. His brilliance as a military commander was accepted almost without question. To Buchan 'as a soldier Montrose ranks by common consent with the greatest of his age, with Cromwell and Condé.'[2] For Sir John Fortescue, historian of the British Army, he was 'perhaps the most brilliant natural military genius disclosed by the Civil War.'[3] C.V. Wedgwood saw him as having 'a genius for guerrilla warfare that was to be the wonder of the age.'[4] Of modern military historians, only Stuart Reid has seriously questioned Montrose's military infallibility.[5]

In the sphere of politics, Montrose's biographers are understandably more circumspect. Buchan conceded that Montrose was:

> a most fallible politician and he was without skill in the game of ... intrigue. He was an optimist about his dreams: he saw the Lowland peasantry looking for a deliverer, when they regarded him as a destroyer ... he did not understand the depths of the antipathy of Saxon to Celt, or how fatally the use of Alasdair's men prejudiced his cause.[6]

It was Montrose's ambivalent political track record which largely coloured the views of his contemporaries. There was always something equivocal about Montrose. Even his portraits provide two contradictory images. Best known is the painting by Honthurst executed during the later years of exile, and showing a haunted, delicate featured man with a piercing gaze, clad in black armour, a figure full of intimations of tragedy. Yet in other contemporary engravings, Montrose is a heavier looking, earthier character.

Montrose's own followers, notably his chaplain, George Wishart, whose account of the *annus mirabilis* of 1644–45 was effectively Montrose's autobiography, did much to create the image of their hero. Patrick Gordon of Ruthven described him:

> of speech slow, but witty and full of sense; a presence graceful, courtly and so winning upon the beholder, that it seemed to claim reverence without striving for it, for he was so affable, so courteous, so benign, that he seemed verily to scorn ostentation and the keeping of state.[7]

This was Montrose in his dealings with his social inferiors, on whom he turned his irresistible charm. With equals he was notably less affable, and frequently both tactless and egotistical, having little time for those who disagreed with him.

Not all who met him succumbed to the Montrose charisma. Bishop Burnet said that he was 'a young man well trained, who had travelled, but had taken upon him the part of a hero too much; and lived as in a romance, for his whole manner was stately to affectation . . . '[8]

Early life

The Grahams were leading Scottish Lowland magnates, and Montrose, who succeeded his father as earl at the age of fourteen in 1626, was automatically in the forefront of Scottish affairs. Montrose married Magdalen, daughter of Lord Carnegie, in what his more romantic biographers have, with scant evidence, attempted to portray as a love match. In fact Montrose never evidenced any great interest in women, and it was probably a dynastic marriage of convenience. He was educated, without particular distinction, at the University of St Andrews, showing a greater flair for gambling, archery and sports than for study. He travelled in Italy and France, where he enrolled in 1633–4 at the military academy at Angers.

Returning to England in 1636, Montrose received a cool reception at the Court of Charles I, mainly because that suggestible monarch had been warned off Montrose by the currently favoured Marquis of Hamilton, who regarded Graham as a potential rival. How far this snub influenced Montrose in supporting the Covenanting party in Scotland in the dispute with the king centred around the proposed new Prayer Book is debatable. Montrose's own political aims seem to have been limited to curbing some of the worst excesses of royal power. In 1638 he opposed the pro-Royalist Marquis of Huntley in the Aberdeen area, and secured the town for the Covenant at the future cost of alienating himself from Huntley.

When the Royalists regained control of Aberdeen, Montrose won it back for the Covenanters at Brig o'Dee (19 June 1639). Montrose was made Lieutenant-General of the Covenanting Army, but he was growing disillusioned with the more extreme aspects of the Covenanters' political programme. As head of the House of Graham Montrose feared the growing power of his neighbour, and leading member of the more radical Covenanting faction, Archibald Campbell, Marquis of Argyll.

By the time the Second Scots War began in 1640, the Covenanting party was diverging into two factions, those who supported the radical ideas of Argyll and his allies and the moderates centred on Montrose. The latter was by now attempting to build bridges with the king, although overtly he remained a supporter of the Covenant, and served with the Scots army during its invasion of England in 1640. He was discovered to be in secret communication with Charles. Argyll, who regarded Montrose as still too influential to move against openly, allowed him to be pardoned, but Graham was henceforward a marked man.

Montrose was imprisoned during the king's visit to Scotland in 1641, but, following the sweeping concessions which Charles made to the Covenanters on that occasion, Argyll evidently regarded Montrose and the weak Scottish Royalist faction a spent force, and allowed him to return home. During the quiet year which Montrose spent on his estates, watching the inexorable approach of civil war in England, he became convinced of the need for the monarchy to provide unifying authority to guard against 'the oppression and tyranny of subjects, the most fierce, insatiable and insufferable tyranny in the world.' In Scotland, Montrose saw this as represented by the regime of Argyll and in England by the more radical elements of the Parliamentarian opposition.

By February 1643 Montrose was convinced that the regime in Scotland was set on intervening in the English Civil War on the Parliamentarian side, and he made a clandestine visit to the queen at York, pressing for a Royalist rising in Scotland. However, Montrose's old rival, Hamilton, with, as it proved, some justification, held that the Covenanting government had such a firm grip over the Scottish Lowlands that only in the Highlands would there be limited support for a rising, which without substantial help promised, but by no means assured, from the Earl of Antrim in Ireland, would be doomed to failure.

Montrose would prove reluctant to work with Antrim, and considerably over-estimated the degree of sympathy in Scotland for the Royalist cause, having alienated by his ambivalent political behaviour most of its leading supporters, including Huntley.

By the summer of 1643, his position in Scotland untenable, Montrose had fled to join the king at Oxford, but his lobbying for support met with no interest until after the Scots invasion actually began in January 1644. Montrose was now given the initially empty title of Lieutenant Governor and Captain General in Scotland, but virtually no troops with which to spark his planned uprising. The Marquis of Newcastle, on whom Montrose had pinned his hopes for military assistance, could spare no more than 100 horse. Graham added to these about 2,000 raw levies scraped together in Cumbria, and in March mounted an abortive incursion into south-west Scotland. He got no further than Dumfries, where, with no sign of a Scottish Royalist rising, and his men near mutiny, Montrose fell back into England. Created a marquis in May, Montrose spent the next few weeks operating against the Scottish line of communications in north-east England, until the crushing Royalist defeat at Marston Moor (2 July) rang the death-knell of his hopes of military assistance.

The rising begins

Disguised as a groom, and with only two companions, Montrose slipped across the Border, and lay low at the home of a kinsman, Patrick Graham of Inchbrakie, waiting for some favourable opportunity.

It remains unclear what prior knowledge Montrose had of what happened next. The extravagant promises made by the Earl of Antrim at last materialized in the shape of 2,000 men under that other leading figure of Montrose's war, Alasdair MacColla. Over the next twelve months, Alasdair and his Irish soldiers would play a key, if often infuriating, role in Montrose's campaigns.

MacColla, a man of considerable physical stature and fighting ability, was a heroic figure of the war in Ireland. He would, however, prove to be less concerned with fighting for the Royalist cause than against the hated Campbells who held many of the ancestral lands of the Irish MacDonnells, who comprised most of his men. There have been many misconceptions regarding the nature of the Irish troops. They were not, as often suggested, variants on the traditional Highland clansman, equipped and using Highland arms and tactics. The majority of Alasdair's men were veteran soldiers, who in many cases had served with the redoubtable Spanish Army of Flanders, and the three regiments into which they were formed were armed, trained and equipped in conventional style with pike and musket.

Though they were formidable soldiers, there were disadvantages for Montrose in using MacColla and his men. As Irish Catholics, they were anathema to the Scottish Lowlanders, and alienated not only wavering Covenanters but also many Scottish Royalists. The use of them and Highland clansman repelled many of the Scottish nobility who might otherwise have assisted Montrose. Opinions also differed on MacColla's own suitability for senior command. One contemporary wrote equivocally of him that he was 'so vigorous in a fight that had his conduct been equal to his valour he might have been one of the best generals in Europe.'[9] The tough old Scottish professional soldier, Sir James Turner, phrased his opinion more succinctly: 'nae soljer, tho stout enough.'[10]

Landing in Kintyre in July, MacColla and his men secured a base of operations, but met with little local support, and were likely to be opposed by the Atholl Stewarts and Robertsons. Alasdair prepared to march through to Lochaber and then link up with Huntley. What happened next is part of the glittering Montrose legend. According to Wishart's version, Montrose, more or less by chance, encountered a messenger from Alsadair seeking his help, and donning Highland dress arrived at Blair Atholl just in time to avert a pitched battle between the Irish and the local clans. Such, according to one Royalist writer, was Montrose's charisma and powers of persuasion, that he 'quickly made a conquest of the hearts of all his followers, so as when he list, he could have laid them in a chain to follow him with cheerfulness in all his enterprises.'[11]

This an exaggeration, and it is impossible to say if the meeting at Blair Atholl had been pre-arranged, but Montrose raised his standard and proclaimed his

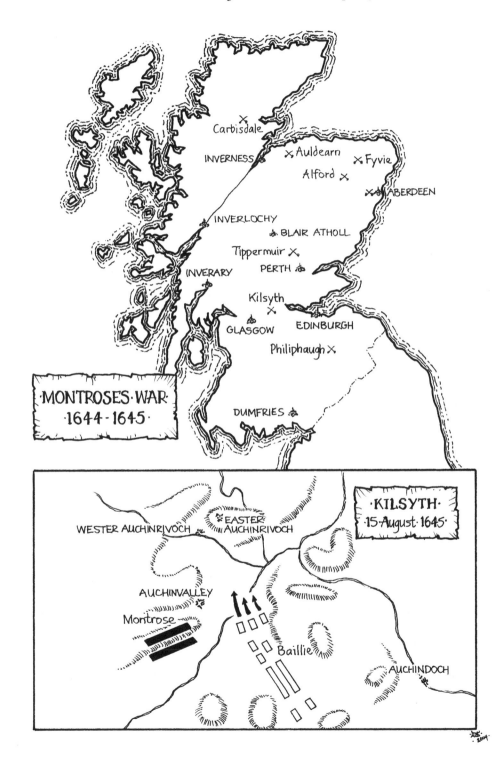

MONTROSE'S WAR
·1644·1645·

×Carbisdale

INVERNESS
×Auldearn
×Fyvie
Alford ×
×ABERDEEN

INVERLOCHY
BLAIR ATHOLL
Tippermuir ×
INVERARY
PERTH
Kilsyth
×
GLASGOW
EDINBURGH
Philiphaugh ×
DUMFRIES

·KILSYTH·
·15·August·1645·

WESTER AUCHINRIVOCH
EASTER AUCHINRIVOCH
AUCHINVALLEY
Montrose
Baillie
AUCHINDOCH

intention to fight for 'the defence and maintenance of the true protestant religion, his Majesty's just and sacred authority, the fundamental laws and privileges of parliament, the peace and freedom of the oppressed and thrilled subject.' An immediate contradiction was that the majority of the troops supposedly fighting for that Protestant cause were in fact Catholic. Montrose would have argued rightly that he had no option but to use anyone who would fight for him, but the result was guaranteed to alienate many potential supporters.

Militarily, Montrose was in a vulnerable situation. Although the bulk of the Covenanters' regular units were absent in England or Ulster, the Scottish military system theoretically allowed for the conscription of the entire male population between the ages of sixteen and sixty. In practice shires and towns were given quotas of men to raise and equip at musters. They varied considerably in training and experience, and for the opening months of the rising Montrose mainly encountered second-rate militia-based forces. Later, experienced troops were brought back from England and Ireland, but shortage of soldiers of some kind would rarely be a problem for the Covenanters.

Montrose was less fortunate. For several months the core of his army would remain his Irish Brigade. At his first two major actions, Tippermuir and Aberdeen, the Irish formed the bulk of Montrose's force, although casualties and desertion reduced their numbers thereafter. The Royalists later raised a considerable number of foot, equipped in orthodox fashion, from among the Gordons of Aberdeenshire. Popular accounts make much of Montrose's employment of Highlanders, but these proved of mixed value. They were unreliable, and tended to go home with their booty after any major success, or if dissatisfied in any way. They also varied in fighting value. The best of them, chieftains, gentry, and their professional soldiers, were useful fighters, but the body of ordinary clansmen were often poorly armed, trained and motivated. The main use of the Highlanders lay in frightening raw levies with their fearsome reputation, and pursuing and killing an opponent who had been broken by Montrose's conventional forces.

Montrose lacked significant cavalry for much of the earlier part of the rising. This prevented him from mounting a sustained campaign in the Lowlands, and meeting larger Covenanting armies on equal terms. It was not until the spring of 1645, after the defection to the Royalists of Lord George Gordon and his regular cavalry regiment, that this problem was to some extent overcome.

Montrose's strategy is also sometimes misunderstood. Although at times hubris following his victories led Montrose to exaggerate his prospects, there was never any real likelihood of his conquering all of Scotland. He lacked the necessary breadth of support and a secure territorial base from which to maintain a sizable conventional army, and had no siege artillery with which to reduce defiant garrisons. A more achievable strategy was to gain enough success to cause the Covenanting authorities to withdraw troops from their units in England. Montrose did partially succeed in this aim, although by then the Parliamentarian victory at Naseby had removed much of the need for Scottish assistance. Naseby in its turn would force Montrose to adopt his own high-risk strategy, which proved fatal. The

Covenanters also had considerably more success than they are often credited with. For several critical months they were able to contain Montrose with home-based units, and rather than withdraw forces in their entirety from external theatres, brought home detachments from seasoned larger regiments.

Following the muster at Blair Atholl, Montrose headed for Perth, where on 3 September his army of 3,000 men, the majority of them Irish foot, encountered on Tippermuir about 2,800 Covenanters, many of them raw levies, under Lord Elcho. After preliminary skirmishing, the battle was decided by a volley, followed by a charge, made by MacColla's men, before which the Covenanting centre collapsed. As usual, Royalist claims of the casualties they inflicted were probably too high, but Montrose was able to occupy Perth and demand from its citizens a £60,000 'ransom' and £13,000 worth of cloth to outfit his ragged soldiers. He was received with understandable lack of enthusiasm, and gained few recruits.

Hearing of the approach of another Covenanting force under Argyll, the Royalists abandoned Perth on 4 September, and headed for Dundee. Finding the town too well-prepared, Montrose moved on towards Aberdeen. Here defending forces were being mustered by Lord Balfour of Burleigh, and consisted of a mixture of regular units and militia, totalling about 2,000 foot and 300 horse. Because of desertions among his Highlanders, Montrose had been reduced to some 1,500 Irish foot and 60–80 cavalry.

Before fighting began, Montrose sent the citizens of Aberdeen a summons to surrender, which was rejected, and the drummer who accompanied the Royalist emissary was shot dead as they were leaving the town. Burleigh had drawn up his forces on rising ground about half a mile to the south of Aberdeen, and opened proceedings with attacks by cavalry stationed on his wings. Despite their superior numbers, the Covenanting horse proved hesitant, and were fairly readily held off by the Royalists. When Covenanting troopers under Forbes of Craigievar attacked MacColla's men in the centre, the Irish veterans calmly opened their ranks and let them through, then about-turned and opened a devastating fire from which 'few or none went back.' Fighting continued for about two hours, with the Royalists slowly advancing uphill, until the Covenanting foot broke before MacColla's disciplined men, a significant number being cut down in the pursuit.

The victorious Royalists poured into Aberdeen. There followed a three-day sack of the town which for Montrose's partisans remains an embarrassing stain on his reputation. Graham laid great stress on his efforts to fight a chivalrous and honourable campaign, once remarking that 'If the meanest corporal in my army had given quarter to their general, I would abide by it.' But the reality of Montrose's war was very different. It was a conflict in which actual or potential opponents were routinely subjected to looting and the burning of their lands and property, and in which the defeated in battle were given no quarter. There may not have been much killing of non-combatants in Aberdeen, for many of the ninety-eight townsmen listed as dead probably fell in the battle, but there was looting on a wide scale. One of Montrose's officers reported that 'the riches of that town hath made all our soldiers cavaliers', while on that first evening it was said that nothing could be heard but 'pitiful howling, crying, weeping, mourning through all the streets.'

Montrose himself entered Aberdeen next day, and, if confirmation were still needed, proclaimed his intention to bring the king's subjects to obedience 'by fair means or by fire and sword.'[12]

The sack of Aberdeen was one of Montrose's gravest errors. The city had not even been predominantly Covenanting in sympathy, but its fate sent a chill of horror through the Scottish Lowlands, and seemed to threaten the same for any other place which fell into Royalist hands. Significantly, Wishart's laudatory account makes no mention of the incident.

On 18 September Argyll placed a reward of £20,000 on Montrose's head, dead or alive. By now the Royalists had headed off into the wilds of Rothiemurchie, with Argyll some three days behind, and then turned south into Atholl. MacColla and 500 of his men went off to pursue their interests in the Western Highlands, and Montrose headed back towards Aberdeen in an unsuccessful attempt to gain the support of the Gordons, although he was joined by various other recruits, giving him a total of about 1,500 men.

Thanks to his recurrent weakness in failing to gather adequate intelligence of enemy movements, Montrose was now caught out because of his ignorance that on 26 October Argyll had left Aberdeen in pursuit with about 2,000 foot and some horse. He caught up with the Royalists at Fyvie, and took Montrose by surprise. However, the Royalists occupied good defensive terrain, and after three days in-decisive skirmishing Montrose pulled back safely into Atholl.

His force was rapidly melting away:

> some of them pleaded ill-health, others declared themselves unequal to such winter marches, through wild, pathless mountains beset with rocks and thickets, and mostly buried in snow, where the foot of man never trod; and therefore, unwillingly, they said, and only through absolute necessity, they begged to be dismissed. He refused leave to none that asked it, but more with an air of indignation and scorn for their degeneracy, than indulgence and approval.[13]

Argyll, encouraged by the defection of Montrose's supporters, apparently believed that the rising would not survive the winter, and called off his pursuit. However, in November MacColla rejoined Montrose, bringing with him about 1,500 men, including many new recruits from the Western Highlands. The resulting strong clan influence in his army forced Montrose to devote the winter to operations against the hated Campbells. MacColla apparently issued an ulti-matum that he would leave unless this was done, but Montrose, expressing his own doubts, hoped that he would be backed by the majority of Lowlanders on his Council of War. Wishart suggests that Montrose was eventually convinced by MacColla's arguments, but it is more likely that he yielded because he had no choice if he were to preserve his army. In the version of events which he sent to the king, Montrose unconvincingly claimed: 'I was willing to let the world see that Argyll was not the man his Highlanders believed him to be, and that it was possible to beat him in his own Highlands.'[14]

In the event the winter campaign, while not entirely relevant to his overall strategy, proved a remarkable success. Assisted by unseasonably mild weather, Montrose pushed through the mountain passes and on 13 December seized the Campbell 'capital' of Inverary, and burnt it, Argyll fleeing ignominiously by galley. He was hindered in his response by a dispute with Lieutenant General William Baillie, commanding the first contingent of regulars to return from England, who was unwilling to commit his men to the rigours of a winter campaign in the Highlands. Nevertheless, by the end of January, Montrose, in the Great Glen with about 2,000 men, appeared to be blockaded there by Covenanting forces at each end, including Argyll in the west at Inverlochy. This was in fact deceptive, as the Royalists could have escaped over the mountains to the south-east, but instead Montrose decided to attack Inverlochy.

After a gruelling cross-country march through the mountains which concealed his movements, Montrose with 1,500 men appeared on the hillside above Inverlochy early on 2 February. The marquis and his officers 'breakfasted on a little meal, mixed with cold water, which out of a hollow dish they did pick up with their knives for want of spoons.'[15] Then in a brief but bloody encounter, the irresistible Royalist charge swept down the hillside against the Campbells. The Highland contingent of the Covenanting force broke almost immediately, and a considerable number were cut down, although two regular foot regiments surrendered on terms.

Auldearn and Alford

Inverlochy was a considerable boost to Royalist morale, although it hardly justified the grandiloquent despatch which Montrose on 3 February penned to the king:

> I am in the fairest hopes of reducing this kingdom to your Majesty's obedience. And if the measures I have concerted with your other loyal subjects fail me not, as they hardly can, I doubt not before the end of this summer I shall be able to come to your Majesty's assistance with a brave army, which, backed with the justice of your Majesty's cause, will make the rebels in England, as well as in Scotland, feel the just rewards of Rebellion. Only give me leave, after I have reduced this country to your Majesty's obedience, and conquered from Dan to Beersheba, to say to your Majesty then, as David's General to his master, 'Come thou thyself, lest this country be called by my name: Sir in all my actions I aim only at your Majesty's honour and interest, as becomes one that is to his last breath, your Majesty's humble, most faithful, and most obedient Subject and Servant.[16]

Exaggerated though these claims were, Inverlochy did bring in recruits for Montrose, most significantly the defection on 19 February of Huntley's eldest son, Lord George Gordon, with his regular cavalry regiment. Montrose now had about 3,000 foot, about one third of them Irish, and most of the remainder conventionally equipped Lowlanders, with about 300 horse. During March further indecisive manoeuvring between Montrose and the Covenanting forces under Baille and Sir John Hurry followed, Montrose evading his opponents while devastating the countryside in an attempt to force recalcitrants to join him, and unsurprisingly having little success. Instead, in another of his failures of intelligence gathering, Montrose, in an ill-judged raid on Dundee, narrowly escaped destruction when Baillie unexpectedly appeared. Largely due to his own presence of mind, Montrose managed to extricate his men in a 48-hour, 70-mile march, but the outcome, rather than the success claimed by Wishart, was nearer to being the 'great and real disaster' portrayed by the Covenanter Robert Baillie. The raid had been without real strategic aim and purpose, and in marked contrast to his optimistic claims of early February, Montrose wrote tetchily to the king on 20 April:

> Had I but for one month the use of those five hundred [horse under Sir Philip Musgrave promised by the king] I could have seen you before the time that this could come to your hands with twenty thousand of the best this kingdom can afford.' [He had] 'continued this half year without the assistance of either men, arms . . . ammunition . . . Howsoever though you have not assisted me, I will yet still do my best to bar all assistance coming against you.[17]

Though Montrose hoped to shame the king into sending support, the reality was that most of the senior Royalist commanders did not share the hopes which their monarch placed in his Scottish champion. They mistrusted Montrose, and saw him as at best a useful distraction against the Covenanters. Even if they had been willing and had the men to spare, it would be difficult for a small force of cavalry to traverse the enemy-held north of England and Scottish Lowlands in order to link up with Montrose, and for the moment Royalist attentions were divided between the threat of the New Model Army and regaining the north of England. Only if the latter were achieved might it be practicable to reinforce Montrose.

In the interim Montrose once again teetered on the edge of disaster.

William Baillie now based part of his force under Hurry at Aberdeen, with orders to operate against the Gordons to the north and east. On 17 April Hurry set out from Aberdeen in a march towards Covenanter-held Inverness. Montrose united his own forces, intending to bring Hurry to battle. However, on 8 May Hurry joined some of the Covenanting troops from Inverness and turned to attack Montrose, who was camped around the village of Auldearn. Once again Montrose's neglect of basic precautions came near to costing him dear.

That night the Royalists slept unaware of the approaching enemy, and their scouts were only alerted at daybreak on 9 May by the sound of Hurry's musketeers discharging their pieces in order to clear damp powder charges. The Royalists had learnt of their peril in the nick of time, but a desperate battle followed around the village, in which MacColla's defensive action bought time for Montrose to muster the rest of his army and make a series of counter-attacks which eventually caused Hurry to retreat. Both sides had lost several hundred men in a narrow and costly victory for Montrose, whose army was too badly mauled to make an immediate follow-up.

Baillie and the remainder of his army avoided contact until rejoined by Hurry on 20 May, and then Montrose once again slipped away into the wilds of Badenoch. His attempt to stage a breakout into the Southern Lowlands was foiled by a Covenanting force under the Earl of Crawford-Lyndsay. Baillie meanwhile resumed ravaging Gordon lands in the north-east, causing Lord George Gordon to head north to their defence.

Indecisive sparring continued for several weeks, with Montrose's promises of marching to the king's assistance from a subjugated Scotland looking ever more optimistic. At length, on 2 July, he accepted battle with Baillie at Alford. Lord George Gordon, at the head of the Royalist cavalry, burning to avenge the attacks on his clan lands, promised Montrose: 'I shall bring you Baillie by the neck from the midst of his party.' Fighting began with a cavalry action, in which the Royalists gained the upper hand, thanks to the intervention of the Irish infantry of Colonel Thomas Laghtman, who used their swords and dirks to hamstring their opponents' horses. Baillie's foot were then broken in a coordinated assault by Montrose's infantry from the front and his horse in the rear, though some of the fruits of victory were lost when Lord George Gordon was killed during the pursuit.

The death of Lord George, with whom Montrose had a good personal relationship, meant that although his younger brother, Lord Aboyne, assumed command of the Gordons with Montrose, their future support could not be relied upon. The victory also persuaded more Highlanders to join Montrose, but their widespread plundering continued to alienate the nobility and gentry whose support Montrose so much needed.

However, the victory at Alford meant that, although the army of Crawford-Lyndsay was still in the field, Baillie was temporarily out of action, and Montrose, with news of the king's increasingly desperate situation adding urgency, felt that the time had come to move into the Southern Lowlands.

KEY ACTION: KILSYTH, 15 AUGUST 1645

By the time he began, a disgruntled General Baillie was back, having taken over Crawford-Lyndsay's men. He had submitted his resignation, and was in effect serving out his 'notice' until a successor arrived from Ulster, at least according to his own version of events, hindered by the presence of a committee of 'advisers' appointed by the government and headed by Argyll. When Argyll asked him his plans, the sulking Baillie replied 'That direction should come from his Lordship and those of the Committee'. Baillie himself, he said, would offer advice but not give orders. In practice he modified this stance, and when Montrose made a customarily incautious raid on Perth, almost caught him, and did succeed in massacring a number of Royalist camp-followers at Methven Woods.

Montrose was joined at Dunkeld by Aboyne with 400 horse and 800 Gordon foot, and, bypassing Baillie's position at the Bridge of Earn, headed for the Mills of Firth, which he reached on 11 August. Baillie, still bickering with the trouble-some Committee, went in pursuit, and crossed Stirling Bridge on 14 August. The Royalists were now heading towards Glasgow, and late on the 14th Baillie's scouts reported them encamped on high ground near Kilsyth.

Early next day, approaching Montrose's position, Baillie made the decision to leave the main road and cut across country until he reached some 'unpassable ground' where he began to deploy his army. His aim was to threaten Montrose's left flank, for the Royalists had formed up parallel to the road, expecting Baillie to continue his march along it. Viewing the ground, Baillie resolved to continue his attempt to turn the Royalist flank by moving northwards to occupy higher ground around Auchinrivoch.

Initially the Covenanters' movements were concealed by a fold in the ground, but once they were spotted a race began for possession of the higher ground. Baillie had about 3,500 foot, including five regular regiments totalling 2,400 men and just over 1,000 raw Fife levies, together with 360 horse. The Royalists, with about 5,000 foot and 600 horse, for once had the advantage of numbers.

Baillie intended the flank of his march to be screened by a composite battalion of 'commanded' musketeers from his regular regiments, and when these troops left the shelter of the fold in the ground they were the first to be spotted by the Royalists. The battalion commander, a Major Haldane, took upon himself to halt and make a stand around some farm buildings at Auchinvalley. Royalist troops under Ewan Maclean of Treshnish began skirmishing with Haldane, and as more Royalists came up to join in, Baillie realized that he would have to stand and fight. He instructed his cavalry commander, the Earl of Balcarres, to form up on the right of Lauderdale's regular regiment of foot, but when he attempted to deploy the rest of the army Baillie discovered that Colonel Robert Home's Regiment had broken ranks and gone forward to assist Haldane.

At this stage neither Baillie nor Montrose seem to have had much overall control of a situation in which subordinate commanders were acting on their own initiative. By now Home's and Argyll's regular foot, together with Haldane's musketeers, had occupied an enclosure, from which Baillie found 'it was im-possible to bring them of'. His army was now split into three distinct bodies. Baillie himself was with the 1,600 men of Home and his fellow officers. Behind them and to the west were the remaining 800 regular foot under Major-General Holburne, together with about 300 horse under Balcarres. To the left rear of Baillie were the Fife levies under Major General Leslie.

Immediately facing Baillie were about 1,600 mainly Highlander troops led by MacColla, on whom Baillie's musketeers opened 'more fire than I could have wished' at too long a range to be effective. Balcarres now tried to move the Covenanting horse around the Royalist flank to attack their rear, but was countered by a small troop of Montrose's horse under Captain Adjutant Gordon. After a brief tussle, Gordon was forced back to higher ground by superior numbers. At this critical stage, Montrose ordered his remaining horse under the Earl of Airlie to assist the Gordons. Some of their officers 'flatly refused the task of supporting them.' In Wishart's version of events, Montrose saved the day by turning to Airlie and saying: 'You see my Lord, those rash men of ours have plunged into desperate danger, and will soon be cut to pieces unless supported', with more in the same vein, which recalled his recalcitrant horse to their duty. He may well have said something of the sort, though briefer and more to the point, and the upshot was that Airlie and the main force of Royalist horse launched a counter-charge which drove Balcarres back down the hill and out of the battle.

The Royalist cavalry now turned against the right flank of Baillie's foot at the same time as MacColla launched a frontal attack. Baillie watched as 'the rebels leapt over the dyke, and with down heads fell on and broke these regiments {Home, Argyll and Haldane].' Resistance was evidently patchy, for Baillie noted that some of his officers were 'careful to save themselves before the routing of the regiments'. As the rest of his army broke, Baillie attempted to join the Fife levies, 'but before we could come at them, they were in flight', evidently routed by the Gordon foot and the Irish.

After a fairly brief action, the whole Covenanting army collapsed. Unable to rally them, Baillie fled to Stirling. While his regulars seem to have escaped relatively lightly, the fleeing Fife levies were cut down in hundreds. The Royalists may also have suffered significant losses in this triumph of the combination of Montrose's quick-thinking leadership and MacColla's fighting ability. They remained on the battlefield for two days instead of pursuing Baillie and then moved against Glasgow.

Triumph and disaster

For the moment, however, Montrose was effectively master of the field in the Lowlands of Scotland. He occupied Glasgow without a fight, and then, to avoid looting, pulled his men back out of the town. But his triumph rested on very unsure foundations. The nobility, while in some cases sending a younger son to join Montrose, continued to hedge their bets, and although large parts of the country, including Edinburgh, nominally submitted to Montrose, without an army with which to enforce his control, this was merely an illusion of victory.

Far from increasing, Montrose's army was actually dissolving. After disobeying orders, and looting Glasgow anyway, most of the Highlanders went home, while early in September Alistair MacColla, despite being knighted by Montrose, took the bulk of his men off to continue their private campaign in the Western Highlands. At the same time Aboyne, feeling that his services had received in-sufficient appreciation, went home with his Gordons.

Montrose was left with only 500 Irish infantry and 100 cavalry. This was not the first time that he had found himself in a similar situation, and the obvious course of action would have been to pull back north of the Forth until he was able to rebuild his forces. But Montrose knew that the Royalist cause in England was tottering, and that Charles's first attempt to march north to join him had failed. It seemed, illogically from a military point of view, that the only chance lay in Montrose going south to join the king. How Montrose can have imagined that the few hundred seasoned troops he had with him could possibly have made any difference is impossible to comprehend. He seems once more, and this time fatally, to have fallen victim to his own propaganda. Writing that 'it may be sensibly seen as to be the Lord's doing, in making a handful to overthrow multitudes', Montrose may have come to believe that divine support for him would overcome all difficulties, or more prosaically, in the view of Edward Cowan: 'He would have been less than human if his spectacular record had not turned his head.'[18]

His original army largely dispersed, Montrose accepted assurances from the Border magnates Lords Home, Roxburgh and Traquir that they would raise their tenants to join him if he marched south. The King's emissary with Montrose, Sir Robert Spottiswood, informed Charles of the defections from Montrose's army, adding 'All these were great disheartenings to any other but him, whom nothing of this kind can amaze. With the small forces he has presently with him, he is resolved to pursue David Leslie, and not suffer him to grow stronger.' On 7 September, at Galashiels, Montrose was joined by about 1,000 Border horse under the Marquis of Douglas, but there was no sign of the other Border lords, who were said to have deliberately allowed themselves to fall into the hands of the Covenanters. And there were reports that on the previous day, David Leslie had reached Berwick upon Tweed with six regiments of horse and four of foot from the army in England.

The situation was plainly hopeless, and Montrose abandoned his march south and turned west, probably intending to withdraw through Clydesdale back into the hills. On the evening of 12 September, Montrose and his officers quartered in the town of Selkirk, leaving their men in scattered quarters around the village of Philliphaugh to the east. As usual unbeknown to Montrose, the enemy were fast approaching. That night the Covenanters surprised a Royalist outpost in the village of Sunderland to the north of Selkirk, but when a survivor carried the news to Montrose he was dismissed as a victim of a drunken brawl among the Royalist troops.

No attempt was made to put the army on the alert, and when 13 September dawned misty, Montrose remained inactive waiting for visibility to clear. Unseen, Leslie was closing in with about 4,000 horse and dragoons, and at 10am launched his attack. What followed was scarcely a battle. Hearing fighting, Montrose hastily mounted and hurried to the scene, where he found 'all in uproar and confusion'. With most of their officers absent, the raw cavalry were already scattering, although Colonels Laightman and O'Cahan were able to form up about 200 of their Irish infantry in a ditched enclosure. The Covenanters completed the rout of the Royalist horse in about a quarter of an hour, and the Irish foot were overwhelmed in a fierce little action. Other than their commanders, the Irish prisoners, together with a number of camp-followers, were slaughtered.

About half of the Irish foot made off in the mist, and by 19 September, Montrose, who had also escaped, had crossed the Clyde with 200 horse and 250 Irish foot, and was back in the fastnesses of Atholl.

Philliphaugh was not a major military disaster; some of Montrose's victories had cost him more casualties. But in practice it was the end of Montrose's hopes. Heading back to Gordon country with 800 foot and 200 horse, Montrose contrived to quarrel with Lord Lewis Gordon, who had commanded his horse until replaced by the Earl of Crawford.

Without the Gordons, Montrose could do nothing, and Philliphaugh had convinced many that Montrose's rashness made him too dangerous to follow. Huntley eventually agreed to cooperate on his own terms, but the winding down of the war in England allowed more Scottish troops to be brought home to counter the Royalists. Montrose spent the winter and spring on Speyside, trying to build up his forces. By the end of April he had quarrelled again with Huntley, and was besieging Inverness, as usual narrowly escaping destruction when he was surprised by government forces.

It was left to Huntley to strike the last blow of the war by seizing Aberdeen. But three weeks later Montrose and Huntley received the king's orders to disband their forces.

Aftermath

Montrose went into exile in Europe. His military reputation was such that he was offered employment and the title of Marshal of France by Louis XIII, but refused. Deeply angered by the execution of Charles I, Montrose returned to Scotland in 1650 at the head of a small mercenary force. He seems to have recognized it as a forlorn hope, telling the young Charles II: 'I can make no other acknowledgement but with the more alacrity to abandon my life for your interests.' His words proved literally true. To Charles, engaged in his political intrigues with Argyll, Montrose was an expendable pawn useful mainly to pressurize the Covenanting regime into an accommodation, and jettisoned when this was achieved. Once Charles had recognized Argyll's regime as the legitimate government in Scotland, Montrose was doomed. In his last fatal act of carelessness, Montrose's little force was surprised and routed at Carbisdale. Montrose was captured, and taken to Edinburgh, where, displaying superb courage, he was hanged as a traitor.

Montrose remains perhaps the most romantic and tragic figure of the Civil Wars. But as a general he was limited. His habitual carelessness and lack of precautions in the face of the enemy repeatedly brought him close to disaster, and Montrose never appears to have learnt from these experiences. While some of his problems, such as the alienation of support by his employment of Catholic Irish and Highlanders, were unavoidable, his lack of political finesse also cost him dear. Undoubtedly a charismatic figure, Montrose was never able to overcome the problems involved in holding together a disparate force of the sort which he found himself with.

The Scottish Royalists arguably lacked the breadth of support necessary for a rising to be successful in any case. But under Montrose's leadership it was never more than the potentially useful diversion which Charles' English generals saw it to be.

Chapter Thirteen
Conclusion

On March 21 1646, at Stow-on-the-Wold, the last major Royalist field force surrendered to the Parliamentarians. Although it would be many months before the last Cavalier garrison fell, King Charles had lost the First Civil War.

Historians still debate the reasons for the Royalist defeat. Here we are particularly concerned by the part played in it by King Charles and his generals, but it is also important to examine the other factors involved.

From the beginning of hostilities, Parliament had a major advantage as result of its control of London. The capital, with its huge financial and material resources, its port and its reserves of manpower, gave a huge material benefit to whoever held it, as well as affording the Parliamentarian leadership a legitimacy which they would otherwise have lacked. Control of the plentiful resources of south east England, with its large population, gave Parliament a compact and relatively easily defended base of operations.

The king was never so fortunate. The Royalist heartlands of Wales, the north and Cornwall were not only significantly poorer in resources of all kinds, but were spread around the periphery of the kingdom, making the use of men and supplies raised there difficult and uncertain. Parliament controlled more of England's manufacturing resources than the king, and one consequence of this was that the Royalists were initially forced to import the bulk of their munitions from abroad. With the only significant ports under his control being in the north-east and west of England, and the Parliamentarian fleet in virtually undisputed command at sea, difficulties in arming his forces adequately significantly both shaped and hindered the king's operations until the second half of 1643. It was only thereafter, with the capture of additional ports, most important of which was Bristol, with its manufacturing capability, that munitions ceased to be such a major problem for the Royalists.

Another disadvantage for the Royalists, which worsened as the war went on, was not only that most of their territory was poorer in resources than that held by the Parliamentarians, but also that much of it was never securely under their control. While Parliament's south-eastern heartlands were largely inviolate for most of the war, a wide belt of the Royalist west Midlands and south-west England was subject to constant enemy incursions, whether from raiding parties or major invasions by field armies. As a result, the king had to employ a larger proportion of his forces in garrison duty than his opponents in order to maintain his uneasy grip on these areas. The demands and depredations of the opposing armies not only exhausted their resources, and disrupted Royalist attempts to establish a stable and effective local administration, but also led to mounting war-weariness, and eventually active hostility, by the civilian population. Although the Royalists had more success in establishing effective local administration than they are some-times credited with, this remained strongly military in nature, and this characteristic increased as the war went on, until increasingly large numbers of Royalist troops were engaged in 'occupation' duties. After Naseby, with the destruction of the main Royalist field army, the king no longer possessed the mili-tary 'muscle' to enforce his control of the dwindling areas in his nominal possession.

Parliament's greater resources meant that the king's opponents were much better able to sustain a prolonged war than were the Royalists. This advantage made itself increasingly felt as time went on. By the spring of 1645 the Parliamentarians probably had roughly twice as many troops in the field as their opponents, and controlled all but three of the country's major ports and thirty-seven of its fifty largest towns.

From the start of the war, the king's best hope lay in achieving a quick victory before Parliament's resources, and a probable alliance with Scotland, could be fully utilized. In practice this meant that Charles's best chance of victory lay in winning decisively the opening campaign of 1642. Not only did Parliament then have only one significant field army, but the defences of London were weaker, and the Royalist party in the city stronger, than they would be at any other time. The Royalist failure to destroy the Earl of Essex at Edgehill and strike decisively at London before the end of the year were far more serious in their long-term consequences than was generally realized.

As a result, Charles and his generals were forced to make 1643 a year of con-solidation, in which they endeavoured to expand and secure their territorial base of operations and strengthen their armies in preparation for an advance into Parliament's heartlands around London. There has been much debate concerning the existence of a Royalist 'grand strategy' including an alleged three-pronged advance on London by the Oxford Army, the Western forces and Newcastle from the north. It seems most likely that this plan never existed in more than hypothetical form. More probably, the king and his Council of War hoped to reinforce the Oxford Army with as many troops as possible from other areas, and then make an advance in strength on London. Thanks to the stubborn resist-ance of regional Parliamentarian forces and garrisons, and the predominantly local interests of many of his own supporters, the king was never able to put this plan into operation.

The last real chance of a decisive Royalist victory was in August and September of 1643. A military conquest of London was still beyond the king's resources. But there was a real possibility, if the Royalists, following a summer of almost broken success, crowned their efforts with the capture of Gloucester and defeated Essex's army, temporarily the only effective major Parliamentarian field force, that enemy will to fight on might have collapsed.

His failure at Gloucester and the First Battle of Newbury can be seen in retrospect as costing Charles the war. Henceforward, particularly after the intervention of the Scots on Parliament's side, the Royalists could only realistically hope to prolong the fight as long as possible against mounting odds in the hope that either the unlikely prospect of foreign intervention on his behalf, or dissensions among his opponents, might afford the chance of reaching a compromise peace. Unfortunately, neither Charles nor most of his counsellors ever seem to have grasped this uncomfortable reality, even after the crushing defeat of Marston Moor cost them the north of England and tipped the scales still further against them.

By early 1644 the Royalists had been compelled to adopt a basically defensive strategy. This was not, as claimed by some contemporary and later analysts, the result of military defeats such as Cheriton, but was brought about by the increasing disparity between the resources of the opposing sides. Even before Marston Moor, Royalist commanders were increasingly being forced to react to ever more frequent enemy threats, rather than initiate offensive operations of their own. By a mixture of good luck, some excellent generalship, and enemy mistakes, the Royalists were able to survive the spring and summer crisis of 1644. But by the time Prince Rupert assumed command of the Royalist forces that autumn, nothing but a near-miracle was likely to save the king's cause. Even Rupert's professed hope of achieving a compromise peace through military stalemate was optimistic, and the battle of Naseby would prove that, whatever his belief in divine support, God was not fighting for King Charles.

This then, was the background against which the Royalist generals should be assessed. So far as the high command in the vital central 'Oxford' theatre is concerned, the two sides were fairly equally matched until the end of 1644. King Charles and Forth, while not particularly bold or imaginative, were of similar ability to Parliament's Earl of Essex, and more than held their own against Sir William Waller and the Earl of Manchester when those commanders appeared in the area. Prince Rupert, and his effective successor, Lord Wilmot and, later, George Goring, proved superior cavalry commanders to any of their Parliamentarian counterparts during the same period. The Major Generals of Foot, Jacob Astley and Phillip Skippon, were both highly competent and experienced professional soldiers who were closely matched during their several encounters.

Elsewhere, a similar pattern was evident. In the north there was little to chose in ability between Newcastle and Parliament's senior commander, Ferdinando, Lord Fairfax. Both came to the war with little previous experience, and both had a tendency towards over-caution and unimaginative leadership. Each relied upon more experienced or dynamic subordinates. In Fairfax's case, his son, Thomas, proved the driving force of the Parliamentarian war effort in Yorkshire. Newcastle was somewhat less fortunate, for among his senior commanders, only George Goring, for a brief period until his capture, displayed similar qualities. It was partly for this reason, as well as the distractions caused to Newcastle by the need to protect the queen and her munitions supplies, that the Fairfaxes were able to hold out for so long, until eventually overcome by Newcastle's numerical superiority rather than better generalship.

The Royalists indeed never gained all the advantages they might have expected from their overall dominance in the north. It is possible that a more dynamic and confident commander than Newcastle might have posed a serious threat to Parliament's Eastern Association during 1643, although if Hull had remained in enemy hands it is likely that any large-scale operations further south by the northern Royalists would have been severely hindered. And an earlier Royalist victory in the north might have resulted in the Scots intervening sooner.

The real causes of Royalist failure in the north resulted, as elsewhere, from their having insufficient resources to meet, in 1644, converging threats from several directions. Newcastle must of course, along with Prince Rupert and to a lesser extent Charles himself, bear the principal responsibility for the ultimate disaster at Marston Moor, which was as much a failure in personal relations as in generalship.

In the other principal theatre of war, south-west England, many of the generals of each side proved a close match in ability during the earlier part of the war. In the Severn Valley neither Prince Maurice nor Sir William Waller were able to gain a decisive upper hand. In Cornwall and Devon, the Royalist Western Army headed by Sir Ralph Hopton, aided by Cornish Royalist gentry, eventually secured Cornwall for the king, but had little real success east of the Tamar. Parliament's Sir William Waller, on the several occasions they met, proved equal to Hopton.

By late 1643, the Royalists were losing the impetus of the wave of successes which had been theirs for much of the year. By now the 'grandees' who had made up most of Charles's initial group of regional commanders were being replaced by in some cases less nobly-born generals. However this was not an unqualified success. Men like Rupert, Maurice, Sir Richard Grenville, and Charles Gerard in South Wales might have a better record as soldiers, but they lacked the knowledge of and respect for the communities in which they operated. Increased military effectiveness, when it was achieved, was all too often gained at the cost of a deterioration in relations with the civilian population, as professional soldiers were allowed to ride rough-shod over them.

By the end of 1644 the Royalist forces were in urgent need of the same kind of root and branch reform which was taking place in the Parliamentarian armies. But instead, following the appointment of Prince Rupert to command the king's forces, the weaknesses already apparent worsened rapidly. Much of the fault lay with Charles himself. His decision to set up a separate Council of the West led to near-chaos in the conduct of military affairs in that region, with confusion regarding the areas of authority of the already top-heavy Royalist command structure there, and individual generals, like Grenville, Sir John Berkeley and Goring, quarrelling among themselves and exploiting the situation to gain more independence from both king and the Council.

Even if Rupert had been suited in other ways for the command which he had been given, the exclusion from his direct control of such a large part of the king's dwindling territory and armies struck what would prove to be a fatal blow at his slim chances of success. At a time when the Royalists needed to concentrate every available soldier if they were to overcome their numerical inferiority and meet Parliament's New Model Army with some prospect of success, nearly half of the king's best remaining soldiers were out of Rupert's command.

The campaigns of 1645 saw Parliament's military machine operating with greater efficiency than ever before. Its directing body, the Committee of Both Kingdoms, having at last found in Sir Thomas Fairfax a commander who was both highly competent and trustworthy, gave him a largely free hand, while regional commanders such as Sir William Brereton in the north-west and Sydenham Poyntz in Yorkshire were both competent and ready to cooperate when instructions or suggestions were sent to them.

On the Royalist side the picture was very different. While the Parliamentarians, belatedly partially recognizing the importance of ability over birth, had gradually brought to the fore men of relatively humble backgrounds, such as Fairfax and Cromwell, on the king's side promotion by merit remained slow and uncertain. For this reason the campaign of 1645 saw the Parliamentarians for the first time with a clear advantage in the quality of their senior generals. It was not that the king lacked able officers, but men such as that excellent cavalry commander, Sir Charles Lucas, were left in the obscurity of minor regional commands, or like George Goring, their talents wasted by being employed in the wrong situations. All too often these appointments were governed by jealousy or Court intrigue rather than for sound military reasons. This culminated in the almost ludicrous situation of the Oxford Army, which had been famed in the earlier years of the war for the quality of its horse, going into the Naseby campaign without a senior cavalry commander. Goring, still nominally General of Horse, had been allowed by Rupert, out of jealousy, to remain, for the most inadequate of reasons, in semi-mutinous inactivity in the west.

As a result, the king's army went into its last major battle with all and more of the weaknesses which had been apparent at its first major engagement at Edgehill in 1642. It still had Charles as an ineffectual Captain General, unable to control or reconcile his quarrelling councillors and commanders. It had lost its competent if unspectacular Lord General, Forth, and replaced him with the near-paranoid and embittered Rupert, who plainly lacked the necessary talents for the post. His failure to appoint a commander for his cavalry forced Rupert to take that role himself, thus abandoning any hope of exercising overall control of the battle. Only the elderly Major General of Foot, Jacob Astley, remained to exercise the competent unspectacular leadership which he had displayed throughout the war. And that would not be enough.

Man for man, the king's generals were as competent and able as their Parliamentarian opponents. The failure to control them, and utilize their talents to the full, lay at a higher level. Two men, more than any others, must share the blame for the Royalist defeat. It is Prince Rupert, and most of all King Charles, on whom the greatest responsibility for defeat rests.

Notes on the text

Chapter 2

1 Charles Carlton, *Charles I,* London, 1991, p.245.
2 S.R. Gardiner, *The Great Civil War,* London, 1893, I, p.41.
3 See pp.30, 152.
4 Sir Edward Walker, *Historical Discourses,* London 1705, p.
5 Clarendon, *History of the Rebellion,* Ed. W. Macray, Oxford, 1884, VII, 82.
6 Clarendon, VII, 284.
7 *Ibid,* VIII, 12
8 *Ibid,* VIII, 17.
9 *Ibid,* VII, 27.
10 See pp.185–6.
11 Walker, *op. cit,* p.16
12 Clarendon, VIII, 47.
13 Richard Symonds, *Diary* (Ed. C.E. Long), Campden Society, 1859, p.8
14 Quoted Peter Young, *Marston Moor, 1644,* Kineton, 1971, p.87.
15 Walker, p.25
16 See p.187.
17 Eliot Warburton, *Memoirs of Prince Rupert and the Cavaliers,* London, 1849, Vol II, p.32
18 Clarendon, VIII, 94
19 Symonds, p.63.
20 *Ibid,* pp.64–5.
21 Clarendon, VIII, 168.
22 *Ibid,* IX, 40–1.
23 *Ibid,* IX, 3.

Chapter 3

1 Richard Ollard, *The War Without an Enemy,* pp.68–9
2 Richard Holmes and Peter Young, *The English Civil War,* London, 1974, p.335
3 Frank Kitson, *Prince Rupert: Portrait of a Soldier,* London, 1994, p.13
4 B.L. Harleian MS, 7379, f.75b
5 Rupert *Diary,* quoted Patrick Morrah, *Rupert of the Rhine,* London, 1971, p.80

6 Quoted Peter Young, *Edgehill 1642,* Kineton, 1967, pp.269–70
7 Quoted Richard Brezezinski, *The Army of Gustavus Adolphus: I Cavalry,* Oxford, 1993, p.23
8 Warburton, II, p.82
9 Sir Philip Warwick, *Memoirs of the Reign of King Charles I,* 17, pp.227–8
10 Morrah, *op.cit.,* p.96
11 Warburton, II, p.106
12 *Ibid.*
13 *His Highness Prince Rupert's Late Beating Up of the Rebel Quarters . . .* Oxford, 1643, p.7
14 See p.88.
15 Thomas Carte, *Life of Ormonde,* V, pp.520–1
16 See pp.128–9.
17 *Ibid,* pp.337–8
18 *Mercurius Aulicus,* 23 March 16434, p.899
19 *Ibid*
20 See John Barratt, *Cavaliers,* Stroud, 2000, p.124.
21 See p.17.
22 Carte, *Ormonde,* V, p.151
23 See pp.172–5.
24 See pp.132–3.
25 Warburton, III, p.8
26 Warburton, III, p.23
27 *Ibid,* p.28
28 Warburton, II, p.148 (wrongly assigned there to 1644)
29 *Ibid,* III, p.100
30 Warburton, III, pp.119–21

Chapter 4

1 Robert Markham, *Decades of War,* p.170.
2 Clarendon, *Great Rebellion,* II, p.161.
3 Peter Young and Richard Holmes, *The English Civil War,* p.337.
4 Ronald Hutton, *The Royalist War Effort,* Chapter 18.
5 Warburton, *op. cit.,* II, p.198.
6 P.R.O. S.P. 16/463/4.

7 Clarendon, VII, 83.
8 Quoted Phillipp Eliot-Wright, *English Civil War,* London, 199, p.94.
9 Clarendon, II, 293.
10 See p.28.
11 H.M.C. *Ormonde MS* N.S. II, p.379.
12 Quoted Peter Young, *Edgehill,* p.163.
13 Clarendon, II, 363.
14 John Gwynne, *Military Memoirs* (Ed. Norman Tucker), London, 1967, p.52.
15 *Mercurius Aulicus,* 2 September 1643, p.486.
16 *Ibid* 31 May 1644, p.1002.
17 Edward Walker, *Historical Discourses,* 17075, p.63.
18 *Kingdom's Intelligencer,* 6 May 1645.
19 Sir Henry Slingsby, *Diary* (Ed. D. Parsons), Edinburgh, 1803, pp.144-5.
20 Glenn Foard, *Naseby: the Decisive Battle,* Whitstable, 1998, p.205.
21 *Ibid.*
22 Sprigge, *Anglia Rediviva,* 1647, p.37.
23 Rushworth p.716.
24 Walker, p.
25 Foard, p.260.
26 *Ibid,* pp.261-4.
27 William Bariffe pp.82-4.
28 Rushworth, p.716.
29 *Kingdom's Weekly Intelligencer,* 10-17 June 1645.
30 Rushworth, p.717.
31 Quoted Foard, p.273.
32 Quoted Foard, p.286.
33 Rushworth, p.718.
34 Clarendon, IX, 161.
35 Walker, p.146.
36 F.A. Hyett, *The Last Battle of the First Civil War* in *Transactions of the Bristol and Gloucestershire Archaelogical Society,* 1898.

Chapter 5

1 Clarendon, *History* VII, 16.
2 Burne and Young, *The Great Civil War,* p.234.
3 Ronald Hutton, *The Royalist War Effort,* especially Chapter Sixteen.
4 Warburton, *op. cit.,* I, p.450.
5 Richard Atkyns, *Memoirs* (Ed. Peter Young), London, 1967, p.21.
6 *Ibid.*
7 Atkyns, *op. cit.,* p.12.
8 *Ibid,* p.15.
9 *Ibid,* p.16.

10 *Ibid,* p.22.
11 *Ibid,* p.23.
12 Clarendon, VII 144.
13 *Ibid,* VII, 155.
14 *Ibid,* 156.
15 Warburton, II, p.307.
16 Drake, p.63.
17 Warburton, III, p.54.
18 *Ibid,* p.59.
19 *Perfect Occurrences,* 14-21 February 1645, (British Library, E.258 (26).

Chapter 6

1 *Bellum Civile,* (Ed. C. Chadwick-Healey,) Bristol, 1902.
2 Burne and Young, *The Great Civil War,* p.230.
3 F.T.R. Edgar, *Sir Ralph Hopton,* Oxford, 1968, p. 203.
4 Clarendon, *op. cit.,* VII, 401.
5 *Ibid,* VI, 296.
6 Walker, *Historical Discourses,* p.50.
7 John Stucley, *Sir Bevil Grenville and his Times,* Chichester, 1983, p.122.
8 Quoted Edgar, p. 60.
9 Hopton, *Bellum Civilie,* p.25.
10 *Ibid,* pp. 27-8.
11 Lloyd, *Memoirs of Historical Personages,* London, 1665, p.343.
12 Atkyns, *op. cit.,* p.23.
13 Hopton, p.30.
14 Quoted Edgar, pp.70-1.
15 Hopton, pp.36-7.
16 *Ibid,* p.43
17 Mary Coate, *Cornwall in the Great Civil War,* p.75.
18 Hopton, p.51.
19 Coate, p.77.
20 Hopton, p. 52.
21 Atkyns, p.33.
22 Walter Slingsby's *Relation,* in Hopton, *op. cit.,* p.97.
23 Quoted Edgar, pp.131-2.
24 Hopton, pp.58-9.
25 Edgar, p.135.
26 Hopton, p.63.
27 *Ibid.* p.62-5.
28 *Ibid,* p.65.
29 Quoted Edgar, p.150.
30 Hopton, p.68.
31 B.L. *Additional MS,* 18980, f.160.
32 C.S.P.D. 1644-45, p.511.
33 Clarendon, XI, 64
34 *Ibid.*

35 Clarendon, XI, 36.
36 Joshua Sprigge, *Anglia Rediviva*, 1647, pp.205–6.
37 *Ibid*, pp.209–10.
38 Clarendon, IX, 84.
39 Quoted Edgar, p.198.
40 *D.N.B.*
41 Clarendon, VIII, 555.

Chapter 7
1 Quoted Mark Bence-Jones, *The Cavaliers*, London 1976, p.88.
2 Clarendon, *Great Rebellion*, VIII, 169.
3 *Ibid.*
4 Richard Bulstrode, *History*, p.134.
5 Peter Young and Wilf Emberton, *The Cavalier Army*, London, 1974, p.98.
6 Peter Young and Richard Holmes, *English Civil War*, p.337.
7 Bence-Jones, *op. cit.*, p.87.
8 C.H. Wilkinson (Ed.) *Poems of Richard Lovelace*, London, 1930, pp.81–2.
9 Clarendon, II, 314–5.
10 Francis Banks (Ed.) *A Royalist Notebook*, London, 1936, p.105.
11 Clarendon
12 *Ibid.* II, 315.
13 *Mercurius Aulicus*, 4 April 1643, p.174.
14 Quoted Warburton, *op. cit*, II, pp181–2.
15 Wakefield Library, 942.815 Wak.W.
16 G. Tyas, *The Battles of Wakefield*, Bradford, 1854, p.36.
17 Sir Thomas Fairfax, *Short Memorials . . .* p.12.
18 *Mercurius Aulicus*, 28 May 1643, p.283.
19 C.S.P.D. 1644, p.192.
20 *Ibid*, f.200.
21 Sir Hugh Cholmley *Account of the Battle near York*, in *English Historical Review*, V, 1898, p. 348.
22 Lionel Watson's *Account*, quoted in Peter Young, *Marston Moor 1644*, p.230.
23 Warburton, II, p.475.
24 *Ibid.*III, pp.2–3.
25 *Ibid*, III, pp.16–17.
26 Walker, *Historical Discourses*, p.47.
27 Clarendon, VIII, 116.
28 Richard Symonds, *Diary*, p.64.
29 *Ibid*, p.65.
30 Walker, p.106.
31 Symonds, p.141.
32 *Mercurius Aulicus*, 28 October 1644, pp.1236–7.
33 Clarendon, VIII, 169.

34 B.L. *Add MS*, 18981, f.346.
35 Warburton, III, p.
36 *Ibid*, p.52.
37 Clarendon, IX, 9.
38 Warburton, III, p/73.
39 *Mercurius Aulicus*, 11 April 1645, p.1547.
40 Bulstrode, p.134.
41 Sandford, p.620.
42 Bod. Lib. *Clarendon MS* 1856.
43 *Mercurius Aulicus*, 12 April, p.1541.
44 Bulstrode, p.120.
45 *Ibid*, p.121.
46 *Clarendon MS* 1868.
47 Clarendon, IX, 20.
48 *Ibid*, IX, 21.
49 *Ibid*, IX, 28.
50 Joshua Sprigge, *Anglia Rediviva*, 1647, p.16.
51 *Mercurius Aulicus*, 8 May 1645, pp.1580–1.
52 Clarendon, IX, 28.
53 *Ibid*, IX, 30.
54 *Ibid*, IX, 31.
55 B.L. *Add MS* 18982, f.59.
56 C.S.P.D. 1644–45, pp. 506–7.
57 H.M.C. *Portland MS* I, p.198.
58 Bod. Lib. *Clarendon MS*, 1883.
59 *Ibid*, 1904.
60 Bod. Lib. *Clarendon MS* 1931.
61 *Ibid*, IX, 101.
62 *Ibid*, IX, 102.

Chapter 8
1 Geoffrey Ridsdell Smith, *Leaders of the Civil Wars 1642–1648*,, p.22.
2 Peter Young, *Marston Moor 1644*, Kineton, 1967, pp.75–6.
3 R.N. Dore, *Letter Books of Sir William Brereton*, Lancashire and Cheshire Record Society, vol. 128, 1990, p.586.
4 Stuart Reid, *All the King's Armies*, p. 150–1.
5 Peter Newman, *Biographical Dictionary of Royalist Officers*, item 230.
6 Clarendon, *Great Rebellion*, II, 161.
7 *Ibid*, II, 248.
8 Eliot Warburton, *op. cit*, vol II, p.526.
9 B.L. T.T.E. 117.11.
10 Bulstrode Whitlocke, *Memoirs*, p.65.
11 *Mercurius Aulicus*, 1 January 1643, pp. 1–2.
12 Peter Young, (ed) *Sir john Byron's Relation to the Secretary of State of the Last Western Action between the Lord Wilmot and Sir William Waller* in *Journal of the Society for Army Historical Research*, vol. XXXI, No. 127, 1953, p.23.

13 Bodleian Library, *Clarendon MS 1738.*
14 *Ibid.*
15 *Ibid.*
16 *Ibid.*
17 see Ian Ryder, *An English Army for Ireland*, Southend-on-Sea, 1987, *passim.*
18 Arthur Trevor to Ormonde, 21 November 1643, quoted in Thomas Carte, *Ormonde,*, Vol.V, p.52.
19 *Ibid*, p.52
20 John Barratt, *Great Siege of Chester*, Stroud, 2003, p.54
21 *Ibid*
22 J. Hall (Ed.), *Memorials of the Civil War in Cheshire and the Adjacent Counties*, Record office of Lancashire and Cheshire, vol. 9, 1889, pp.94–6.
23 J.R. Phillips, *Memoirs of the Civil War in Wales and the Marches*, London, 1874, Vol.II, pp.116–7.
24 *Mercurius Civicus*, quoted Philips, *op. cit.* I, p.189.
25 Major Connock, however, in 1654, would be tried at Chester for murder, found guilty, and executed.
26 John Lewis (Ed.), *Your Most Humble and Obliged Servant: Ten Secluded Letters of the Lord Byron*, Newtown, 1995, p.2.
27 John Barratt, *The Battle of Nantwich*, Bristol, 1994.
28 For Nantwich see Barratt, *op. cit;* John Lowe, *The Campaign of the Irish-Royalist Army in Cheshire, November 1643–January 1644*, in *Transactions of the Historic Society of Lancashire and Cheshire*, vol.111, 1959.
29 Quoted in S.R. Gardiner, *Great Civil War*, vol.I. p.296.
30 B.L. *Harleian MS* 2125, f.320.
31 Lewis, *op. cit.*, pp.5–6.
32 Bod. Lib. *Carte MS* 12, f.43.
33 J.S. Clarke (ed) *Life of James II*, London, 1816, Vol. I, p.22.
34 Quoted Peter Young, *Marston Moor, op. cit*, p.214.
35 Bod.Lib. *Carte MS* 12, f.43
36 Philips, *op. cit.*, Vol. II, p.213.
37 Thomas Carte, *Collection of Letters*, London, 1739, I, p.67.
38 *C.S.P.D. 1645–7*, p.457.
39 John Byron, *Account of the Siege of Chester* in *Cheshire Sheaf*, 1971, p.7.
40 see Barratt, *Great Siege of Chester*, pp.84–6.
41 Byron, *Account*, p.8

42 Randle Holmes, *Journal*, quoted Barratt, *Great Siege . . .*, p.60.
43 Byron, *op. cit*, p.8.
44 *Ibid.*
45 *Ibid*, pp.14–5.
46 *Ibid*.p.17.
47 Dore, (Ed.) *Letterbooks*, II, item 928.
48 Byron, *op. cit*, p.20.
49 William Cower, *Account of the Siege of Chester*, 1764, C.C.R.O. DCC 26.
50 Byron, p.21.
51 *Ibid.*
52 Bod.Lib. *Clarendon MS* . 31; reprinted in *JSAHR* vol. XLIX, no 199, 1971.

Chapter 9
1 'Rogue'
2 R. MacGillivray, *Restoration Historians and the English Civil War*, the Hague, 1974, p.216.
3 Roger Granville, *The King's General in the West*, London, 1908., p.v.
4 Amos C. Miller, *Sir Richard Grenville of the English Civil War*, London, 1979, p.164.
5 *Ibid*, p.163.
6 Mary Coate, *Cornwall in the Great Civil War*, Oxford, 1933, p.131.
7 Peter Young and Wilfred Emberton, *The Cavalier Army*, London, 1974, p.104.
8 Mark Stoyle, *The Last Refuge of a Scoundrel: Sir Richard Grenville and Cornish Particularism, 1644–46*, in *West Britons: Cornish Identities and the Early Modern British State*, Exeter, 2002, p.92.
9 Clarendon, *History*, VIII, 143.
10 B.L. *Add. MS* 18982, f.32.
11 Clarendon, *History*, VI, 244.
12 Clarendon, *op. cit*, VIII, 134.
13 *Ibid.*
14 *Ibid*, 135.
15 *Ibid*, 136.
16 *Ibid.*
17 Miller, *op. cit*, pp.42–3.
18 *Carte MS* III, f.124.
19 Clarendon, *op. cit.*, VIII, 137.
20 John T. Gilbert (ed) *A Contemporary History of Affairs in Ireland*, London, 1879, I, p.600.
21 Thomas Carte, *Ormonde Papers*, III, 59–63.
22 See Charles Carlton, *Going to the Wars*, London, 1992, pp. 34–6.
23 Miller, pp.61–2.

24 *Carte MS* III, f.126.
25 quoted Miller, p.65.
26 *Perfect Diurnal*, 20 December 1643 (BL. 252[12]).
27 Clarendon, VIII, 138.
28 John Rushworth, *Historical Collections*, V, 23.
29 *Mercurius Brittanicus*, 20 March 1644.
30 Clarendon, IX, 55.
31 Clarendon, VIII, 141. The Parliamentarian version was that two men were captured. One was forced to hang his comrade, then in turn hanged by Grenville's men.
32 *Continuation of a True Narrative of the Most Observable Passages at Plymouth*, London, 1644.
33 *Ibid.*
34 *Perfect Occurrences*, 5 June 1644, B.L. E 254(6).
35 *Mercurius Brittanicus*, 5 August 1644 B.L. Burney 19.
36 *Scots Dove* 9 August 1644, B.L. E.6 (12).
37 Sir Edward Walker, *Historical Discourses*, London, 1705, p.49.
38 quoted Miller, p.85.
39 Walker, *op. cit.*
40 *Ibid*, p.59.
41 *Clarendon*, VIII, 133.
42 Grenville in his highly unreliable *Narrative of the Affairs of the West* (*Clarendon MS* XXVII, f.76) claimed the lower figure.
43 Clarendon, IX 134.
44 Mark Stoyle, *Sir Richard Grenville's Creatures: the New Cornish Tertia 1644–46*, in *Cornish Studies, 4*.
45 Miller, p.55.
46 *Mercurius Aulicus* 16 October 1644.
47 B.L. Add.MS 18981 f.340.
48 Joseph Jane, *History*, ff.154–5.
49 Clarendon, IX, 32.
50 Granville, p.75.
51 Stoyle, *Last Refuge*, pp.93–4.
52 T.W.Webb (Ed.), *Military Memoirs of Colonel John Birch*, Camden Society, N.S. 1873, pp.14–5.
53 Bod.Lib. *Tanner MS* 286, f.103.
54 Quoted Miller, p.101.
55 See John Barratt, *A Drubbing for Skellum: Sir Richard Grenville's Attack on Plymouth, 1645*, in *English Civil War Times*, No.55, pp.23–6.
56 Grenville, *Narrative*, ff.77–8.
57 Clarendon, IX, 12.

58 SP/16/507, f.23
59 *Scots Dove*, 11 April 1645, B.L. E.277 (15).
60 *Clarendon MS* XXV, f.6.
61 Clarendon, *History, IX, 65.*
62 Stoyle, *Last Refuge, passim.*
63 *Clarendon MS* XVII f.310.
64 *Modern Intelligencer* 23 April 1646.

Chapter 10

1 Sir Philip Warwick, *Memoirs of the Reign of King Charles I.*
2 Clarendon, *History*, VIII, 85.
3 Margaret, Duchess of Newcastle, *Memoirs of the Duke of Newcastle*, (ed. C. H. Firth)., London, 1908.
4 *Diary*, 18 March 1668.
5 Burne and Young, *Great Civil War*, p.181.
6 Austin Woolrych, *Battles of the English Civil War*, London, 1961.
7 Morrah, *Prince Rupert*, p.107.
8 Stuart Reid, *All the King's Armies*, Staplehurst, 1998, Chapter IX; Peter Newman, *The Royalist Armies in the North of England*, unpublished Phd thesis, University of York, 1963, *passim.*
9 Clarendon, VIII, 82.
10 Firth (ed), *Life*, p.13; Reid, p.77
11 Ellis, *Original Letters . . .*, London, 1830, I. iii, p.291.
12 Stuart Reid (ed) *Declaration of the Earl of Newcastle 1642*, Southend-on-Sea, 1983.
13 Firth, p.190.
14 *Ibid*, p.191.
15 Sir James Turner, *Memoirs* (Ed. J. Thomson, Edinburgh, 1829, p.45.
16 Firth, p.x.
17 Firth, pp.22–3.
18 Sir Henry Slingsby *Diary* D.Parsons (Ed.) 1803, p.95.
19 Firth, pp.23–4.
20 Sir Thomas Fairfax, *Short Memorials*, p.22.
21 M.A.E. Green (ed) *Letters of Queen Henrietta Maria*, London, 1857, p.225.
22 Warwick, p.265.
23 *Ibid*, p.245.
24 Reid, *op,. cit*, p.94, n.17.
25 Warburton, *Memorials*, II, p.368.
26 Firth, p.34.
27 Warburton, II, p.481.
28 Firth, p.201–2
29 Warburton, *op. cit.*, p.397.
30 *Ibid*, p.399.

31 Mark Napier, *Memorials of Montrose,* Edinburgh, 1859, ii, p.124.
32 Firth, p.29.
33 Peter Wenham, *Great and Close Siege of York,* Kineton, 1971, p.16.
34 *Pythouse Papers,* p.19
35 Sir Hugh Cholmley, *Memorials Touching the Battle of York,* in *English Historical Review,* V, 1898, p.347.
36 *Rupert 'Diary",* quoted Peter Young, *Marston Moor,* Kineton, 1970, p.214.
37 Cholmley, p.348.
38 *Ibid.*
39 *Ibid.*
40 See p.
41 Firth, pp.38–9.
42 Cholmley, p.348.
43 Firth, *op. cit.*
44 *Ibid.*
45 *Ibid,* pp.40–1.
46 Cholmley, p.350.
47 *Diary,* quoted Young, p.214.
48 Clarendon, VIII, 82.

Chapter 11

1 See p.
2 Clarendon, VIII, 30.
3 G. Ridsdill Smith and M. Toynbee, *Leaders of the Civil Wars,* Kineton, 1977, p.182.
4 H.M.C. *Middleton MS,* p.193.
5 John Cruso, *Militarie Instructions for the Cavalerie,* 1635, p.7.
6 Peter Newman, *Biographical Dictionary* . . . item 1585.
7 David Eddershaw, *Civil War in Oxfordshire,* Stroud, 1995, p.87.
8 Peter Young, *Edgehill 1642,* Kineton, 1967.
9 Warburton, II, p.74
10 Clarendon, VIII, 101
11 Atkyns, p.
12 *Relation, op.cit.*
13 Atkyns, p.26.
14 Warburton, II, p.273.
15 Clarendon, VIII, 30.
16 *Ibid,* 31.
17 Sir Edward Walker, *Historical Discourses,* p.16.
18 Ivor and Eileen Carr, *Battle of Tipton Green,* in *English Civil War Notes and Queries,* 31, pp.2–5.

19 Warburton, II, p.415.
20 *Ibid,* p.416.
21 Clarendon, VIII, 61.
22 *Ibid,* VIII, 62.
23 Quoted Peter Young and Margaret Toynbee, *Cropredy Bridge,* Kineton, 1970, p.129.
24 29 June 1644, p.1501.
25 Clarendon, VIII, 95.
26 *Ibid,* VIII, 96.
27 *Ibid.*
28 *Ibid.*
29 *Ibid.*
30 Warburton, III, p17.
31 Clarendon, *op. cit.*
32 Richard Symonds, Diary (Ed.) C. E. Long, Camden Society, 1859, p.109–10.
33 Clarendon, *op. cit.*
34 Richard Ollard, *The Escape of Charles II,* London, 1986, p.30.
35 Clarendon, XIV, 135.

Chapter 12

1 Bence-Jones, *Cavaliers,* p.140.
2 John Buchan, *Montrose,* London, 1936, p.334.
3 Sir John Fortescue, *History of the British Army,* I, p.228.
4 C.V. Wedgwood, *The King's War,* London, 1957, p.364.
5 Stuart Reid, *The Campaigns of Montrose,* Edinburgh, 1990.
6 Buchan, p.332.
7 Patrick Gordon of Ruthven, *Britaines Distemper,* pp 6–8.
8 Bishop Burnet, *History of Own Times,* London, 1724, I, p.30.
9 Edward J. Cowan, *Montrose:For Covenant and King,* London, 1975, p.155.
10 Quoted *Ibid,* p.156.
11 Gordon of Ruthven, *Ibid.*
12 Cowan, p.168.
13 Wishart, p.77.
14 Mark Napier, *Memorials of Montrose,* II, pp.175–6.
15 Gordon of Ruthven, p.100.
16 Napier, pp.175–9.
17 Gardiner, *Great Civil War,* II, p.160.
18 Cowan, p.229

Bibliography

Manuscript Sources

Bodleian Library
Carte MSS (papers of 1st Duke of Ormonde)
Clarendon MSS, 1738 (Civil War papers of 1st Earl of Clarendon)
Firth MSS (transcripts mainly of Prince Rupert's correspondence collected by C.H. Firth),
    XXVII (Sir Richard Grenville's Narrative)

British Library (BL)
Additional MSS, 18990–93 (Letters to Prince Rupert. Some are transcribed, not always fully
    or accurately, in Eliot Warburton, *Memoirs of Prince Rupert and the Cavaliers*, London,
    1849)
Harleian MS, 2125

Historical Manuscripts Commission (HMC)
Portland MSS I

Printed Sources

Primary Sources
Anon (Bernard de Gomme?) *His Highnesse Prince Rupert's Late Beating up of the Rebel's
    Quarters and Victory at Chalgrove Field,* Oxford, 1643
Anon, *Prince Rupert's Burning Love for England,* London, 1643
Anon, *A True and Fuller Relation of the Battell Fought at Stow in the Wold, March 21 1646,*
    London, 1646
Atkyns, Richard, *The Vindication of Richard Atkyns,* in Peter Young (ed), *Military Memoirs:
    the Civil War,*London, 1967
Banks, Francis (Ed.), *A Royalist Notebook,* London, 1936
Barratt, John (Ed.) *A Royalist Account of the Relief of Pontefract,* in *Journal of the Society for
    Army Historical Research,* vol.XLVI, 1973
Barriffe, William, *Militarie Discipline: or the younge artillerieman,* London, 1635
Bulstrode, Sir Richard, *Memoirs,* London, 1721
Byron, Lord John, *Account of the Siege of Chester,* in *Cheshire Sheaf,* 4th series, No.6, 1971
Calendar of State Papers: Domestic, 1641–7
Carte, Thomas, *History of the Life of James, First Duke of Ormonde,* 6 vols, Oxford, 1853
————*Original Letters,* 2 vols, London, 1739
Carr, Ivor and Eileen, *Battle of Tipton Green,* in *English Civil War Notes and Queries,* No.31

Cholmley, Sir Hugh, *Memoirs*, (Ed. C.H. Firth), in *English Historical Review*, V, 1890

Clarendon, Edward 1st Earl of, *History of the Great Rebellion*, (Ed. W.D. Macray), 6 vols, Oxford, 1888

Continuation of the Most Observable Passages at Plymouth, London, 1644

Corbet, John, *Military Government of Gloucester*, London, 1647

Cruso, John, *Militarie Instructions for the Cavall'rie*, London, 1632

Day, W.A., *The Pythouse Papers*, London, 1879

Dore, R.N. (Ed.) *The Letterbooks of Sir William Brereton*, 2 vols, Record Society of Lancashire and Cheshire, Vols 123 and 128, 1983–4 and 1990

Drake, Nathan, *Sieges of Pontefract* (Ed. Richard Holmes), Leeds, 1887

Fairfax, Sir Thomas, *A Brief Memorial of the Northern Actions in which I was Engaged*, London 1985 edn.

Firth, C.H. (Ed.), *Life of William Cavendish, Duke of Newcastle by Margaret, Duchess of Newcastle*, London, 1886

Green, M.A.E., *Letters of Queen Henrietta Maria*, London, 1857

Gwynn, John, *Military Memoirs of the Civil War, being the Military Memoirs of John Gwynn*, Edinburgh, 1822

Hopton, Lord Ralph, *Bellum Civile*, (Ed. C.E.H. Chadwyck-Healey), *Transactions of the Somerset Record Society*, vol.18, 1902

Kingdom's Weekly Intelligencer, 1643–45

Lewis, John (Ed.), *May It Please Your Highness*, Newtown, 1996 (letters to Prince Rupert, mainly of 1644)

———*Your Most Humble and Most Obliged Servant: Ten Secluded Letters of the Lord Byron*, Newtown, 1995

Lloyd, David, *Memoirs of the Lives, Actions etc of those Excellent Personages*, London, 1668

Malbon, Thomas, *Memorials of the Civil War in Cheshire*, (Ed. James Hall), Record Society of Lancashire and Cheshire, Vol.19, 1889

Mercurius Aulicus, 1643–45

Mercurius Brittanicus, 1644

Miller, Amos C. (Ed.), *Joseph Jane's Account of Cornwall during the Civil War*, in *English Historical Review*, vol.90, 1975

Ollard, Richard, *The Escape of Charles II*, London, 1986

———*This War Without an Enemy*, London, 1976

Ormerod, George (Ed.), *Military Proceedings in Lancashire*, Chetham Society, II, Manchester, 1844

Perfect Diurnal, 1643–4

Perfect Occurrences, London, 1644

Reid, Stuart, (Ed.), *Declaration of the Earl of Newcastle, 1642*, Southend-on-Sea, 1983

Robinson, Edward, *Discourse of the Warr in Lancashire*, (Ed. William Beaumont), Chetham Society, LXII, Manchester, 1864

Roy, Ian (Ed.), *The Royalist Ordnance Papers*, Parts I and II, Oxfordshire Record Society, 1964 and 1974

Rushworth, John, *Historical Collections*, 8 vols, London, 1688–1701

Scottish Dove, 1644

Slingsby, Sir Henry, *Diary*, (Ed. D. Parsons), Edinburgh, 1836

Spalding, John, *History of the Trubles of Scotland*, 2 vols, Edinburgh, 1850–1

Sprigge, Joshua, *Anglia Rediviva*, London, 1647

Symonds, Richard, *Diary of the Marches of the Royal Army*, (Ed. C.E. Long), Camden Society, London, 1859

Tibbutt, H.G. (Ed.), *Letterbooks of Sir Samuel Luke,* London, 1963
Turner, Sir James, *Memoirs* (Ed. J. Thomson), Edinburgh, 1829
Walker, Sir Edward, *Historical Discourses upon Several Occasions,* London, 1705
Warburton, Eliot, *Memoirs of Prince Rupert and the Cavaliers,* 3 vols, London, 1849
Warwick, Sir Phillip, *Memoirs of the Reign of Charles I,* Edinburgh, 1825
Whitelocke, Bulstrode, *Memorials of English Affairs,* London, 1862
Wishart, George, *Memoirs of James Graham, Marquis of Montrose 1639–50,* (translated by Revd G. Murdoch), London, 1893
Young, Peter (Ed.), *Sir John Byron's Relation of the Last Western Action between the Lord Wilmot and Sir William Waller,* in *Journal of the Society for Army Historical Research,* Vol. XXXI, 1953

Secondary Sources
Abrahams, Andrew, *The Battle of Montgomery, 1644,* Bristol, 1994
Adair, John, *Roundhead General,* 2nd ed., Stroud, 1997
Atkin, Malcolm, *The Civil War in Worcestershire,* Stroud, 1995
Barratt, John, *The Battle for York: Marston Moor 1644,* Stroud, 2002
———*The Battle of Langport, 1645,* Bristol, 1995
———*Cavaliers: The Royalist Army at War,* Stroud, 2000
———*A Drubbing for Skellum: Sir Richard Grenville's Attack on Plymouth, 1645,* in *English Civil War Times,* No.55
———*For Duty Alone: Hopton's Account of the Last Campaign in the West,* Birkenhead, 1995
———*Great Siege of Chester,* Stroud, 2003
———*A Happy Victory: the Siege and Battle of Nantwich, 1644,* Birkenhead, 1996
———*The Last Blow in the Business: Royalist Strategy in the Naseby Campaign,* Southend-on-Sea, 1995
———*The Siege of Liverpool and Prince Rupert's Campaign in Lancashire, 1644,* Bristol, 1994
Bence-Jones, Mark, *The Cavaliers,* London, 1976
Brezezinski, Richard, and Richard Hook, *The Army of Gustavus Adolphus: Cavalry,* London, 1993
Buchan, John, *Montrose,* London, 1928
Bull, Stephen, and Mike Seed, *Preston, Bloody Preston,* Preston, 1998
Burne, A.H, and Peter Young, *The Great Civil War: a Military History,* London, 1959
Carlton, Charles, *Charles I: the Personal Monarch,* London, 1983
Coate, Mary, *Cornwall in the Great Civil War and Interregnum,* Oxford, 1933
Cooke, Dave, *The Forgotten Battle* (Adwalton Moor), Heckmondwyke, 1996
Cowan, E.J, *Montrose: For Covenant and King,* London, 1977
Darman, Pete, *Prince Rupert and the Swordsmen,* in *English Civil War Notes and Queries,* Nos 31 and 32
Donaghan, B., *Atrocity, War Crime and Treason in the English Civil War,* in *American Historical Review,* 1994
Dore, R.N, *The Sea Approaches: the Importance of the Dee and the Mersey in the Civil War in the North-West,* in *Transactions of the Historic Society of Lancashire and Cheshire,* vol.138, 1986
Eddishaw, David, *Civil War in Oxfordshire,* Stroud and Oxford, 1995
Edgar, F.T.R., *Sir Ralph Hopton: the King's Man in the West, 1642–52,* Oxford, 1968
Edwards, Peter, *Dealing in Death: The Arms Trade and the British Civil Wars, 1638–52,* Stroud, 2000

Eliot-Wright, Philip, *The English Civil War,* London, 1997
Firth, C.H. *Cromwell's Army,* 4th ed., London, 1962
Fissel, Mark Charles, *The Bishops' Wars: Charles I's Campaigns against Scotland, 1638–40,* Cambridge, 1994
Foard, Glenn, *Naseby: the Decisive Campaign,* Whitstable, 1995
Fox, George, *Three Sieges of Pontefract,* Leeds, 1887
Gardiner, S.R., *History of the Great Civil War,* 4 vols, London, 1886
Gilbert, J.K., *Contemporary History of Affairs in Ireland,* Dublin, 1879
Godwin, G.N., *The Civil War in Hampshire,* London, 1904
Granville, Roger, *History of the Granville Family,* Exeter, 1895
——— *The King's General in the West: the Life of Sir Richard Granville,* London, 1908
Hutton, Ronald, *The Royalist War Effort,* London, 1981
Hyett, F.A., *The Last Battle of the First Civil War* [Stow on the Wold], in *Transactions of the Bristol and Gloucestershire Archaeological Society,* 1898
Kenyon, John, and Jane Ohlmeyer, (Eds), *The Civil Wars,* Oxford, 1998
Kitson, Frank, *Prince Rupert: Portrait of a Soldier,* London, 1994
Lowe, John, *The Campaign of the Irish-Royalist Army in Cheshire, November 1643-January 1644,* in *Transactions of the Historic Society of Lancashire and Cheshire,* vol.111, 1959
Lynch, John, *For King and Parliament: Bristol and the Civil War,* Stroud, 1999
Miller, Amos C., *Sir Richard Grenville of the Civil War,* Chichester, 1979
Morrah, Patrick, *Prince Rupert of the Rhine,* London, 1976
Morris, R.H., and Lawson, P.H., *The Siege of Chester,* Chester, 1923
Napier, Mark, *Memorials of Montrose,* 2 vols, Edinburgh, London, 1848
Newman, Peter, *The Battle of Marston Moor,* London, 1981
——— *Biographical Dictionary of Royalist Officers in England and Wales, 1642–1660,* New York, 1981
——— *The Old Service: Royalist Regimental Colonels and the Civil War, 1642–46,* Manchester, 1993
——— *The Royalist Armies in the North of England,* PhD thesis, University of York, 1978
——— *The Royalist Officer Corps, 1642–46: army command as a reflection of the social structure,* in *Historical Journal,* 26, 1983
——— and P.R. Roberts, *Marston Moor 1644: the Battle of the Five Armies,* Pickering, 2003
Parker, Geoffrey, (Ed.), *The Thirty Years' War,* 2nd ed., London, 1997
Peachey, Stuart, *The Battle of Stratton, 1643,* Bristol, 1993
Phillips, John Rowland, *Memoirs of the Civil War in Wales and the Marches,* 2 vols, London, 1874
Porter, Stephen, *Destruction in the English Civil Wars,* Stroud, 1994
Reid, Stuart, *All the King's Armies: a Military History of the English Civil War, 1642–1651,* Staplehurst, 1998
——— *Auldearn 1644: the campaigns of Montrose,* Oxford, 2003
——— *Campaigns of Montrose,* Edinburgh, 1993
——— *Officers and Regiments of the Royalist Armies,* Southend-on-Sea, nd.
——— *Scots Armies of the 17th Century: 1. The Army of the Covenant,* Southend-on-Sea, 1988
——— *Scots Armies of the 17th Century: 2. The Royalist Armies, 1639–45,* Southend-on-Sea, 1989,
Ridsdell Smith, Geoffrey, *Leaders of the Civil Wars,* Kineton, 1967
Roberts, Keith, *Battle Plans,* in *English Civil War Times,* No.51
——— *Soldiers of the English Civil War: 1. Infantry,* London, 1986
Roy, Ian, *England Turned Germany? The Aftermath of the Civil War in its European Context,*

in *Transactions of the Royal Historical Society*, 4th series, 1978

———*The Royalist Army in the First Civil War*, MA thesis, University of Oxford, 1963

———*The Royalist Council of War, 1642–46*, in *Bulletin of the Institute of Historical Research*, 35, 1962

Ryder, Ian, *An English Army for Ireland*, Southend-on-Sea, 1987

Stevenson, David, *Alaistair McColla and the Highland Problem in the 17th Century*, Edinburgh, 1980

———*Revolution and Counter Revolution in Scotland, 1644–51*, London, 1977

Stoyle, Mark, *Last Refuge of a Scoundrel: Sir Richard Grenville and Cornish Particularism*, in *Historical Research*, 71, No. 144, 1998

———*Sir Richard Grenville's Creatures: the new Cornish Tertia, 1644–46*, in *Cornish Studies*, 4, 1996

Stucley, John, *Sir Bevil Grenville and his Times*, Chichester, 1983

Sunderland, F.H., *Marmaduke Lord Langdale and His Times*, London, 1926

Tincey, John, *Soldiers of the English Civil War: 2. Cavalry*, London, 1990

Toynbee, Margaret, and Peter Young, *Cropredy Bridge, 1644*, Kineton, 1970

Tucker, Norman, *Royalist Major-General: Sir John Owen*, Colwyn Bay, 1959

Underwood, David, *Royalist Conspiracy in England, 1649–1660*, New Haven, 1960

Wanklyn, M.D.G., *Royalist Strategy in Southern England*, in *Southern History*, V, 1985

Wedgwood, C.V., *The King's Peace*, London, 1955

———*The King's War*, London, 1957

———*Montrose*, London, 1952

Wenham, Peter, *Great and Close Siege of York*, Kineton, 1971

Williams, Ronald, *Montrose: Cavalier in Mourning*, London, 1975

Willis-Bund, J.W., *Civil War in Worcestershire*, Worcester, 1905

Woolrych, A, *Battles of the English Civil War*, London, 1961

Young, Peter, *Edgehill 1642*, Kineton, 1967

———*Marston Moor 1644*, Kineton, 1970

———*Naseby 1645*, London, 1985

———*Newark: the Civil War Siegeworks*, London, 1964

———*The Northern Horse at Naseby*, in *Journal of the Society for Army Historical Research*, Vol. XIV, 1964

———*The Royalist Army at the Relief of Newark*, in *Journal of the Society for Army Historical Research*, Vol. XXX, 1952

———and Wilf Embleton, *The Cavalier Army*, London, 1974

———and Richard Holmes, *The English Civil war: A Military History of the Three Civil Wars, 1642–1651*, London, 1974

Index

Aberdeen, 192,200, 205;
  battle and sack of (1644), 196, 197–8.
Abingdon (Berks), 15, 16, 50, 185.
Aboyne, James Gordon, Lord, 201–3.
Acton Church (Cheshire), 130.
Adwalton Moor (Yorks), battle of (1643),
  166–7
Airlie, John Ogilvie, Earl of, 203.
Alford, battle of (1645), 201.
Alton (Hants), 90.
Andover (Hants), action at (1644), 104–6.
Antrim, Randall Macdonnell, Earl of, 193.
Argyll, Archibald Campbell, Marquis of,
  192–3, 198, 199, 201, 205.
Arundel (Sussex), 90–1.
Ashburnham, John, 31, 41, 42, 80, 113.
Astley, Sir Bernard, 51, 54.
Astley, Jacob, Lord, Chapter 4 *passim*, 2,3,
  5,10, 12, 26, 28, 42, 209, 211:
  and Prince Rupert, 46.
Aston, Sir Arthur, 48.
Aston, Sir Thomas, 124–5.
Atkyns, Richard, q.63–4, 66, 67, 68, 82, 87,
  182–3.
Auldearn, battle of (1645), 200–1.

Baillie, William, 199, 200–3.
Balcarres, Alexander Lindsey, Earl of, 202–3.
Barriffe, William, q.56.
Balfour of Burleigh, Lord, 195.
Balfour, Sir William, 48, 104, 106–7, 150.
Banbury (Oxford.), 58, 106.
Bartholmley Church (Cheshire) 32, 128–9.
Basing House (Hants), 50, 89, 146.
Bassett, Francis, 82, 83, 85.
Bath (Somerset), 22, 87, 110.
Beacon Hill, battle of (1644), 150.
Beeston Castle (Cheshire) 127–8.
Belasyse, John, Lord, 48, 52, 169, 170, 171.
Bennet, Sir Humphrey, 106.

Berkeley, Sir John, 80, 83, 85, 155, 210.
Berwick-on-Tweed, 47, 204.
Birch, John, 22, 59, 154.
Birmingham, 59,
  sack of (1643), 30.
Blair Atholl, 194.
Blake, Robert, 71.
Bodmin, 79, 82, 149.
Bolden Hill, battle of (1644), 171.
Bolles, Richard, 90.
Bolton (Lancs), 36.
Brackley (Northants), 120.
Braddock Down, battle of (1643), 82–3.
Bradford (Yorks), 166–7.
Breda, siege of (1637), 26, 62, 95–6, 177.
Brereton, Sir William, 59, 74, 128, 136,
  138–9.
Brett, Sir Edward, 21.
Bridgnorth (Shrops.), 17, 33.
Bridgwater (Somerset), 71, 86, 116, 117.
Brig O' Dee, action at (1639), 192.
Bristol, 37, 38, 68, 87, 203;
  Royalist capture of (1643), 9, 31, 88;
  Parliamentarian capture of (1645), 43.
Broadway (Worcs.), 59.
Buckingham, George Villiers, Duke of, 7, 142.
Bulstrode, Sir Richard, q.27–8, 94, 108, 110,
  112.
Burford (Oxford.) action at (1643), 122–3.
Byron, Lady Eleanor, 134, 136, 140.
Byron, John, Lord, Chapter 8 *passim*; 2, 7, 4,
  5, 36, 180–1;
  and Prince Rupert, 28, 32, 38, 123;
  regiment of horse, 120, 122, 123.
Byron, Sir Nicholas, 48, 124.
Byron, Sir Richard, 140.
Byron, Sir Robert, 128–30.

Cadiz, 142.
Caernarvon, 139.

223